Italy: I Love You!

Here's to our children who were fortunate enough to study in Siena!

Best wishes,

Jeralyn Peterkin

Italy: I Love You!

A love letter from

Geralyn Peterkin

To order additional copies of this book, contact:
Xlibris Corporation
1-888-795-4274
www.Xlibris.com
Orders@Xlibris.com
56280

CONTENTS

INTRODUCTION

"Open my heart, and you will see 'Graved inside of it, 'Italy.'"

Robert Browning—De Gustibus, st. 2

"... the Lotus-Eaters, who live on a flowering food ... any ofthem who ate the honey-sweet fruit of lotus was unwilling ... togo away ... and forget the way home."

THE ODYSSEY. Book IX,
trans. Richard Lattimore

"... the Sirens by the melody of their singing enchant ..."

THE ODYSSEY, Book XII,
trans. Richard Lattimore

This is not a guide book, nor is it a directory for works of art, hotels, restaurants, places of interest or "things to see" for Italy. It is not an historical tract or a political lecture.

So, what am I writing about? In simplest terms, I suppose one could call it a love letter; a statement of my love for this country. In real terms, Italy is more, much more than a country. Browning described this condition perfectly; Italy becomes a part of your heart, a state of mind, an emotional experience. But, even human love affairs can have down sides, and therefore, occasionally so can my love for Italy. Honesty compels me to include the few things that are not so lovable.

Psychologists and religious leaders remind us that we cannot love that which is incapable of returning our love. One cannot truly "love" ice cream, golf, a book, a house, or a car, but Italy is different from these entities. It can return your love, and as real lovers do, it can occasionally hurt you. But, if the love is true and good and real on both sides, it repairs itself and often becomes better and stronger.

Therefore, to me Italy is like a lover; one who tempts you, thrills you, often satisfies you, sometimes annoys you, confuses you, and, not often, but sometimes, fools you. But it is a lover whom you are able, but choose not to live without. I've been visiting this land for more than thirty years and of course it has changed; what or who doesn't in that amount of time? But it retains enough of the character and flavor of the years of the past to charge the taste buds of the memory with reminiscences of sheer delight.

I have visited fourteen countries through Europe and the Americas and have greatly enjoyed their different cultures, histories, cuisines and ways of living. But only Italy inspires in me this intense passion for place; no other land has ever affected me and touched my heart, even in a small way, as Italy has. How did this happen? It's as mysterious as explaining how one falls in love. Perhaps, as the men with Odysseus were tempted, the first pasta I tasted in Rome in 1971 was infused with lotus blossoms, or possibly while sailing off Porto Ercole near the island of Giglio my senses were assailed by the song of the Sirens, making me forget, at least temporarily, all thoughts of home. Whatever the cause, passion, pasta or song, Italy is a magnet and I am made of stuff forever attracted.

Therefore, this is my love letter to and for my favorite place; the "nursery of arts" Shakespeare writes in THE TAMING OF THE SHREW, that mesmerizes, magnetizes, and holds me in its very large, warm and accepting heart.

ITALY! I LOVE YOU!

Italy is bells. Church bells that don't quit. Especially at midnight or very early morning. They define hyperbole, outlast the centuries, and nudge one about eternity.

Italy is gelati! The best ice cream in the world! Flavors you've never dreamed possible—fig, melon, grapefruit, blueberry, Malaga and chocolate that makes a chocolate afficionado weep. After all, the Italians invented the stuff.

Italy is flowers. A riot of color. Honeysuckle odor. Pungent herb. Red, pink, violet, white. Pots of color on each balcony whether on crumbling flat or posh villa. Fat geraniums, like Vesuvius in action, bursting. Light through the prism, blooming.

Italy is wine. Chianti, Bardolino, Valpolicello, Soave, Marsala, Orvieto, Frascati, Montepulciano, and so much more. Red, white, golden, amber, dry, sweet, fruity, good, poor, great, fantastic. Ubiquitous. Acqua Vitae. Blessed is the grape.

Italy is heat. The crushing, pulsating, unrelenting heat of summer. Sun that flattens. Only for mad dogs and you know who. Makes possible the beautiful pomidoro!

Italy is pasta. A thousand shapes in a thousand dressings. One better than the previous—an ambrosial gorge. To each district its specialties. Enjoy!

Italy is fruit. Baseball sized peaches, but juicy and sweet beyond sugar. Strawberries, raspberries and glorious figs that make agnostics think there might be a heaven. Watermelon that is life-saving in its properties—water, sucrose, salt; and brilliantly colored!

Italy is inconsistency. Consistently. From the price of a straw handbag to the response of "tea, please" it is always a surprise to see the result. Rather like a marriage that's not dull because it's not predictably programmed. Keeps one a tad unbalanced; keen to receive life's signals.

Italy is churches. Too many to count. Mostly old, some ancient, some "important," others more "important." Some only there. Coolness and incense and statues; some marble. Steps and crosses, mosaics and golden reliquaries; others stucco and wood. Gothic and Renaissance, Florentine, Byzantine; lots of "neo-" and even, . . . early Mussolini.

Italy is traffic. The stench of diesel; the verve of driving. The insanity of passing; the danger of a *"far bella figura."* Eight rows of vehicles in a three lane road; motorbikes, tour busses, Fiats, Vespas, three-wheeled trucks, cars all over. Pedestrians strolling nonchalantly through the din. The Inferno?

Italy is the café'. Coffee, wine, beer, Campari, soda, gelati, whatever you wish and whenever you wish. For the price of a minerale' you are left undisturbed for as long as you wish. To dream; to recover; to read; to gape!

Italy is graffiti! This too their invention—look at the etymology! Not much "John loves Mary" or "Kilroy was here" but politically motivated. And before an election, inundation.

Italy is water. Salt sea washing the surrealistic shoe. Lombard lakes, Alps tears. Naples Bay, panoramic and a bit polluted; Calabrian coast, gray purple, well-named "Mauve." The almost phony postcard blue of Portofino and Port'Ercole; geysers from marble! Roman fountains! Wow Bernini! Neptune's Muse! Muddy, shallow and seemingly insignificant Tiber and Arno! Are you the fabled rivers of nearly forgotten geography primers? The canals of Venice; faded, sinking, occasionally odoriferous, but always sinfully splendid. Italian H2O, catalogued.

Italy is art. Fresco and sculpture, mosaic and oil; architecture and acrylic. In Florence a surfeit; too much, we cry, too much. A rest. My mind aches; I never dreamed . . . To live in its midst? No wonder the Italians are so smug about art. They have it all. Michelangelo and all the rest.

Italy is people. The best; they are warm, kind, generous, hospitable and interesting; open to others. No where do you find persons who are more full of the joy of living; more loving of family and children; respectful of their heritage, art and history.

ITALY! Life is what's happening here. A celebration of life to live.

I LOVE YOU!

IN LOVE

"A man who has not been in Italy is always conscious of an inferiority."

Samuel Johnson, quoted in Boswell's
LIFE OF SAMUEL JOHNSON

My husband Roger and I fell in love in 1971; at that time we had been married for almost sixteen years, and, to each other! The reason for this new passion was that we discovered Italy. The intense emotion we felt was classic love at first sight, perhaps infatuation, but, like a solid marriage, this love has grown, matured, and become ever more fulfilling with each visit.

If Hemingway considered Paris his "moveable feast," then I must say that Italy is my moveable picnic on a magnificent beach, Thanksgiving dinner, fireworks on the fourth of July, circus, perfect SAT score, hole in one, parade, a matchless sunset after an impeccable day, the satisfaction felt from a sympathetic lover, the pride in a child's accomplishment, an inspiring symphony, a well-acted Shakespearean tragedy, and the joy given by a grandchild. Honesty compels me to add that at times this wondrous country can also be as frustrating as an endless line at the Motor Vehicle Bureau, as annoying as a letter from the IRS, as exasperating as a loyal but drooling dog, or as confusing as badly translated directions from Japanese to English on an electrical appliance.

Feeling life strongly is happening here; passion about everything from politics to religion, from cooking to driving is exhibited. Conversation is constant and exhibits compelling beliefs as well as the idea that others will understand and agree. A visitor can be satiated, exhausted, delighted, dizzied, angered, thrilled, amused, excited, dazzled and/or confused by the Italian ambiance, but never bored. Despite Antonio's weariness in THE MERCHANT OF VENICE, who, as Shakespeare's creation, was actually an Englishman in Venetian clothing, Fellini's post-war characters created from a subculture on the fringes of Italian life, the propensity to change governments ever so frequently, the fascinating yet mysterious conundrum of Church and State, a consistent inconsistency, this is the place where I am most content; my mind, soul and body are nurtured. This land is a moveable celebration! Life in all facets is happening here, and to share in that life, however briefly or fractionally, is worth more than the sum of all other travels and experiences! If we compare our relationship to Italy as a love affair and marriage, it is no longer the honeymoon, yet it retains enough of the character and flavor of the beginning years to charge the taste buds of the memory with sheer delight! Italy, I love you!

So, what is Italy? Italy is art, church bells, traffic, *gelati*, flowers, wine, sun, pasta, fruit, cheese, the café', water of the lakes and sea, history—the Etruscans, Greeks, Romans—and so many more, the bustle of the North, the deceptive languor of the South, and the often delightful inconsistency. Being in love with this place, or more accurately, the spirit of this land, is akin to combining the best of marriage with the excitement of a love affair. A predictably programmed journey it is not; one is slightly off balance and therefore keen to receive life's signals, antennae up!

The beginning of our first romantic Italian odyssey happened in the summer of 1971. Our four children were safely ensconced in excellent camps in Vermont. This gave us a limited amount of free time. Our cash was also limited but we had heard that T.W.A. offered a two week package called, "Fly-Drive" at an affordable price. Having been on an escorted tour the year before to another European country, we wanted no part of bus transportation, meals shared with groups in touristy restaurants, lecturers no matter how learned expatiate on the local history, instructions about having one's bags packed and put outside the bedroom door by 6:00 A.M., or other such orders which made a vacation holiday more like a military maneuver. We, rightly or not, have never been "joiners" and have avoided the herd mentality whenever possible. We knew we wanted the freedom to explore and drive when we chose, avoiding the necessarily strict schedules of a group. There are many excellent tours which have served and pleased thousands of contented tourists; this just wasn't our cup of tea—or, *cappuccino*, as it turned out.

The T.W.A. offering included round-trip air fare, a rental car for the two week period, maps, and hotel vouchers for each night. There was an itinerary, but it was up to you to decide how early or late you would travel, arrive or depart. Except for included hotel breakfasts, it was up to you to find restaurants for all other meals. One was free to explore. For many years I had dreamed of going to the fabled cities of Florence and Venice, and yet, impulsively when it was time to choose destinations, we picked the one that would take us on the longest journey, Sicily.

Perhaps it was the memory of my grandfather who had been born there which influenced my decision. His image, still strong in my mind, is of a small, white-haired man who played the guitar, sang, cooked some of the best food I had ever eaten and listened to opera by the hour—I still have many of his old records—and was invariably cheerful, compelled the choice, perhaps unconsciously. My husband was extremely fond of him too. When we were high school sweethearts my grandfather "baby-sat" for me while my parents were away for a month. Each night Grandpa would ask in his thick accent, "Is 'Rojah' coming to dinner?" If I answered negatively because it was a school night, he was always disappointed. He was inordinately fond of Roger, and therefore, destination Sicily was a logical response from us both.

Against the well-meaning and seemingly practical advice of many who were no doubt misinformed about Southern Italy, we left Rome and drove south, stopping first in Naples in Campania, and then to Cosenza in Calabria as we had hotels reserved there in our itinerary. The weather was clear, sunny and as hot as Italy can be in July; the Autostrada of the South was not yet finished, we were in a tiny Fiat, and so began a journey that would not end in two weeks, or two years, or thirty; it was the start of an adventure and pilgrimage we hope will never end for the rest of our lives. Each trip is special, exciting, sometimes frustrating, and often amusing; we have learned of Italian culture, past and present, of art and artists, of architecture, and about its history, as well as watching the evolution of this country from the early 1970's into the third millennium.

Clearly, I am an American, born and bred; I am loyal, patriotic and proud. I am awed by my country's history, of its democratic experiment which made dreams come true for millions of people who came to its shores, either recently or awhile back, as most of my ancestors did. I am awed by the gigantic achievements of so many of our people and of my country which not only permitted, but encouraged this. Although far from perfect, I see my country trying, at least some of the time to be better, cleaner, and more equitable to people of different races, religions and backgrounds. I look at history, even recent history and I am proud of the advances we have made. I cringe with shame when I remember being driven to Florida as a young child and having seen restrooms and drinking fountains labeled, "colored" or "white." Even with "miles to go" as Robert Frost wrote, we are getting better and I am glad that the "United States of America" is imprinted on the cover of my passport.

However, just as one loves a parent, but is passionate about a lover, I freely admit that I am moved in the most secret place in my heart by this country called Italy. Something in or about this land, which I admit is really more of a state of mind than a tangible, describable entity, tweaks my brain and runs barefoot across my soul. America is my platonic love; Italy, the erotic.

I am not able to succinctly describe Italy anymore than one can succinctly describe a lover. First of all, there is no one Italy. Lombardy is as different from Calabria as Mississippi is from Massachusetts or as Florida is from Oregon. And, as one might prefer Maine to Arizona, so also one might prefer the Veneto to Molise; everyone has preferences, if not favorites, whether in place, food or friends.

My heritage is Scots, German and Sicilian; the Sicilian part reflecting who knows how many other ancestries considering the numbers who have invaded, ruled or conquered that island, whether Greek, Roman, Arab, Norman, Spanish, or others. That notwithstanding, both Roger and I feel we have become Italians in heart, if not by birth or passport. If we were infatuated with this varied land in 1971, we have grown into mature lovers of a country which rarely fails to satisfy one's reason for being, and zest for life.

Heraclitus, a 5th century B.C.E. Greek philosopher, stated that you couldn't step into the same river twice. Water changes constantly and therefore the river is not the same second after second. This is true of modern Italy; it endures, it charms, it inspires love, yet it is changing. This is another fascinating aspect of this country. Many older Italian people are not altogether thrilled with many of the changes; and although many tourists would like the countryside unchanged since the time of the Caesars, but at the same time insisting on air conditioning, computer access, international telephones and the accouterments of a five star hotel, change is happening.

Who or what doesn't change? Certainly the United States is not the same place it was when I was a high school student or later a young mother. Children change, friends change, technology changes, yet, the changes in Italy seem more dramatic perhaps because there was so little change for so long.

When we first went to Italy we were amused by the lack of regulation in parking cars. Sidewalks, crosswalks, wherever—it didn't seem to matter; if one could fit his car in an empty space almost anywhere, he did it with impunity. Now we have noticed that cars are frequently ticketed for illegal parking and often towed away. There are zebras for pedestrian crossing, but it is still wise to look both ways! Many stores now have Sunday openings which was totally unheard of several years ago. Restaurants have increased food portions but we have observed few "doggy bags" as yet. Nursery schools have proliferated as the work force now includes thousands of young mothers. Heretofore if a young woman was employed there were always grandparents to babysit. Many of course still do, but the increased mobility of young families has rendered this difficult if not impossible. Historically, very few people ever left the village or town of their birth; however, now when the corporate world offers positions to the educated young, they must leave the family town for economic success.

Women are now police persons, postal workers, and taxi drivers in addition to the more traditional kinds of feminine employment.

Roger and I have joked that fifty per cent of Italians work in construction. Building is ubiquitous and never seems to cease; legions of cranes pierce the skyline. Earth movers, tractors and what I used to call "steam shovels" when a child, appear all over. New structures, industrial complexes, apartment houses and individual homes are being erected seemingly everywhere. Old buildings are being restored at an unprecedented rate; as we often return to the same towns and cities year after year, we are aware of these structures newly cleaned, or in the process of being spruced up. Italian law is strict about this process; the preservation of the architectural heritage of the country must be strictly observed. No one is permitted to destroy an edifice with any historical importance. When a structure is either being built or restored and evidence of archeological material is discovered, all current work is immediately halted until historians can identify and preserve the ruins. We have seen this happen firsthand in Urbino at the University. Similar situations have occurred all over Italy.

A huge change has happened with telephone service. During the seventies we often had to go to a "Postal-Telegraph" office in order to make an international telephone call. One would tell the person in charge who was seated in a booth much like the teller in a bank, the country and the number wanted. After a wait of between ten and twenty minutes, the supervisor would point to you and loudly pronounce a number. That meant that you were to find the booth with the identical number, enter it, pick up the telephone and wait for the connection to the number you wished to speak to. It was a process which could easily fill more than an hour by the time a "P-T" office was located, the call made, and the return. No more! Now telephone booths have proliferated, simple 'phone cards are widely available and excellent service is typical. Of course hotel telephones then as now could provide the same service, but, in the seventies at least, at fairly exorbitant prices.

Many rental accommodations have a telephone system, which operates on a "click" system. The landlord will state the going rate per click—a timing device that is audible—and at the end of the rental period, the amount owed will simply be added to the bill. We have found this to be fair, convenient and very useful.

Every Italian is equipped with a cell phone, which is used with great facility and regularity. I do not recall ever seeing any during the seventies but since then and much before they became a virtual appendage to the average American, Italian people universally adopted them. These telephones do not usually have international access, although at added cost some do mainly for people involved in business across national boundaries. Several years ago we purchased an Italian cell phone which is useful twenty-four hours a day for contacting anyone in Italy or at a very reasonable rate for calling the USA. A card is purchased and inserted into the 'phone and the price paid decreases with each call. When the amount becomes low, another card is purchased and one can continue to telephone friends, family or business contacts. Great system and convenience!

Changing or unchanged, mobile or static, mercurial or constant, pleasing or occasionally annoying, in countless ways we loved you at first and we continue to love you now. Italy, our pleasure, our passion.

My paperback Merriam-Webster dictionary defines the word "addict" as: "to devote or surrender oneself to something habitually or excessively," and the word "addiction" as "the quality or state of being addicted." Despite the usually negative implications of these words, addiction itself is not necessarily bad depending on what one is habitually surrendering to. Thus, we have decided that we are "Italy addicts." Fortunately, no one has suggested this is detrimental, and more fortunately for us, there is no re-hab for this particular and delightful addiction. And so, we return as often as possible.

We take hundreds of photographs which are methodically placed in albums marked "Italy" followed by the particular year. Frequently we take them down from the crowded shelves and gaze with love at the memory inducing scenes. Soon after, we begin planning another journey; I think of Geoffrey Chaucer's memorable line from the Prologue of the CANTERBURY TALES: "Thanne longen folk to goon on pilgrimages." Our favorite pilgrimage, first, last and we hope as long as possible, is to Italy!

FLIGHT TO MILAN

From thirty-one thousand feet, the lakes are
Rorschached, sprinkled, undulated across
The green-black landscape I believe is Maine.
The sun has dwindled from the blinding, bright
Blaze of a ninety degree New York day
To the orange scarlet fire of near set.
The steely horizon line neatly slices
Across the pink and black. The whole land mass
Dissolves and darkness envelops all as
Eastward we roar across the Atlantic.

We peons swill Pepsi and three dollar
Vodka. Up front, peeking between curtains
I spy the privileged, sipping Bordeaux and Graves,
Furnished, gratis, by the airline. Except
For a brief, reckless flight of envy, I
Begrudge them nothing. Their fare, five times mine
In American dollars, would buy a
Lagoon of fine wine. On the other hand,
Tax-wise, business smart, its cost is footed
By, bottom line, the government. That's me. And you.
Ah well, *C'est la vie.* Thus it's ever been.

On minute islets below, infrequent
Lights glow. Such remoteness is not for me.
I admire and imagine I desire
The almost unreachable, but really
I desire not to be too far removed
From the pavements. Children, traffic, sirens.

Dinner. So called; a waste. Salad dressing
Made of seventeen ingredients; nine

Unpronounceable—DuPont or Monsanto.
"Corn oil spread" not butter; dessert, a "gel"
Of chocolate resembling mousse "as an
Apple doth an oyster," SHREW's words remind.

I muse, "Why not knock twenty dollars off
My ticket, give the attendants a break,
Let me feast on my own corned beef on rye?
Why is it deemed so important to serve
This meal, however foul and/or ersatz?

Not a happy flyer, I want only
To arrive safely; as eating well in
Italy I shall do. I savor that.
As long as this craft continues to surge
Safely through the sky sans political
Upheaval by men sporting box cutters
Or hidden plastic Glock pistols, failures
Mechanical or human, I will be
Silent, and not complain, gastronomically.

The surreal darkness and sound of motors
Combine to star-trek me across all space.
Intellectually, I understand.
Emotionally, no way. This bird is
Too heavy to fly; only butterflies,
Dust-motes and bubbles are yet capable
Of flight; not huge seven forty sevens
Filled with people enough to populate
A village, or thirty nine-man softball
Teams. Six hours and forty-seven minutes
Seat-belted in a magic compartment
And then, Milano! (How do they find it?)
Thank you, Captain! You've wrought a miracle.

SICILY

"To have seen Italy without seeing Sicily is not having seen Italy at all. For Sicily is the key to everything."
Johann Wolfgang Goethe

THE FLIGHT TO ITALY: DIARY AND SELECTED LETTERS
Ed. and translated, T.J. Reed

"In Sicily it doesn't matter whether things are done well or done badly; the sin which we Sicilians never forgive is simply that of 'doing' at all. We are old, . . . very old. For more thantwenty-five centuries we've been bearing the weight of a superb and heterogeneous civilization, all from outside, none made by ourselves, none that we could call our own."

From THE LEOPARD, by
Giuseppe di Lampedusa
Chapter 4, "Love at Donnafugata"

When I was in graduate school my Chaucer professor had a suggestion for his students. This had nothing to do with THE CANTERBURY TALES or TROILUS AND CRISEYDE; in the manner of many interesting people he often got sidetracked from his planned lectures and would tell us fascinating stories and anecdotes from his own graduate studies many years before both in the United States and in Europe. His suggestion on one particular day was that at some time in the future, each of us should go to Sicily in February just as the almond blossoms emerged, and then follow those blooms up the Italian peninsula as they unfolded. I never forgot this.

Although we had been in Sicily several times, we had never had the opportunity to be there in February. In late 1999, as we planned our next Italian journey, it seemed logical; begin in February in Sicily and follow those blossoms! So we did.

The essence of Sicily defies ordinary description; it delights, it maddens; it explains, it confuses; it exhilarates, it saddens; it awes, it exhausts; mostly, it endures and endures and endures as it progresses in the twenty-first century.

Sicily is the largest island in the Mediterranean Sea; beautiful and fruitful, it has been used and often abused for thousands of years. Guarding the entrance to the Mediterranean insured its importance in the ancient world as well as in the modern age, and thus it was a desired conquest and a target for invaders. The Greeks, Romans, Carthaginians, Arabs, Byzantines, Normans, French, Spanish and Germans either occupied, subdued, fought over, raped, stole, terrorized Sicily, or infrequently, made it a haven of tolerance, gentility and culture. This unique land could best be described as a living library of history telling of the heroism and noble vision of man, as well as of his degradation, decadence and greed. All of Italy has felt the crush of invasion over and over again; perhaps more than any other land the history of Sicily resounds with the anguish felt by oppression, not only from without, but from the often cruel exactitude of tyrants within. The inhabitants are a proud people with fiercely strong love ties to the land. How could they not be deeply, and perhaps permanently affected by the cataclysmic events which have been part of their heritage? This is Sicily.

My paternal grandfather left Sicily for the United States in 1904, and as I grow older, each visit to this beguiling island is more emotional. I know little about his circumstances there; unfortunately as is often typical, one is not curious enough about ancestors until it is too late to inquire directly from them. I know that in his new country he was a barber. Did he learn that trade in Sicily or in the USA? I don't know. He retired while still in his fifties and from then on seemed to earn his pocket money by playing pinochle. He once told me that when he was very young he was sent to be trained as a priest. What happened? Did he run away from that possibility? Was he asked to run away? Again, I don't know. He sang and played the guitar. Where did he learn music and under what conditions? Sometimes late at night I fantasize that he was escaping from a cruel landlord, or from the Mafia, or from the Church, but most likely, as thousands of other Sicilians and Southern Italians did during the same time period, he was leaving his homeland for economic opportunity. My logical mind reasons that there was nothing romantic in his exodus, as my imagination wants to drift off into the mysterious, the sentimental, and the stuff from which bodice-ripping novels, soap operas and GODFATHER films are made. I sincerely doubt whether any of these were the scenario that brought him to New York more than one hundred years ago.

Roger and I visited the place that was written in the *Certificato* or official paper needed for immigration to the United States, as Grandpa Pietro's place of origin, Valguarnera, in the province of Catania. I knew the name of the town as I had acquired this certificate as well as a few others years ago. These documents stated that he was in good standing as a citizen, did not owe military service to the government and wasn't a criminal. His date of birth and parents were also listed.

We decided to find this town where Grandpa was born. Parking in front of the impressive municipal building of Valguarnera, which was closed as it was the lunch hour, we soon found a small mamma and pappa trattoria for our noon meal. After a delicious meal of *penne e pomidori* (a quill shaped pasta with a plain tomato sauce), *insalata mista* (mixed salad), and *petto di pollo* (a fillet of chicken breast) cooked over a wood fire the proprietor started after we ordered, I wrote on a sheet of notebook paper in my primitive Italian, that my grandfather had been born here in 1882 and had emigrated to the United States in 1904. I wasn't totally certain of the owner's reply, but I believe he said that the priest at the local church, *Chiesa San Giuseppe*, had the same last name as Grandpa's, "Longo."

After lunch we walked to the church, but it seemed deserted. Sicilians take the *"riposo"* or rest hour after the midday meal seriously. Then we walked through the cemetery for an hour, but gave up. I could have pursued the search afterward, but the more I thought of it, I decided, what for? Just to have been there was something special for me, and I think for Roger too, who was very fond of him. I wish I had known more of his background, but as a youngster I was never encouraged.

The landscape on the way to Valguarnera is composed of the stuff landscape artists dream of. Rolling mountainous hills, some cultivated, many with cattle and sheep grazing and almost no houses to break the spectrum of greens, browns and red-browns are the textures and colors of this eye-compelling scene. Photographs cannot quite capture this construct; we've tried.

We first visited Agrigento in 1971. The temples literally took my breath away! I couldn't imagine anything like this outside of Greece. As I studied more history I learned that indeed the Greeks had colonized Sicily in the 8th century B.C.E., building exquisite temples, altars and impressive fortifications. In the Valley of the Temples in Agrigento, the outstanding monument is the Temple of Concord; this is the temple found most often on postcards. I saw this first as we drove in to this city more than thirty years ago and I have never forgotten the dramatic effect it had on me as I encountered its majesty. I have a photograph of this incredible structure taken in 1971 and another of the same building in 1997. Except for the scaffolding in the later photo, they are virtually identical. The difference lies in the area around these ancient ruins, as well as in the visits by throngs of tourists. There were comparatively few visitors in the early 70's; now, many. Another drastic change was the obvious building boom from the time of our first visit. Scores of apartment buildings dot the surrounding area. Despite the fact that the land surrounding the temples was named by the government to be a protected archeological area, prohibiting construction, these rules were flouted and more than six hundred structures were built. In the winter of 2000, despite the protests of many locals, bulldozers razed most of the illegal buildings. These demolitions were covered by the Italian press throughout Italy. A retired carabinieri officer from the north of Italy we have come to know well, told us that he had been assigned to duty in Agrigento years before and that he and his fellow officers had witnessed the illegal building, but were powerless to stop it. Without actually incriminating himself or anyone else, he suggested that it was the "favors" received by politicians and the judiciary that allowed it to survive for as long as it did. These injustices are practiced all over the world, but in Sicily, for so long this was a way of life, the only way to get along. People expected it, were never surprised, and simply, the shoulder-shrugging attitude was incorporated into the Sicilian character.

Anyone who has been aware of the international scene in the past ten or fifteen years can appreciate the strides the Sicilians have made against the corruptions which have drained so much of the life and joy from the majority of their hard-working and law-abiding citizens. The thorough and extremely well-documented book, EXCELLENT CADAVERS, by Alexander Stille depicts this battle, and covers the murder of the two leading fighters, Paolo Borsellino and Giovanni Falcone against the Mafia and the politicians "owned" by this nefarious and lethal criminal group, as well as a gripping account of the famous maxi-trial of the alleged criminals in Palermo. The airport in Palermo is now named as a memorial to these two heroic gentlemen.

Agrigento, as well as being famous for Greek temples, is also home to an almond festival in February. We intended to begin our "almond journey" there, but Roger was incapacitated by a badly strained back and we could not reach Sicily until after the celebration. Having missed that, we decided to begin that year's odyssey in the important city of Siracusa, where to our delight, we found the blossoms in full flower.

If I had to pick a favorite place in Sicily, I think it would be Siracusa. The city is located on the Ionian Sea in the southeast part of the island. Colonists from Corinth founded this city around 700 B.C.E. and it grew rapidly, even founding colonies of its own. With a large population and a vigorous economy, it rivaled Athens. During the two hundred years between 400 and 200 B.C.E. culture flourished; Pindar and Archimedes lived here; Plato visited, and in the Greek Theater, located in what is now known as the Archeological Zone, Aeschylus premiered some of his dramas. This spectacular theater is an incredible sight. One of the largest in the world, it seated almost 15, 000 people.

Later, after having defeated the Siracusans, the Romans also built a theater, but I do not think it is as impressive as the Greek one.

Fascinating is the Ear of Dionysus, an artificial cave with peculiar acoustics said to have been used to house prisoners so that whispered secrets could be heard by the particular tyrant in power!

Perhaps beside the point in one's quest for history, but for old Sicilian travelers who have noticed so many changes for the better, I must mention that the Zone was totally and perfectly immaculate. Not one gum wrapper or cigarette stub marred the walks and trails throughout this huge area. Sicily has not always been noted for public tidiness and great strides have been made in the more recent years to improve and thereby attract tourists. Mainland Italy depends on the tourist trade, and in past years, Sicily was behind in this effort. They are catching up!

In Siracusa, the old part of the city is located on the island of Ortygia. Special efforts at restoration have made this a most attractive area. The Cathedral in the Piazza del Duomo, a gorgeous square filled with architectural gems, was the Temple of Athena during the Greek period. We were seated outside in the front of a restaurant in this piazza directly across from this edifice during our maiden Sicilian journey in '71. I remember noticing the Doric columns encased within the cathedral walls and thinking, not only of the upheavals in religious beliefs in several millennia, but of the efficient and clever restoration of a building fronting on this lovely site.

Piazza Archimede is graced with a lovely fountain at its center; we visited it often, not because it was a delightful spot, which it is, but because it was very near our favorite restaurant. Getting to and from dinner, we had to pass through this piazza.

Fish, quite naturally, is a specialty of all coastal Sicily and Siracusa is no exception. On Ortygia I saw the largest outdoor markets of finned and shell fish I have ever encountered. Each display was beautifully and artistically presented, decorated with lemons, cucumbers and tomatoes. Nearby were the vegetable and fruit markets, and they too are a bouquet to the eye; to those of us who love to cook, an inspiration is felt to buy everything in sight and rush home to prepare it. A pleasant frustration however, if one is residing in a hotel. Wandering further along, the cheese, oil and olive stalls appear with their mouth-watering and visually exciting wares. Finally, the flower and plant sellers emerge nearer to the main thoroughfare.

At the risk of sounding like a fanatically neat person which I assure you I am not, I could not help noticing the total tidiness and order on the streets and sidewalks of all of Ortygia. It would put most American cities of that size in second place if a contest of neatness and order were held between them and Siracusa. What a delightful improvement it is.

Although I love to cook and am the owner of thirty-three well-used cookbooks on Italian food alone, I have never been comfortable cooking fish. I once read that cooking a small fish was like ruling a large kingdom—I think it came from an old edition of THE JOY OF COOKING—and I guess it influenced me, as I knew I could never rule a small kingdom, a puny town or even a hamlet. Hence, in Siracusa, although we were residing in an apartment on this particular visit, we tended to dine in restaurants when we wanted to enjoy local fish specialties. There were many excellent places, but one became our favorite and we returned there three times in one week and frequently on each subsequent foray to Siracusa. Since the beginning of our many Italian odysseys we found that ninety-nine per cent of the time, a first time client is treated with respect and courtesy at restaurants. If one returns for a second time, the respect and courtesy become almost familial and the genuine joy from the staff reflecting your choice is apparent. However, by the third visit, you are singled out and very special. Perhaps a *"focaccia"* will be given to you to nibble on while you choose from the menu, or an after dinner *"digestivo."* The best part is the warmth and recognition felt from the entire staff from busboys and waiters to the managing staff or owners. After our third visit in one week to our favorite Siracusan dining room, we were not only treated like first cousins to all the employees, we were given an incredibly beautiful calendar of scenes of Sicily. Between the dining room and the kitchen, there was a small window opening. After our first visit, the chef, recognizing us, would wave a greeting, and we would tell him how delicious a certain course was after finishing it.

At the end of a sumptuous meal, after handshakes and photographs, we departed, happily thinking about the spaghetti *vongole* (spaghetti with clam sauce), *tagliatelle con spada* (a flat noodle with pieces of swordfish in a delectable cream sauce), *zuppa di pesce* (a kind of bouillabaise with clams, calamari, mussels, three other kinds of shell fish I didn't recognize, a fresh anchovy, and an entire small fish complete with head, all "swimming" in a broth made by cooks who must have been children of mermaids), *frutta di mare* (an antipasto of cooked shellfish in a vinaigrette dressing), *cassatta* (the sweet, rich dessert), and all the other incredible specialties of the fish as well as the dessert chefs of Siracusa.

Driving through the countryside around Siracusa we found the almond blossoms which had set us on this winter journey in the first place. Through Noto, Avola, Augusta and on the side of almost every country road we wandered by, we saw the snowy white perfection of these flowers. Much of the southeastern part of Sicily has unique landscapes; I gape in wonder and admiration, but Roger, with the eye of the artist, truly appreciates their grandeur. Rock, mostly grey colored stone, sternly, yet serenely sits on all the high hills and mountains. Siracusa itself is surrounded by a necklace of quarries which have been the substance of the great buildings of this area since ancient times and even before, or during the period known as "pre-history." Drama lies in the color of the fields as well. Here, in the middle of February there is a shade of green, so new, so fresh, it made me think that this would have been the green of

Eden. Never, ever have I observed a green just like this. Between the lush verdant patches are fields of brown, newly plowed and seeded. The eye is filled, but not satiated, ever seeking more.

Orange trees in beautifully lush groves are laden with golden fruit. As is my wont, I worried that all might not be harvested. Did I doubt for a moment that the farmers of Sicily didn't know what they were doing after cultivating for millennia? There are different sizes, shapes and varieties in the fruit; many are sold by vendors in small stalls along the side of the road, and often, directly from the back of a truck. Lemon trees and their fruit are also found in great abundance, and always, the ubiquitous olive trees, silver-grey, graceful, and surprising to me, often extremely large in the Italian South as compared with those in Umbria, Toscana and Abruzzo.

The Paolo Orsi Archeological Museum in Siracusa is not to be missed. Incredibly organized, it begins with the paleolithic and neolithic data of the peoples before the Greeks, and then continues on to subsequent civilizations and cultures. It is detailed with explanations in clear English—unlike many museums in the North—excellent photographs of the sites, and chronologically arranged displays. The building itself is ultra-modern, well-lighted and heated. I have not come across a more impressive museum in Italy, and I have been in many.

Outside of the city of Siracusa is Castello di Euryalos; these are enormous ruins of what is left of a huge fortress complex built to defend the city against the Romans. A system of walls, castles, trenches and tunnels extending for about sixteen miles were built. As the Scottish poet Robert Burns sadly noted many years later in his 1785 poem, "To a Mouse:"

> "The best laid schemes o' mice an' men /
> Gang aft a-gley" (Go often awry).

And so it went for Euryalos and ultimately, Siracusa. Those wily Romans attacked on a major holiday and the guards were probably off partying with the rest of the citizens of Siracusa, or else not paying as much attention as they should have been. So, the Romans conquered. The ruins here though are well worth viewing, and the splendid scene of the land below the ridge is justification alone for the drive out of town. We happily trudged among the fallen stones for more than an hour on several different trips, thinking of the enormous amount of labor that created this huge but failed enterprise. One cannot help but muse at how tourists in the year 3000 will look at our successes and failures whether in architecture or human relations. On a more pleasant and optimistic note, the almond blossoms we spied throughout the land below the ruins dispelled any more depressive thoughts.

The apartment we once rented a few miles outside of Siracusa was actually reflective of the two faces of Sicily; the first face like a patterned quilt of beauty and diligence, while the other face mirroring a small but significant segment of this island which has not caught up with, or may actually be purposely impeding progress.

The exterior of the building housing six apartments was most attractive with white stucco walls, a red tile roof, and surrounded by palm trees, flourishing plants and lush flowers. Facing the sea we observe fishermen at night from our balcony; they work in small boats glowing with intensive lights, harvesting what we guess are shellfish from the bay. During the daylight hours, parts of the city itself can be seen in the distance across the water; behind these stand white colored mountains which look snow covered, but in reality are the very pale grey of the local rock. When the wind is up, the bay waters stir up in a froth of white caps, reminding me of a highly decorated Sicilian cake. That is the reflection of the good part!

We have rented houses and apartments in Italy many, many times. We have not been disappointed or unduly surprised. Not until now. The refrigerator in this unit was moldy, and I mean on the inside; naked electric light bulbs hung from bare wires in the kitchen. The dishwasher was unusable; I could live with that, but it would have made any typical Board of Health official resign his position or order several arrests were he to peer into it. The owner tried to hide the small electric heater as she did not want it used. We understand that energy is terribly expensive in Italy, but it was understood in our contract before we left the States that we would have its use.

The bathroom had a shower, but the shower curtain closed in only a small part of it and missed the bottom by four inches. Hence, when one showered, even quickly which was actually necessary as the hot water heater was VERY small, the commode and surrounding walls got soaked, as did the floor. A marvel of design and engineering it wasn't. The base was less than two inches deep, resulting in a bathroom in which Noah would have felt at home.

This rental, I must admit, was the only one we have ever felt was totally unrepresentative of the company's catalogue description; we have rented from them many times before with no problems, but I guess no one bats a thousand! Roger's comment as we departed was that this was as close to camping as he would ever get. Obviously we are not of the tent and campfire crowd. On our next trip to Siracusa six months later, we resided in a hotel. I would rent again in Siracusa, but probably would retain the option of eye-balling it first. A post script to this experience is that when the new catalogue of rentals arrived, we observed that this particular unit is no longer listed with them. No doubt other renters were as disenchanted as we. But, that too is part of the adventure of travel!

The Villa del Casale just outside of the town of Piazza Armerina is a site no visitor to Sicily should ever miss. This Roman villa, covered by a landslide for centuries, was re-discovered in 1950; it houses forty mosaics from the third century C.E. Incredibly huge and stunningly beautiful, these works of art created from tiny stones or tesserae, depict Hercules, Odysseus and the Cyclops, huge African animals, local animals, a children's hunt, chariot races, and the "Bikini Girls," which by *Playboy* standards, is quite innocent. Archeologists write that this building is the best preserved as well as the largest Roman structure in Sicily.

Although I took many pictures of the fantastic and incredibly wrought mosaics, I found that the dozens of postcards of these works of art were infinitely better than my photographs, and I would suggest that anyone who would like picture souvenirs of these unique creations might be better off investing in some cards photographed by professionals.

We made several afternoon excursions to Caltagirone, the city of ceramics, as we tend to re-visit places we have enjoyed, some, many, many times. Within the town center is a famous staircase, *La Scala,* which is vast and replete with ceramic tiles; its one hundred and forty-two steps lead up to the town's cathedral. Begun in 1606, the stairs were re-done in 1884 and finished in historic tiles in 1954 and represent the town's history from the tenth century.

The staircase tiles are colored with vivid yellows and blues and reflect not only the Christian and the Moorish history of Caltigirone, but the political history as well. The ceramic arts are said to have begun in this area about four thousand years ago. The Moorish influence is readily recognized throughout this interesting, artistic city by the ubiquitous display of ceramic "Moor heads," one male and the other female. Throughout the city at various places, ceramic pieces are inserted into public places, villas and the cemetery.

Many stores, including one which was the size of a large supermarket representing many individual workshops, offer thousands of pieces of ceramics for sale. I am very fond of Italian ceramics, too fond perhaps, as I invariably end up hand-carrying pieces back to my home, especially if the pieces are not expensive. Naturally, for very large and/or expensive pieces, there are many excellent transport services which efficiently take care of this. These capable companies have often delivered the purchased treasures to our home before we have returned. As I think of this, I look around our house and see more than one hundred items from Italy collected over thirty years; oil paintings, prints, posters, ceramic pitchers, platters, dishes, bowls, vases, items designed to be hung on walls, busts of Dante and David, small statues of the Capestrano Warrior, the Venus of Siracusa, the Etruscan "Ombra Della Sera," three sculptures of *cinghales* or wild boars, and embedded in the walls of our kitchen, twenty-seven tiles collected from centers throughout Italy.

Our next destination was Palermo, but we planned on stopping in Enna en route, located in the center of Sicily. The highway from Siracusa to Palermo through the heart of *Triarcia*, which is the word often used to describe this triangularly shaped island, is nothing short of fantastic. Bridges over land, supported by hundreds of concrete pillars as high, or seemingly as high as the Washington Monument, convey the cars through scenery as old as mankind.

The guide books were effusive in describing Enna as an almost impregnable city, which, because of its location, managed to fend off invaders many times through history; it is the highest provincial capital in Italy. From its perch one is able to see for miles in all directions. Populated long before the Greeks, it took great effort for many years to subjugate these people to Greek rule. On the day of our first visit it was cold and the wind was howling. A friendly, older man approached us and although the language barrier was difficult, we both managed to communicate. He was an amateur collector of foreign currencies; taking his wallet from his jacket, he showed us money from Japan, France, Germany, Denmark, the United Kingdom and Canada. He asked us if we had a coin with President John F. Kennedy's image. We didn't, but we took his name and address, and we sent him one when we returned home. From the *belvedere,* or a high point which overlooks the scenery, he pointed out the neighboring city of Caltanissetta across the valley as well as of Lake Pergusa, site of the classic tale of Persephone's abduction.

This charming man, a self-appointed helper and guide to tourists, recommended a local restaurant and we had yet, another super meal. The owner of what we think is the best restaurant in Rome and who is also a very good personal friend of ours, suggested that when in Sicily we should emphasize all kinds of fish, eggplant, pizza and pasta in our diets as no one does these things better than the Sicilians.

I ordered the special of the day, a rich lasagne containing small pieces of eggplant, and to me the most exciting, peas! This brought back happy memories of my grandfather's lasagne. He always put peas in this dish, although I have never seen this in any recipe or cookbook, nor have I had it in any restaurant in Italy in thirty years of visiting and touring in that country. I used to insert peas into the lasagne I made when my children were young, but abandoned the practice when I realized they spent more time separating the tiny green vegetables from the pasta than eating it. I decided on the spot in that restaurant in Enna that from now on, peas would be a part of this dish in my kitchen!

Palermo, a city almost impossible to describe, is at once, ethereal and eerie; beautiful and mysterious; opulent, luxurious, full of art, juxtaposed with decay. The process of restoration and expunging detritus is slow, but very apparent to those who have been there three or four times. Progress, big time, is being made.

Arab and Norman are obvious and continuous influences in architecture, habit and menu. The Greek influence so predominant in eastern Sicily and especially Siracusa, does not exist here in this city of contrasts and remembered splendor.

We had reservations at a comfortable, large hotel facing the sea. We had stayed here on our first trip many years before, as well as having had a most happily remembered dinner in the beautiful dining room when we were renting a house in nearby Terrasini two years before, so we knew what to expect and were ready to be pampered! And we were. It was more than comforting with excellent dining, a lobby with soft upholstered chairs and couches, a lavish bathroom with no end of the hot water supply, and moreover, a wonderful view! This to soothe us after our somewhat stressful rental apartment accommodations in Siracusa! The staff were all so friendly, warm and helpful. Another stay here seven months later however found the hotel in somewhat of a chaotic period. It was being restored and refurbished and the facilities were minimal. I am certain that by now its condition is not only improved, but is better and more attractive then ever. Such are the experiences of travel, and those who journey must expect setbacks from time to time. We've made reservations for this hotel for four months from now and we're confident that it has returned to excellence.

The beach in front of the hotel was immaculate; after we returned home two months later, I looked at the photo album from our first journey to Palermo in 1971. The views were remarkably changed. Previously the beach was littered with refuse and cluttered with unsavory huts housing vagrants. Now it was empty of anything unclean or tacky. This is one example of the strides taken by the local government to improve the quality of life for the residents as well as the encouraging of tourists, which, most importantly, boosts the local economy.

I had compiled a list of sites and monuments we had not seen in Palermo on our previous expeditions in this city, and we decided that the most efficient way to visit these places would be to hire a guide. The hotel arranged that we meet with "Jake." It was a fortuitous encounter. He was a fount of knowledge, had a sense of humor, spoke excellent English, knew the ins and outs of the wild traffic patterns of the city, drove a comfy, amply sized Fiat, and took us directly to each destination.

We first went to the Cathedral, or *Duomo*. Begun in 1185, and drastically restructured in the eighteenth century, it was a tad disappointing. I began to think that perhaps I was getting jaded from an overdose of the splendors of Italian art, architecture and antique monuments, but abandoned that thought as we next stopped at the Norman Palace. Although much of the building is used by the regional parliament, the Palatine Chapel is a jewel!

I must interrupt myself at this point to mention that my husband Roger's ancestry is almost wholly Anglo-Saxon, with perhaps a touch of French. Not one drop of Italian blood! But, don't ever mention that as you will incur his deep displeasure; more than that however, you will subject yourself to a lecture on the genealogical studies on which his late uncle labored, which shows that his ancestors, or at least one of them, supposedly crossed the English channel with William the Conqueror. Those Normans really got around in the Middle Ages and when they

ruled Sicily, both the first and second kings were named, "Roger!"
From that, with much more than a gigantic leap of faith mixed
with a suspension of disbelief, my Roger is convinced in his own
mind that somewhere in his background he has Norman/Sicilian
blood. Recently he has even added Tuscany to that combination!
He is so enamored of Italy that he convinced himself that his
small French part is actually Norman, and that somehow, way,
way back, his own forebears came to Sicily. One of our daughters
attributes this kind of reasoning to the fact that for many years
we lived in an old Victorian house which probably had water
pipes made of lead, and we all know what lead can do to the
brain! But, I digress.

The man responsible for the Norman Palace was King Roger
II, a person without peer in his toleration and acceptance of
other races, religions and cultures. One notably visible part of
this broad-mindedness is his use of Arab, Greek, Roman and
Norman artisans to create the exquisite chapel with its mosaics,
carved wood ceiling, inlaid floors and pulpit of marble.

Monreale was the high point of our day's tour. This cathedral
was built by William the Good; (there was also a William the
Bad, but that's another story). The "Good" William was married
to Joanna, the daughter of Henry II of England; I think Henry
is one of the most interesting historical figures of the medieval
period, but that could be because my favorite film has always been
THE LION IN WINTER which deals with him, his incredible
wife, Eleanor of Aquitaine, and their passel of squabbling sons,
Richard the Lion-Hearted, Geoffrey, and John, who years later
was forced to sign the Magna Carta.

"Good" William told of a vision he experienced of the Virgin
at Monreale, and in gratitude decided to build this magnificent
edifice. He had gotten permission from Pope Alexander III, but in

doing so had gone over the head of the local Archbishop, Walter of the Mill, who was so angered by this flagrant omission of observing the chain of command that he began building his "own" cathedral in Palermo. Politics yet again; nothing ever changes.

The mosaics in Monreale are stupendous and cover areas so huge that they are hard to imagine without actually being there to view and experience them. Old and New Testament stories are portrayed as well as wondrous figures of Jesus, Mary, angels and saints. The colors glow; the burnished gold remains forever in the eye of the observer. I would return there again and again. And, we have.

Magnificent is the only apt adjective to describe the cloister of Monreale. It was partially swathed in scaffolding for restoration, but even that did not detract from the beauty of the harmonious design. Each column is decorated with entwined mosaics twisting upward in a serpentine design. The carved capitals use a motif of nature; these are a tribute from the sculptors and artisans who used the world about them as inspiration.

Now for the macabre. I had heard of the Catacombs of the Cappuccini, but frankly I was totally unprepared for the spectacle presented there. Approximately eight thousand bodies are mummified and on permanent display. These corpses were preserved beginning in the 1500's, with the last one processed in the 1920's! The remains are creatively and imaginatively arranged, if that could be an accurate description, and are displayed in categories. Thus, there are rooms containing only the bodies of priests, or rooms of lawyers and other professionals, or of friars, of men, or women. Many infants and children are among the preserved in this strange panorama. Jake told us that it was very expensive to be mummified, and that only the most affluent families afforded this special treatment. I was half afraid I would dream of these leathery, skeletal and very bizarre bodies when I went to sleep that evening, but fortunately, whether from the excellent pasta or fine Sicilian wine, I slept the almost dreamless sleep of the contented.

We inquired about the opera; ever since seeing the film, JOHNNY STECCHINO, starring the extremely talented man, Roberto Benigni and his wife, the beautiful Nicoletta Braschi, in which an hilarious episode occurs in the opera house, we have wanted to attend the Palermo opera. Unfortunately there were no performances scheduled for the time we were there, but that gives us one more reason to return again, as if we needed any!

An hour or two spent at the International Museum of Marionettes, established in 1975, is a joy. Displayed are figures from the major areas of Italy where these kinds of shows were once a major source of entertainment; additionally, there are puppets from Asia, Africa and Oceania. The puppets or marionettes varied in size as well as in how they were manipulated. Some were twenty-four inches high while others were nearly life sized. Strings controlled many while others were moved by rods held by their handlers from the sides of the stage. The most popular stories dramatized by these shows were those of medieval knights in the requisite shining armor as they pursued what they perceived to be chivalric causes, and of their always, or almost always, virtuous ladies. The "good" guys fought the "bad" guys; in entertainments from puppetry to popular cinema, it seems only the technology changes from era to era. We enjoyed the visit here very much, and although we missed a real performance, we intend to see one on our next visit. Another reason to return.

I recently had become interested in the work of the late Sicilian artist Renato Guttuso and wanted to see his painting of the markets of Palermo, the famous, *Vuccirria,* where everything is bought and sold from fish to vegetables and bicycle parts to chickpea pancakes. I knew that the *Galleria d'Arte Moderna* in Bagheria was the gallery most associated with him and contained many of his paintings. After leaving Palermo we drove to Bagheria and found the impressive old villa that housed the art. The paintings were spectacular, but the one I most wanted to see, "The *Vuccirria*" was not here as it was held by the University of Palermo. One of the curators sniffed as she told me that the university just wouldn't give it up, although it really belonged here. There was a small bookshop next to the gallery, but, alas, no books with Guttuso's work. Postcards of his paintings were not available or didn't exist, nor did they have any prints. This is an example of where the Sicilians must catch up. I cannot imagine a museum without a supply of items for sale in its bookstore; if for nothing else, good income is derived from these shops which must help to defray the cost of upkeep and insurance so necessary for the preservation of the often priceless art. Galleries in the Italian north have learned this and at each I've been to in the past ten years or so, there are items for sale from postcards to very expensive reproductions of some of the most famous works in that particular museum. Not until 1993 were Italian museums permitted by law to have concessions for tea rooms or book and souvenir shops within their confines. Since these have been added, the income from these businesses has been adding great amounts of money to the culture ministry. Italy was slow to enter this trend, so widespread in the United States and the United Kingdom, because the Italian government always funded the museums; this type of funding, for the most part was non-existent in the US and UK. My guess is that this will happen in Sicily before much more time elapses; the revenues generated are difficult to resist.

A fortuitous note on my quest for a book of this artist's work: Four weeks later as we were walking through Rome, I spied a large book in the window of the Rizzoli bookstore. Eureka! GUTTUSO on its cover! We immediately went in and purchased it, and finally I got to see the painting I had wanted to for so long. Its fabulous depiction of the food in the market includes swordfish, squid, shrimp, eggs, Romano cheeses, mortadella, mozzarella, olives, fennel, peppers, a hanging carcass of meat, bananas, oranges, pears, and so much more. Women in the market are carrying bags of items they have purchased; the men are the vendors—one is slicing off a piece of meat from the carcass. Naturally, seeing the reproduction is not the same as viewing the original painting, but that's another reason, probably about number five hundred and seventy-two, I believe, that we must return, and in the time between, I can always get the feeling of the famous market by looking at my Guttuso book.

Having just written about all that attractive and delectable food, I must confess to having abandoned this text for about four hours so that I could prepare twelve quarts of my pasta sauce, or as my grandchildren call it, "Nanny's sauce." In Tuscany it would be called *ragu,* and in many homes of people with Italian ancestry in New York, New Jersey and New England, it's known simply as "gravy." Then I made another *ragu* with *porcini* mushrooms recommended by Frances Mayes in the May, 2000 edition of BON APPETIT, and pleased with these efforts, followed up with a pot of pasta *fagioli,* or pasta and bean soup. The sauce and soup should keep us happy for more than a few days! Both will be put into plastic quart containers and then into the freezer for quick, delicious dinners especially during the next month when we expect most of the ten grandchildren to visit.

The idea of food brings another super memory; about five years ago we rented a lovely villa on the Castellammare del Golfo, a sparkling bay so blue, so perfect, it was difficult to look away from it. Nonetheless, one must eat and I found myself in a small supermarket in Terrasini. After choosing such things as I felt I needed for making a picnic lunch for the following day, I decided that boneless chicken breasts, sauteed in oil and flavored with white wine, lemon and capers would be perfect for sandwiches. I walked to the meat section, which in reality was like a butcher shop from the past; as a young child I remember going with my Scottish grandmother to a similar shop in Paterson, New Jersey. I pointed to the breasts of chicken in the glass case and indicated by holding up fingers, that I would like two. The butcher, by clever gesturing, asked me if I would like them sliced. I would, and he did. It was an unbelievable and marvelous scene; he took a huge knife in hand, and quickly and seemingly effortlessly, sliced each breast in almost paper thin, horizontal slices. I had never seen such artistry; I had watched a master! I thanked him, we exchanged big smiles and I went back to our rental and cooked them. The best part was in the eating; tender, fresh, delicious chicken; no hormones, antibiotics or tricks. Simply chicken the way chicken should be!

Many first time tourists to Sicily visit Taormina. This town survives on the tours as well as on the individuals who visit here. Without sounding like a crank, or hoping I don't sound that way, as lovely as Taormina is, and its views are truly breath taking, to me it isn't the real Sicily nor is it genuinely Italian. I am sure it used to be. We heard more French, German and English spoken than Italian. Nevertheless, each time I return to the magnificent Greek theater overlooking the water, with Mount Etna in the background, I am ready to change my mind. It is so outstandingly gorgeous that it boggles my mind and stirs my soul. Standing at the top of the theater where the uppermost seats are carved, I believe it would not have been necessary for a patron to see a drama; the view is enough. It is all.

On one trip to Taormina our hotel room overlooked the Bay of Schiso; as I stared down at its exquisite blueness, a strange feeling overcame me. This began to happen each time I quietly watched the sea, so ethereal and mysterious. I knew that I would not be surprised if Odyssesus' ship were to appear, in fact, I expected it to appear. The clever Ithacan, should he materialize, would be a natural in these Ionian waters. Although I live by the sea in Massachusetts, I would never, ever expect to see him sail by and show up there. Although known as the inveterate traveler, simply he is not the Cape Cod type. So, I look out to the Sicilian waters and dream and fantasize about his sails becoming visible on the horizon. No Penelope I; one who barely manages to hide her sentimental side under a very thin veneer of intellect. This is a confession from one who has never admitted publically that each time she sees the film, the play, or reads ROMEO AND JULIET, she secretly hopes that this time Friar Laurence's message will get to Romeo before his servant Balthasar does. So far, in our many stops in Taormina, Odyssesus has remained elusive. Perhaps next time his ship will appear.

I had read of the town, Erice, in Alfonso Lowe's fascinating book of Sicily, THE BARRIER AND THE BRIDGE—HISTORIC SICILY, and after telling Roger about the mystery and unique qualities of this place, we decided to go there. First of all, it is very high; a long, but perfectly built road wends its way to the town almost 2500 feet above sea level. Lowe states that it is enveloped in fog at least eighty days every year, fog thick enough to barely see anything in front of you. He was correct. Although it was totally clear with bright sunshine when we began the ascent, the fog crashed in as we hit the top. There are a number of very tall communications towers in the town, and though we were directly in front of them, they were totally blocked out by this cotton-ball vapor.

As we began to walk through the town, it was immediately apparent that this was like no other place we had ever been.

I remembered seeing science fiction movies in which towns, though standing, are totally without inhabitants. This was Erice; it seemed totally devoid of people. The quiet was other-worldly. Italian towns are not quiet; life is going on. Children play soccer in the streets, women gossip, men discuss politics, often loudly. Not here. No kids, no adults, no noise. Then I noticed something else that made this place again totally different from anything I had ever seen in Sicily or Italy. There was no laundry hanging to dry on any line anywhere. Clothing and linens on ropes hung from windows is constant all through Italy; dryers take too much expensive electricity to operate for the vast majority of people, so everywhere, clothing, sheets and towels flap in the breeze. Not here. Where were the wet clothes? Were they sent to laundries in Trapani? Were there special rooms to hide these damp items? A mystery wrapped in an enigma.

The streets were composed of stones in the most unusual and startling pattern I had ever encountered. The guidebooks described them as an intricate style designed in the 19th century by a German engineer. The design could have been created or used on quilts, table linens or draperies—it was that beautiful and it continued throughout all the streets.

It was time for our morning ritual of *cappuccini,* but we couldn't find a bar. This is almost unheard of in Italy; every tiny hamlet has at least one bar, often more, and Erice was not that small. Finally, we spied not a bar, but a restaurant; it was closed, but generously they agreed to serve us our morning coffee treat. It was very good; the price was quite a bit more than we usually paid, but they went out of their way to do us a favor. It was understandable.

As we further explored the town we finally did find a bar. Over a second coffee, we began chatting with the barman who became ever more friendly when he found out we were Americans. This is a common phenomenon we have discovered; I don't know the exact percentage, but an enormous number of Southern Italians have relatives in the United States, and therefore they tend to be friendlier toward Americans than they are to people from countries in Europe. Many Italian nationals, even those from the north, have told us that generally, we from the USA, tend to be friendly and straight forward; many Europeans tend to be class conscious and shy away from chatting on an equal basis with people such as barmen, waiters, and chambermaids. Americans tend to assess others on competence and personality and not on "class." Being a nation of immigrants, most of us have only to look back two, three or more generations to see where we have come from. With very few exceptions, it was the poor, the downtrodden, the hungry and those looking to better their lives who left homelands to come to the New World. The European aristocracy, the wealthy, the comfortable did not journey to Ellis Island.

Our genial barman told us that Erice was a scientific center and that scientists from all over the world convene here to study such things as seismological events, mad-cow disease, global warming and other topics which affect all world populations. We thought he was exaggerating a bit to promote the excellence of his town, but after leaving his establishment, we found a building, "*Centro Di Cultura Scientificae Maiorama*" and paper notices on the wall which stated, often in English, the dates and titles of upcoming seminars and conventions. There are one hundred "Schools" covering different branches of science. These are attended by scientists from all over the world. I imagine it would be an interesting place for specialists to spend time and listen to others in various fields of study. This international study center was named for the Italian physicist who was born in Sicily in 1906.

I must admit that although we walked around this town extensively, we did not examine the recommended churches. At this point we both were feeling a bit of artistic mental indigestion, and being neither art historians nor archeologists, we began to get a bit foggy on the origins of the lesser known church art works. Was this a fresco by a visiting Byzantine, or was that the one done by Fra Fillipo's younger cousin's pupil?

After we left Erice we drove down the western coast of Sicily to an area where sea water is evaporated for salt just as it has been done for centuries. Huge piles of salt are stacked by the score, and some have tiled roofs covering this recovered product of the sea. Graceful windmills used for grinding salt, and large pens containing sea water were fascinating, and I kept snapping the shutter on my camera. This salt center was located between Trapani and Marsala. Near Marsala at the westernmost point of Sicily, there is a monument showing where Garibaldi landed to begin his quest for freeing and uniting Italy, "Rome or Death."

A day trip from anywhere near Palermo might be to the majestic, if mysterious temple at Segesta. This Doric temple was never completely finished, but is very well-preserved. The columns are not fluted, nor were the stairs finished. No one knows for certain why work was abandoned about four hundred years, B.C.E., but it was. This ancient city was a long-standing rival of Selinus, or Seliunte, and some historians have argued that the cause of its not being finished involved a political fiasco involving the Siracusans, the Athenians and the Carthaginians; however, it is a magnificent structure and one that although incomplete, has withstood the ravages of countless wars and earthquakes; if Greek, or at least temples of Greek design are of interest to one, Segesta should not be missed.

While on the subject of temples, the ancient ruins of Seliunte must be mentioned. This is the site of another prosperous ancient city on the southwest coast of Sicily which was originally founded by colonists from a city near Siracusa. Totally devastated in 409 B.C.E. by the Carthaginians and Segestans, it was rebuilt and then again destroyed in 250 B.C.E. and again by the Carthaginians. The ruins, lost for centuries, have gradually been uncovered, although most of the buildings not destroyed by conquest, have been, if not demolished, severely damaged by earthquakes. We were there for the first time of several visits on a gorgeous day, sunny and warm, but not too hot, happily wandering among the ruins. Below, the sea glistened in the sun; it was a perfect day in Sicily; I wondered what the day might have been like at the moment it was annihilated and its citizens slaughtered more than two thousand years ago.

The excavated ruins include the remains of five temples on the acropolis and three more on the east part of what was the ancient city. These are excellent examples of Doric Greek architecture from the Archaic period. One huge monument is among the largest known. Looking out into the water, we suddenly spotted a huge water spout; its hugeness and intensity bordered on the supernatural, and so, it seemed perfectly in harmony with the devastated majesty of Seliunte.

Sicily is a most worth-while destination. It will confuse and at times annoy you, but you will never forget its beauty, its sensuality, its mystery. An overflowing dumpster or plastic bottles washed up on a deserted, but otherwise perfect beach will cause you anger, but, at the same time, just around the corner, you might find a bar replete with marble counters, crystal chandeliers and yards and yards of glistening glass cases filled with the most opulent pastries, cakes, sweets, and confections you have ever dreamed of, and then discover ice creams in more flavors than you ever knew existed. This will give you pause. What is the real Sicily? Can you believe marzipan candies shaped and colored to look exactly like fruit, even to the half peeled skin on a banana? Chocolates created in shape and color to look like screw drivers, wrenches, hammers, files and keys? And vegetable and fruit markets which are arranged as if done by an old master, or at the very least, an impressionist. My photo albums are filled with as many pictures of the opulence of Sicilian food displays as they are of monuments. Many are framed and remind me to return as soon as possible!

And then it dawns on you. A people who have been so invaded, repressed, robbed and hurt by thousands of years of ever-changing governments have not developed as much concern for what is public as for what is private. In the classic novel of Sicily, THE LEOPARD, Giuseppe Lampedusa writes:

> ". . . we Sicilians have become accustomed, by a long, a very long hegemony of rulers who were not of our religion, and who did not speak our language, to split hairs."

Therefore, one's own table, or home, or land is cherished, cared for, nurtured, just as one's children are, while perhaps, what is not mine is not my concern. These attitudes were not created in a day or a year, but over centuries, and just as they were not made quickly, they will not disappear quickly. In fact, however, they are disappearing, and as we've noticed in repeated visits, the public officials together with the people are making a major concerted effort at making public places as attractive and perfected as the homes of the inhabitants. For even deeper meanings one must again go to Lampedusa.

> ". . . The Sicilians never want to improve for the simple reason that they think themselves perfect; . . . having been trampled on by a dozen different peoples, they consider they have an imperial past which gives them a right to a grand funeral."

Many new billboards adorn the highways on the mainland promoting tourism to this special island. Often, but not always in English, they proclaim:

"SICILY: ISLAND IN A SEA OF LIGHT."

It is, and is also an experience one will never forget, nor want to. Goethe lived and wrote here and his words still ring true about Sicily being the key to the rest of Italy.

A word of advice: Hurry if you want to see Sicily without the masses of tourists common to Florence, Rome or Venice. Sicily has lagged behind these popular destinations, but change is occurring and it's happening quite rapidly. We noticed this in the mid 1990's after an absence of more than ten years and even more in the following years; the billboards on the mainland were appearing more often and beckoning holiday seekers, and now tour groups are frequently seen. The changes began moderately, but recently, new hotels are being built, others renovated; archeological sites are being made more "tourist friendly;" main roads have been improved; the city streets are tidier; extra flights have been scheduled from northern cities; Sicily is constantly getting ready for the next invasion. Fortunately this one will be by tourists who will invigorate their economy. This enterprise will benefit so many from the major players to the postcard and ceramic vendors, the restaurant workers, and all the people who have worked so very hard to give this beautiful and often unfairly maligned island a piece of the tourist dollar, pound and euro as we go forward through the new millennium.

The time had come once more for us to say *"arriverderci"* to this unforgettable island, but not the end of our original quest.

There were almond blossoms to follow.

SICILY—THE UNFATHOMABLE

Sicily, largest island in the sea
Mediterranean, is real and yet
Surreal, but historically unreal.
Blasted by invasion, occupation,
But blessed by sun, the sea and fertile lands,
It endures and endures; an enigma
Puzzle, conundrum. It's experienced
Cruelty and kindness; evil and good;
Blemish and beauty; poverty and wealth;
Exhaustion and endurance; dark and light;
Abomination and tolerance. All
Words describing this unique, special niche.

Earliest known settlers, the "Siculi"
Erased by Greeks, then Carthaginians,
Romans, Byzantines, Arabs, and Normans.
The dynasty of Frederic II,
Brought literature, poetry, science.
The House of Aragon, Savoy and more
Descending to corruption and misrule
Begat Sicilian peoples, so repressed,
To become outcasts, bandits without law.
Not until great Garibaldi arrived
And made Sicily part of Italy
Did unity, peace and some prevailing
Order arrive. Live on, blessed island!

The temples of Agrigento, Greek made,
As well as those of Seliunte, and
Segesta inspire awe, and honor to
Those who conceived and built them eons past.
Grand Palermo, still reminiscent of

The past Arab and Norman peoples who
Lived and ruled here and enriched the arts, laws,
As well as diets of the populace.
The Cathedral inspires; Monreale's
Majesty happily removes one's breath.
Siragusa is Greek in origin;
The Theater, the Ear of Dionysius,
Euryalos Castle and Ortygia Isle
Are all inheritances of the Greek.
Sicily is more; Caltigerone,
Ceramic city; Erice, high, and
Notably scientific. Mosaics
Within Piazza Armerina will
Never be lost within one's memory.
The macabre is not omitted; visit
The Catacombs of the Cappucini!
This visit will create shivers, perhaps
Even nightmares! For an interesting
And pleasant antidote, *Vucciria*,
The vast, amazing market, with food,
Clothing, tools, spices, electronics and
Everything else one could want or desire.
Sicilian ice cream is like none other,
The pastries, seafood, and pasta Norma
Would make an ascetic question his choice.
For the pleasure seeking tourist, there is
Taormina filled with deluxe hotels,
Restaurants, the intact huge Greek Theater
Looking out to views and magnificence
Of the surrounding and glorious sea
Sicily is all that and so much more.
It must be seen and lived to be believed
And worth every exciting moment there.

ITALIAN CHILDREN

"One always hopes that the children—that things will turn out better for them. That's what children are."

From GOAT ISLAND by Ugo Betti

"'Tis not good that children should know any wickedness."

From THE MERRY WIVES OF WINDSOR,
II, 2 by William Shakespeare

"If men do not keep on speaking terms with children, they cease to be men, and become merely machines for eating and for earning money."

From "A Foreword for Younger Readers,"
ASSORTED PROSEby John Updike

At a party several years ago I overheard a middle-aged man say that after he died, he hoped to be reincarnated as an Italian baby. This caused a thought pattern to emerge in my brain about a book I had been assigned to read in Modern British Fiction class about thirty years ago.

I had not thought about E.M. Forster's novel WHERE ANGELS FEAR TO TREAD in ages, but obviously the theme remained in my consciousness; not until I became a regular visitor to Italy, did Forster's central idea, that children in Italy are loved deeply and truly, become a vivid reality.

In this sad and somewhat grim tale, written when the author was still in his twenties, the relatives of an English woman married to an Italian man of whom they never approved, decide to kidnap the infant boy born to this couple after the young English mother died in childbirth. Arrogantly believing that only in England could the child be brought up "correctly," which no doubt he deserved since his mother was English, prompted their decision. Assuming that what they considered to be proper child rearing would be impossible in their imaginative notion of Italy's sensuous atmosphere, which would preclude the formation of the stiff upper lip of the archetypal Englishman, these two British in-laws embark on their nefarious journey to Italy in hopes of "buying" the child from the father at best, or "stealing" him if necessary.

A young English woman who becomes involved with these strange two poses the central question after spending some time watching the father of the baby relate to his son. She sees the baby being lovingly bathed by his father, who simultaneously happens to be smoking a cigar. A few ashes actually drop into the water. In spite of this, when the reality of the situation becomes blatantly apparent to her, she says to the would-be abductors:

> "Do you want the child to stop with his father, who loves him and who will bring him up badly, or do you want him to come to Sawston (England), where no one loves him, but where he will be brought up well?"

Chapter VIII, p. 150

It is a given that in Victorian and early post-Victorian England, British subjects believed that only they were capable of "bringing up" a child properly. Even Forster, who recognized the difference between those who can love a child and those who cannot, still gives the edge to the British educational style. Perhaps in the matter of education that might have been true eighty or ninety years ago, but in the area of love, the Italians, who are not afraid to display affection and have always been the givers of love, are seen in the novel as kinder and more generous with children.

Italians adore children! How I have admired the intense affection and pride these people have always had in their children! Presently, as the economy is better than ever before, these lucky kids are beautifully dressed, given good, positive attention, are valued and treasured. In every city and town babies are paraded in the finest of strollers, covered with the most attractive blankets, and are stopped by admiring relatives, friends and even strangers who effusively praise the child and his parents on the beauty and excellence of this wondrous little being. They "talk" to the child with a cooing, comforting sound and often are rewarded by a smiling infant. The baby "knows" he is a *principe* (prince) or she is a *princippessa* (princess). May it ever continue!

I certainly do not mean to imply that the millions of loving parents in the rest of the world are negligent, but it is often apparent their love is reserved in nature and not joyously proclaimed. This is a result of a culture difference, but the results are enormous and so apparent. Italian infants and children are thoroughly steeped in affection and saturated with praise; their foibles are tolerated and accepted.

Many years ago Roger and I were in a hotel in Taormina, Sicily. We were sitting at a small table on a huge veranda which overlooked the sea. Sipping a before dinner *prosecco* and enjoying a taste of the olives and crackers the waiter thoughtfully had brought out for us, we were enjoying the ambiance of the early summer evening. Suddenly a large wedding party came out on to this attractive, cantilevered deck. Everyone was exquisitely dressed. After a few minutes we noted that four young girls, about six or seven years old and as elegantly attired as the adults, were among the guests. They kept eyeing what I thought at first was us, but what turned out to be the snacks on our table. They edged nearer; finally I caught the gist of their maneuvers and offered them olives. Two of the braver ones came slowly forward, then quickly snatched up the contents of both dishes and dashed off to share the "loot" with the other two. None of the adults seemed to notice, though they probably did. It simply was not important. How refreshing that anyone who did notice, realized that they were children and that they were hungry! I wondered how many children in other countries would have been scolded for this behavior. I then realized how wonderful it was that these youngsters were included in this wedding party and felt free of guilt for begging a few olives! This was the first time in my life that I had even seen children at a wedding. And why not? Is this not a part of life, and especially, if it is a relative's wedding to whom they will relate for years?

I am proud to disclose that when our youngest child was married, both she and the groom included their very young niece and four young nephews among the wedding guests. One six year old boy and the four year old girl were part of the wedding party as ring bearer and flower girl and both discharged their duties with distinction. And, I might add, with great enjoyment and pride! It added to the happiness of the entire celebration, not only for me as grandmother, but for the parents of these children as well. How can children become real parts of an extended family if they are systematically excluded from its important celebrations? The Italian people, bless them, have always understood the real, and not the phony meaning of true family values!

We were thrilled and privileged to have been invited to a
wedding in Urbania, Italy a few years ago. We had not planned on
a trip at that time as we had recently returned, and furthermore,
we were planning an extended trip seven months later. But this
was a once in a lifetime opportunity we reasoned, and off we were
for a quick ten day jaunt. I shall be grateful for that experience
forever! Among the wedding guests were two infants, each
about one year old, and more beautifully attired babies no one
could imagine. These two were passed around among parents,
grandparents, aunts, uncles, cousins and friends during the course
of the day. Neither baby cried or fussed; they weren't stressed and
neither were the adults who related to them. They were fed, and
when tired, happily slept in the arms of a doting relative, secure
and loved. Being incorporated into family events, whether joyous
ones or sad, is a part of their lives, and age does not preclude being
with those who celebrate or who mourn.

Among other wedding guests, we were seated at a table with
a young couple. Their then six year old daughter was with them;
no one would have imagined that she would have been excluded.
Not only are the child relatives of the bride and groom invited,
but so are the children of friends.

We were privileged once again to be included in a wedding, or
"matrimonio" in Tuscany. Among the two hundred guests were
children from three months of age to some in their late teens.
The babies were wheeled into the church in strollers, the toddlers
moved freely about during the ceremony and no one appeared
to notice that this was anything but simply a typical happening.
At the reception, which lasted for more than eight hours, I never
heard a child cry or complain. The pre-teens danced, the nursery
school age children danced with their parents, the teens thoroughly
enjoyed themselves and the parents, grandparents, aunts, uncles
and various cousins wore expressions of vast contentment and

pride as they surveyed the happy scene of a delightful celebration. I attempted to speak to a boy of about ten but was thwarted until his nineteen year old cousin, fluent in English, translated for us. We ended our "conversation" by dancing to the music of the talented and lively musicians. I was amazed at the composure, grace and confidence of this youngster who felt no embarrassment while dancing with a grandmother of ten!

I once heard a mother of the bride in the United States go on and on about her own daughter's wedding plans, to the point at which I wondered if she thought it was she who was to be married and not her daughter. She was so concerned, almost obsessed, that considering the amount of money she was spending on the bride's dress, the decorations, flowers, food, wine, music, and all the other accouterments, that inviting children would somehow detract from the lavish display and show she was producing. Well, if she were arranging this wedding only for the purpose of ostentatiously displaying her wealth, she got it wrong, and the Italians have got it right. Yet again!

Wherever we have traveled through Italy I carry photos of my grandchildren. Of course I have some of my offspring too, but as they are no longer children, they are not as interesting. But my ten grandchildren—or "*dieci nepoti*"—well, I believe that about twenty per cent of the population of Italy have seen them! And they have "oohed" and "aahed"! Those sounds were genuine and filled with admiration. An empathetic feeling is at once apparent, and therefore an immediate compatibility emerges.

One evening before we were scheduled to fly home, we were seated at a family oriented restaurant near the airport Malpensa in Milan. While we were there I enjoyed a delightful grandmother experience. There were four dinner parties among the patrons as well as many couples like ourselves simply out for dinner or between planes. I was fascinated by one large family seated close by celebrating the birthday of a young girl of eleven or twelve. She looked so much like one of my granddaughters, not only in appearance, but in action and expression. Seated next to her was a little fellow of about four who was absolutely adorable. At Roger's urging I went over to say hello to the grandparents and to show them photos of our grandchildren. We both lacked much ability in each other's language, but the ideas and feelings for the *nepoti* or grandchildren, were universally understood. I greeted the birthday girl and said a few words to the small boy before I blew a kiss at him. At the end of the evening when we were ready to depart, I returned to their table, wished them well and said good-night. The young boy had his father bring him out to the front door so that he could kiss me good-bye at the door. I shall never forget that! A great gesture!

Children dine at restaurants with their parents and this includes all children from birth on. Babies are ensconced in strollers, or if unhappy, on someone's lap. Young children are always a part of the family life. We spent a wonderfully gastronomic evening with our good friends Daniella and Paolo and their two youngsters. The specialty of this elegant restaurant where we dined was fish, and fish we had, for six courses. These children, whose ages were five and seven, sat relaxed, devoured every variety of fish served, smiled and exhibited the demeanor of adults. Since that evening, we have spent two more evenings at different restaurants with this family and the results were similar.

Before the sobriety of the Lenten season, festivals occur in various parts of Italy; they are called "*Carnevale.*" Children are an integral part of these occasions, dressing up exactly as American children do on Hallowe'en. We happened to be in the city of Monopoli in Apulia on a Sunday around noon. Not being aware of this custom before, we were astonished at finding hundreds of people in the main piazza, almost all of whom were attached to a child or infant in spectacular costume. There were tiny Zorros, Supermen, Mickey or Minnie Mice, rabbits, tigers, leopards, Spanish dancers and little girls in huge hoop-skirted dresses who looked as if they were in a local production of GONE WITH THE WIND. Even toddlers and babies too small to walk were dressed in costume. Because it was still February and quite cold, although not nearly as cold as it would have been in Massachusetts where I live, these little people had special outfits which included heavy leg coverings as well as coats and hats appropriate to their chosen personas. Vendors were selling confetti which the kids were tossing around with gleeful abandon. Gluey, gummy substances, shot from aerosol cans, were delightedly aimed at each other by the pre-teen boys, who looked as if they ranged from eight to twelve years old. After emptying their cans, they then began impromptu soccer games with the containers as ball substitutes. No parent seemed uptight; the only shouts were of glee, and those were from the children. Then, suddenly at around one P.M., the piazza emptied, almost as if by a hidden signal; all the mothers, fathers and children left for Sunday dinner, probably at the grandparents' houses. The parents probably looked forward to enjoying a wonderful meal, and the children anticipated being admired in their resplendent costumes. Recently a young man from Rome visited us and related how many good memories he has of this event. His father had friends in Monopoli and as a young boy he celebrated *Carnevale* there with them for many years.

We were having dinner one evening in a very small *trattoria* in Calabria; this was during our first Italian trip many years ago but I shall never forget the human comedy of the episode. It was summer and it was hot! A child of about three years old sat alone at a table with a dish of macaroni in front of her. She proceeded to eat about half of it and then said something to her mother who was the only person waiting on tables at the time. I did not understand what she said, but evidently she told her mother she was thirsty and wanted something to drink. Mom brought her a glass of what looked like orange juice. The child screamed. Her mother tried to reason with her, but became frustrated. It continued. Finally, the father of the child appeared from the kitchen; he was the chef. He approached the child and in rapid Italian he asked her what the trouble was and evidently she told him. He then stormed over to the large, glass-fronted refrigerator, removed a bottle of beer, opened it, and put about one inch in a glass; he then filled the rest of the glass with mineral water and put it in front of the little girl who thanked him and immediately drained nearly all the liquid in the glass. The father then turned and scolded the mother, I suppose, for not seeing to his baby girl's wishes. It was a scene fit for a movie. We shall never forget the wonderfully satisfied look on the child as she had outwitted Mom and then Dad had come to the rescue!

Italian fashion has always been a hallmark feature known throughout the world. Exquisite design is apparent in clothing, shoes, handbags, leather goods, jewelry, furniture, ceramics and in so many other items. No where is this more apparent than in the proliferation of stores carrying clothing for infants and children. These stores are brimming with items so gorgeously wrought they defy the imagination. This is blatantly obvious as so many babies and young children are dressed as if they were going to be photographed for a magazine cover. Older children, especially teenagers, are seen in designer jeans, blouses and jackets;many of the high fashion jeans are worn by Italian teens a full season or even a year before they become the "in" mode in the United States.

One evening, seated next to a large family at a restaurant overlooking Lake Como, we enjoyed part of their fun. There were three young people among them; two teenagers and a boy of approximately ten. The youngster had something in his hand which one of the older children took from him and then passed to an adult who in turn passed it until it was impossible to know who had it. Everyone was laughing; the boy ran from person to person to examine their hands as each pretended that he had the object. We decided to join the fun; Roger pretended he had the secret item, then I did and so on until finally the child retrieved it from a grandparent's hand. We were curious to see what this "precious" object was. A chestnut! We all laughed including the young boy who recovered his prize. I told them I thought it was a gold piece the way he went after it. Children are fully indoctrinated as well as always included in all family activities. The family is content, the children are content, and the restaurant managers are never stressed when family is involved. Again, refreshing! True family values, or the value of family!

A young Italian couple together with their five year old daughter and two and a half year old son recently visited us. We constantly hear of the dangerous trend toward childhood obesity fueled by the ingestion of high calorie and low nutritionally endowed snacks swallowed by American children. We were amazed that these children also snacked, however, what they ate between meals and after meals was fruit. No cookies, chips, or candy. The children asked for apples, tangerines, oranges, and bananas. The little fellow had an unbelievable capacity! One afternoon I watched as he devoured two apples and five clementines, neatly peeled and cut into small pieces by either his father or mother.

If one travels extensively through Italy, especially in the spring of the year, groups of school children will be seen as they are taken on field trips. The important historical monuments and archeological sites are explored, as well as the hundreds of museums of all kinds. Art history is naturally paramount in a country that is preeminent in this endeavor, but other museums dedicated to Italian invention, science, the Etruscans, pre-history, and lesser known crafts are not excluded. The hundreds of architecturally important basilicas are not forgotten in these tours. These incredible buildings filled with frescoes, mosaics, oil paintings, marble and bronze statues, wood carvings and so many other embellishments, all part of the cultural history of this country, are not only shown to the children, but explained with pride. We have observed student groups in Modena, Urbino, Rome, Florence, Palermo and Siracusa, to mention only a very few, as they are methodically instructed in their heritage. The value of this kind of education is immeasurable, both to the children and to the society as a whole. The youngsters know that they are worth the time, trouble and money for these expeditions, and it certainly creates a future citizenry with the utmost respect for its heritage.

In fairness I must include some criticism which I have heard from several Italian people. Because so many parents and grandparents grew up either in poverty or in an economy wrecked by war, or often both, they have been overly generous to children to the point at which some feel the youngsters have been "spoiled." A typically one child family, which has been the norm until very recently, will lavish material possessions on that child to the point at which he is rarely satisfied with nothing less than the best and newest in electronic equipment, clothing and even automobiles. However, I have noticed so much of the same happening in the United States in the last twenty years. Toy stores have proliferated providing a surfeit for the very young; electronic devices for music or games are standard equipment for those a bit older, and for some, a computer for each family member. One big difference is the employment factor. American teenagers frequently are employed in part-time jobs, especially during the summer school vacation; Italian teens are not. When I inquired about this I was told that there simply are not enough jobs available in Italy; in our country it is rare to see a supermarket or a fast-food restaurant without a "Help Wanted" sign.

Italian children are indeed fortunate. What an incredibly different world we might have if all the world's children were as loved and cared for as much as these kids are!

CHILDREN—THE BEST!

For the most part, I prefer all children
To adults. I don't dislike grown people-
The simple facts are, that I relate and
Enjoy the under twenty-one group best.

Kids are honest, direct and usually
Sincere, with occasional brief lapses.
I love my four children; twenty-five years
Of high school teaching was rewarding joy
And happily recognized when the State
Of New York's English Council decided
To name me, "A Teacher of Excellence."

The ultimate happiness arrived with
My ten grandchildren—six boys and four girls!
A mutually loving society,
Proven true again from the mouths of babes
When a nine year old granddaughter firmly
Admonished an indecisive adult
By emphatically stating: "My grandmother
Likes kids better than people her own age."

They are without prejudice, whether that
Involves race, religion or Shakespeare's works!
I've never been a religious person,
And often describe myself as "Druid,"
But I truly understand Jesus' words
As He wisely and theologically
Said: "Suffer the little children to come
Unto me." He knew that kids are more fun!

APULIA

"For thou shalt be in league with the stones of the field: and the beasts of the field shall be at peace with thee."

The Book of Job 5: 23

Continuing on our quest for the white almond blossoms, we left Sicily en route to Apulia. We stopped for the night in Catanzaro, a large city in Calabria which is perched on a high cliff, but separated in the middle by a deep canyon-like ravine. This crevasse is connected to the opposite sides of the city by a huge bridge supported by towers, each of which seemed as high as a mountain peak.

This city seems marred by apartment buildings seen as huge concrete hunks as well as unending traffic; there was much building going on all over the town because of expanding industry, but we had not come to be tourists. According to the local brochure there are lovely public gardens, but after dinner and a good night's sleep we moved on in the morning. We had a quest.

On our way out of this busy, growing metropolis, we drove along the sea and the *lido* or beach; it was a large, typically Italian resort. Although we love Italy thoroughly and deeply, we are not especially fond of the beach resorts here. Perhaps we are spoiled by the relatively informal and uncrowded beaches in Cape Cod, but then, we have never been beach people anyway; probably since we saw JAWS in 1974!

Driving on we were delighted to see many almond trees in full blossom and for me, to remember once again the professor who first suggested this pilgrimage. We always stop for a morning cappuccino and as soon as we spotted a likely place we did. This was in a small town called Isola Capo Rizzuto, known in Europe as a beach resort; the date was February 25th. I mention that because only several days later as I was reading the INTERNATIONAL HERALD TRIBUNE, I saw a headline, "Calabrian Crossfire Claims Another Bystander." The article described the murder of an innocent person who was sitting in a pizzeria and coffee bar in this town as the Calabrian Mafia, known as the 'Ndrangheta, entered, intent on eliminating a member of a rival clan. That was apparently accomplished, but in the crossfire a young man, a leading citizen known for his outstanding volunteer work with the handicapped, as well as with other charities, was killed.

I don't believe that this bar where the shooting occurred was the one where we had coffee, but one never knows. As Roger always tells me, you must, *"Carpe Diem,"* or seize the day. There are many perils wherever one may be, so live each day as if it will be the last. Even crossing the street might be eventually hazardous, and it matters little whether that street, coffee bar or amusement park is in Cape Cod, London, Oklahoma City, Buenos Aires, New York City, Beijing, Johannesburg, Cairo or Miami. *Carpe Diem!!*

After our coffee we stopped along a deserted part of the beach and enjoyed a snack we had carried along; pecorino cheese, bread, and blood oranges which are incredibly delicious; orange colored on the outside but the hue of pink grapefruit on the inside. As we continued along the road we saw much perfect agriculture as is typical in all of Italy. There were grape vines, orange groves, olive trees and fields of growing vegetables. Many of these are held under plastic sheeting or netting. This is not lovely to look at, but

I can understand the need to increase the crop yield in order to feed as many people as possible. Not only have so many workers left the agricultural areas, but so much of Italy is mountainous and nearly impossible to be used for farming. The plastic increases the yield; I worry more about all the used stuff going into the landfills around the world than the aesthetics. The half-life of plastic is probably higher than I can count. Let's hope it can be re-used over and over.

Finocchio, or fennel, seems to prevail in the vegetable markets at this time in late February. We passed many large trailer trucks filled with nothing else, and every green grocery is piled high with this celery looking, but licorice tasting veggie. It's great sliced and added to salads.

Continuing on to Metaponto in Basilicata, we stopped to see a 6th century B.C.E. Greek temple to the goddess, Hera. There are only fifteen majestic columns remaining of this once huge temple; the entire area was immaculate—no discarded papers or plastic flotsam in sight. After we walked and took the usual enormous number of photographs, I spotted two carabinieri on the edge of the parking area. Walking up to them, I told them we were American tourists. They were pleased, had broad smiles and were quite surprised. Apparently very few American tourists have appeared in Basilicata, especially in Metaponto! Wanting to practice his English and perhaps to show me that he was aware of our country and its leader at that time, one officer said: "I know your President, Bill Clinton."

I replied, "I know your President, Massimo D'Alemma." He was obviously pleased I knew something about his country, but he then put the thumbs down sign and in halting English said:

"I don't like him."

Technically D'Alemma was not the president but the prime minister. He was rather left-leaning and I suppose as police officers in this part of the country which has had such difficulties with illegal Albanians as well as many from the former Yugoslavia, they would be more conservative and opposed to many of the policies of that prime minister. We then exchanged, *"Arriverderci"* with big smiles from all of us and we drove on.

Apulia is the "heel" of Italy's boot and as a Mediterranean pivot, it has weathered innumerable foreign invasions. It is a land in which superstition and the power of magic continue to have a place in the lives of many of its inhabitants. Food, trees, and even houses are often thought to have something of the supernatural within them. Entering Apulia we drove to a hotel in the city of Gioia del Colle, which means "precious stone of the hill." Our rental began on the following day in Alberobello, only a short drive away. This lovely hotel was pleasant, had a great dining room and restaurant, and a most congenial staff including the delightful waiter Francesco who served us dinner.

On Saturday morning after checking out of our hotel, Roger decided that he must have a haircut. In January he had been ill with back trouble for a month and couldn't sit for more than a few minutes, so he had neglected to do this before we left the States, and by now we had been in Italy for three weeks. He was afraid that he was beginning to look like Rip Van Winkle. So, off we were to discover a barber shop!

He found one quickly and fortunately there was a spot nearby where we could park our car. I decided to stay in the car and read a fascinating book I had just begun the night before, A TUSCAN CHILDHOOD, by Kinta Beevor.

Although I did read at first, I became fascinated with watching the local scene; the streets were alive with people on a Saturday morning. This town was up and about as men and women were shopping, talking, and moving with purpose, but with a relaxed demeanor. I saw a man, probably in his mid-forties, emerge from a bar two stores away from our car; he was carrying a small tray on which three espresso cups with saucers on top of the cups were placed. Holding this tray in his right hand, he climbed on a fairly dilapidated bicycle, grabbing the handlebars with his left hand. Calmly he pedaled off through the narrow street filled with Saturday traffic. I was fascinated. Ten minutes later he returned; the tray in his hand now held empty cups with the saucers under them and after leaning his bicycle against the wall, he re-entered the bar. A few minutes later he again came out with two large cups and one small one, all saucers on top, got on the bike and pedaled off. I couldn't take my eyes away. Frankly, I would have hesitated to walk across the traffic congested street, let alone ride on an old bike I managed with one hand as I balanced three cups of coffee in the other. This scene reoccurred over and over again. Sometimes there were pastries to accompany the coffee or mineral water. This was "espresso delivery" in Gioia del Colle style!

Roger returned smiling and looking five years younger with his tonsorial improvement. Often a haircut will do that to one! He couldn't wait to tell me about the barber shop, so I had to wait to tell him about the coffee delivery service.

The barber shop was packed on this Saturday morning with most men coming to be shaved rather than shorn. Absolute fairness was demonstrated by taking each man in turn according to his time of arrival. When it was about to become Roger's turn, all the barbers, almost simultaneously, put down their razors, scissors and towels. One man asked Rog if he would like a coffee. "*Grazie, no,*" or "no thank you," replied my husband; at that point all the barbers left the shop and went out for morning coffee; they returned about ten minutes later. It was a wonderful and totally natural scene—partly operetta and partly real life, Southern Italian style—or is that redundant?

Although rental properties are not available until four o'clock on Saturday, or as the Europeans say, sixteen hundred, we drove into the tiny town of Alberobello much before that to look around and get a feel for what we had contracted for, sight unseen except for a picture in the catalogue of rental units. This town is known as the *Trulli* capital for the very unusual buildings found here. Protected by the Italian government as national monuments and singled out by UNESCO, they are unique in every way.

These buildings have outside walls of white stone covered with stucco and topped with dark stone, steep, conical roofs; except for pictures, we had never seen anything so unusual. Originally built without mortar, supposedly so that they could be disassembled quickly, today many have been modernized inside, and according to law, except for the outside stucco, the exterior may not be changed in any way. Another exception I imagine is that almost all have television antennas adorning their roofs, but, these are not considered permanent. Obviously a tourist center, many of the *trulli* now are shops where souvenirs of the area are displayed and sold; a few have been made into restaurants, and one was a rental agency from which we rented "our" *trullo*.

I had been fascinated by these unusual buildings for years and when I found that some were available as short term rentals we booked one for a week. Some *trulli* stand alone, but others are connected by interlocking roofs. Near to our little dwelling there was a shop known as the "*Trullo Siamese,*" so named because of the twin, but joined roofs. Painted on the top of some of these *trulli* are unusual symbols; there are primitive signs, Christian emblems, and magic symbols. In the town these structures are in good condition, but in the outlying areas some are in disrepair. Many are obviously being restored or have been recently restored as relics of history and as weekend houses for city dwellers who wish to have a country house.

At four o'clock we were greeted by Dino, the rental agent, a gregarious, delightful, helpful and smiling person. He was a pleasant change from a *strega* from whom we had recently rented. (That word, *strega* in Italian is "witch," made fairly common by the wonderful children's story, "Strega Nona" by Tomie de Paola, which I have often read to my grandchildren and to my grandson Kenneth's first grade class when I was the designated, "mystery reader!"). However, in that story, the grandmother witch is a warm-hearted, kind woman who does "good" magic. I was thinking of the word "witch" in the context of what Roger's very proper aunt used to say, "Witch, spelled with a 'b'."

Dino had heated up the *trullo* as much as possible in a non-insulated stone structure, and to welcome us, he left a huge bowl of excellent fruit and a good bottle of white wine. There was a gas space heater, but Roger, having spent years in the gas business, feels they are dangerous and will not use unventilated ones, so Dino brought us two baskets of wood for our fireplace. There were also two electric heaters in the walls, one in the living/bedroom and the other in the kitchen. Amazingly, none in the bathroom! It was quite frosty stepping out of the shower, but then again, as citizens of a country who are the world's greatest consumers of energy, we are simply spoiled, and I would have bitten my tongue before I complained. After all, it was February, and by April, it would have been perfect.

That night, tired and full of the ambiance of this most unusual house, we snuggled down in the good bed; it was next to the fireplace and its glowing embers, and so we slept the deep wonderful sleep that, ". . . knits up the ravelled sleave (sic) of care." (MACBETH II, ii)

After breakfast the next morning, Sunday, refreshed by our fireside sleep, we drove to the town of Monopoli where the pre-Lenten *Carnevale* was taking place. We did the usual touristy thing; looked around, admired the children on parade in their colorful outfits, had *cappuccini* and drove around admiring the perfect order of agriculture in the countryside. Back in Alberobello, we saw many tour buses; numbers of people walk through the *trulli* zone; there are many more on weekends than during the week as most are Italian nationals, often retired, on one or two day trips. The shops do a brisk business; we bought a small painting of a *trullo,* a decorated tile, and a plate for a daughter who collects them from different parts of Italy. At one point it began to rain and Roger helped the older man who had a shop across from our little house. Many wares are hung outside of these souvenir shops; towels, sweaters and embroidered works act as advertisements to entice customers, but which must be quickly brought under cover before they are drenched. This store owner was so appreciative; he became our local "friend" for the remainder of the week we were there.

When Dino next returned with more firewood, we chatted and asked him if he had ever come to our country. He said he was coming to the USA in seven months. We have spoken to many Italians who have visited or who plan to visit the United States; the three most mentioned destinations within our country they hope to see or have already seen, are: Boston, New York City, and California. These three places are cited more than any others. Knowing this, we fully expected one of those replies from Dino when we asked him where he was going. His answer took us totally by surprise; his destination was Bismarck, North Dakota! He explained that his best friend had moved there and also that he was extremely interested in the history, life and culture of the North American Native Americans, or, as he stated, the American Indians. Roger took out a map of the United States we always carry with us and Dino pointed out each area of our country and stated which tribes had lived there; Iroquois, Comanche, Seminole, Sioux, Lakota, Algonquin, Apache, Navajo, and he continued on. He was extremely well informed; how interesting that in this tiny, historical town in Apulia, a young Italian man was so knowledgeable about an important aspect of American culture.

The countryside in the parts of Apulia we have driven through is a joy to behold. Particularly fascinating are the miles and miles of perfectly formed stone fences, or low walls, marking boundaries of fields and properties. I could not begin to fathom the years of labor as well as the skill of building these barriers; between these meticulously made fences are groomed plots of growing vegetables, olive trees, almond trees in blossom, and cows, horses, sheep and some pigs grazing on verdant plots. The fruit and olive trees had recently been pruned and stand gracefully above their shorn branches; February must be the month for this activity in Apulia.

I was especially delighted to see the almond blossoms as this was part of our quest. From Sicily, to Calabria, Basilicata and now in Apulia, these beautiful white blossoms are right on time; or actually, we are!

So that Dino would not have to continue to bring firewood to us, we asked him where we could buy it ourselves. He made a date for us to meet a man who would sell us the wood. We drove into the center of the small town and the wood seller was waiting for us in his red truck. He spoke to us in the local dialect and we understood nothing. He kept trying with hand signals to indicate that he wanted us to do something; we were clueless. Finally we understood one thing; he said something which resembled, "three kilometers." Roger immediately picked up on the rest. This man wanted us to drive him to his house where the wood was stored! And we did! He had a large and beautiful house on a huge area of land. A locked gate he had to open allowed us to drive up the driveway; behind his house he had stacks and stacks of perfectly cut wood in several sizes, and huge bundles of twigs neatly wrapped for kindling. We filled the trunk of the car, he fed his cats, and then the three of us drove back to his truck in town. His charge was fair and honest. Although we couldn't communicate, I believe that both parties were satisfied with the transaction.

Next on our agenda in Apulia was going to the Baroque town of Martina Franca. It is lovely; the architecture splendid and it was worth the unexpected wait we experienced to get there. This delay, interesting by itself, was caused by a dairy farmer's protest. As we got near to the town, we found we were driving necessarily slowly behind approximately one hundred farm tractors, each waving a white flag with the words, "MILK WARRIORS" written on them in black letters, and interestingly enough, in English. We didn't know the exact nature of the argument of their protest, but it had something to do with the sanctions of the European Union on dairy farmers which they felt to be unfair. The tractors were large, and Roger said, expensive. In the town itself, the streets were filled with city police and carabinieri, the national police, but all seemed very peaceful. After stopping for coffee, we continued on toward Taranto and passed a building where the tractors were parked. We guessed that the farmers were inside for a meeting, or at least for coffee.

The kitchen in our *trullo* was quite well appointed; ample refrigerator, good stove, many dishes and an ample supply of hot water. I found the stock pot furnished by the rental company was of marginal quality though, as the interior was chipped Teflon and I would not use it. To be fair, I do not think many tourists would have a use for it. I love to make soup anywhere I happen to be, and Roger always enjoys eating it; it always seems to be more fun in Italy for some reason and I do this in Tuscany, Lombardy, Abruzzo or wherever we find ourselves with a few days and a kitchen. I decided that I must have a new pot, and thus began our "pot search." My first mistake was looking up the word "pot" in a dictionary that was really more British English than American English. The entry was "*vaso*" for pot. We decided to go to the nearby larger city, Gioia del Colle, to search for our pot, rather than the tiny town of Alberobello and so the search began. Driving up and down streets through the town we saw nothing that looked like a kitchen supply store. We parked the car and continued on foot. Stopping into a hardware store to inquire where I might buy a "*vaso,*" the gentleman smiled and showed me exactly what I had asked for. Unfortunately, the dictionary translation I used meant a "flower pot," of which he had many. I explained that I wanted to cook soup in the "*vaso,*" and he frowned and looked perplexed. Pointing to the hole in the bottom of the clay pot, he shook his head, shrugged his shoulders and looked askance. I suppose he thought I was mildly, if pleasantly deranged.

Continuing our walk through the attractive streets we found computer stores, cell 'phone stores, jewelry shops, gift shops, scores of clothing stores for all people from infants to the elderly and including some ultra fashionable designer emporiums, green groceries, butcher shops, tobacconists, bars, sporting goods stores, hardware stores, car dealers, car accessory shops, florists, barbers, ladies hairdresser salons, and many more besides. But, nothing we wanted; no kitchen supply stores carrying stock pots or kettles anywhere!

Daunted, we decided to return to the lovely hotel where we had spent the night before our rental was available. We were ready for a lunch break and also remembered that many of the staff there spoke English and that they might point us in the right direction for our pot. In the dining room we again chatted with Francesco our waiter, and I explained to him our search and frustration. After thinking for a minute he asked if we could return at six o'clock that evening when his shift was finished and he would take us to a kitchen store. We heartily agreed and thought how very considerate it was that this person would take the time to show two people, probably older than his parents, where they could buy a pot to make soup!

Promptly at six he arrived with his fiancee in tow. She spoke excellent English, was adorable and totally friendly. Directing us to the store she had chosen, we picked out not one, but two pots. They were well designed and not unreasonably priced, but that wouldn't do for this young woman. She bargained with the owner until the items were discounted! They had plans for the evening so we parted before dinner, but not before making a date for Friday evening when he did not have to work at the hotel. They were so personable and had taken time to help us, and we wanted to take them to dinner to show our appreciation, but also because they were quite delightful to be with.

I'm happy to say that we had a most enjoyable evening on that Friday! A great dinner, wonderful wine, and yet again, a promise to them from my romantic husband, that when they were going to be married, if they invited us, we would come!

The Age of Information together with an attempt to be politically correct, led me into a situation I hoped would be harmonious. Even in Italy which has always been overwhelmingly Roman Catholic, there are many people of different faiths. The world is becoming ever more international and one is made constantly aware of diverse and often strong feelings about religion, governments, political movements and culture. I remember being sensitive to these feelings when I was teaching in a large high school; some of my students were fairly recent arrivals from China, The Philippines, Ghana, India, Pakistan, Korea, Russia, Colombia and most likely many other places I am neglecting to mention. The other students were "Americans," which meant that their grandparents or great-grandparents had arrived in the United States from Germany, Ireland, Italy, Great Britain, Scandinavia, the Netherlands, Belgium, Asia, South or Central America and so on more than a few years ago, unless they were Native Americans. Respect for different ways of life and backgrounds was the only correct way to proceed as we examined MACBETH, A TALE OF TWO CITIES, LORD OF THE FLIES or the thousands, or what seemed like thousands of SAT prep vocabulary words. The students who had lived in the United States for generations also represented great diversity in religion, abilities, goals, family incomes, and interests. Our school served a city and two adjoining townships and I always felt it was a microcosm of our country. All of these things ran through my mind as we took an after dinner walk.

We paired off as we walked; Roger and Francesco, and I with the young woman. Seemingly out of the blue she asked me if I believed in a Supreme Being. Not knowing exactly in what direction she was heading and not wanting to upset her by saying the wrong thing although I didn't have any idea of what that might be, I mumbled something lightly about not being very religious. She then continued and asked what I believed happened to humans after death? Did I think there was a heaven? Trying to think quickly, and still not certain of where she was going intellectually and/or theologically, and definitely not wanting to tread on any of her beliefs, I said, "Well, let me tell you what Roger believes."

"He is of the mind that if a person lives as good a life as he is able, if he doesn't steal, if he doesn't hurt other people knowingly, if he shows charity to others, and all in all tries to be as good as he can at least most of the time, that after he dies, he goes to Italy!" Apparently, and thankfully, this was the perfect answer for her. She shrieked with happiness and immediately ran off to tell Francesco what I had said. I guess I passed that quiz! I am certain that she has deep personal convictions typical of those from the deep south of Italy, but her religious beliefs were superceded, if only momentarily, by her patriotic fervor and pride in her country.

The epilogue to the pot/kettle search was that I crammed not one, but both of them into my suitcase for the trip back to the USA; they now comfortably reside in my large, ample kitchen, where, from the four windows, the water in front of our Cape house is soothingly apparent. Each time I use one of these vessels, I smile with the memory of a delightful adventure and the pleasure of knowing some charming young people in Apulia.

We drove to see Bari, a principal city, and although we did not spend a great deal of time there, what we did see was impressive. The port area is as tidy as a small town in New England; the stores in the center are elegant; the fortress walls are being restored; there was a notable police presence. I fully expected to see illegal immigrants assail our car with offers to wash the windows or to try to sell us those ubiquitous packages of tissues, as we have experienced in Sicily, Calabria and Campania, but not once did this happen. Illegal immigration into this part of Italy has been a horrendous problem, but evidently it has been controlled here; there was no outward evidence of it that we could see; order prevailed. Some guide books we had from earlier trips had warnings about thieves in this city, but I don't think it would have been any more of a problem than in any other major city in Europe or the United States.

Back in our "*trullo,*" we sat in front of the fireplace, sipping wine before going out to dinner. At the restaurant which was nicely appointed, had good food and an excellent waiter, we were seated near a party of ten persons. They were extremely friendly toward us and at the end of dinner, they sent over a plate of cookies and dessert wine for us. Another kind gesture from strangers! Another reason to say, "Italy, I Love you!"

We walked back to our little stone residence, sat in front of the fire for awhile, and then partook of sleep, ". . . Chief nourisher in life's feast." (MACBETH, II, ii)

In the morning it was time to bade farewell to Apulia, to Alberobello, to Dino whom we invited to visit us on the way to North Dakota, and to the kindly shopkeepers across the way. We'd like to return, but now it was time to move on—our reservation had expired and we were due in Abruzzo that afternoon. Etched in my memory are the endless, perfectly wrought stone fences which are like nothing I've ever seen before; the unique *trulli,* and yet again, happy memories of so many kind and gracious people.

FOOD!

"Sit down and feed, and welcome to our table."

AS YOU LIKE IT, II, vii Shakespeare

"'Tis an ill cook that cannot lick his own fingers."

ROMEO AND JULIET, IV, ii Shakespeare

Fabio, our very dear friend and restaurant owner in Rome, explained to us that there are only three great cuisines in the world; Chinese, French and Italian. I don't pretend to know much about the first two, but have thrilled to the last for more than three decades.

To Italians, food is more than a necessity of life; it is an extremely important part of the family experience, and therefore it is expected to be of excellent quality, perfectly cooked and served with pride. Meals are to be enjoyed, and not considered merely sustenance. Italian cooking is not only an art, nor is it only a science; it is a labor of love combining both art and science. Food and family are so intertwined by affection and devotion they literally cannot be separated. To cook for those you love is to honor them, please them and demonstrate their worth to you.

Within a family the cook can be mother or father and often is both. Many Italian men are great cooks and take understandable pride in what they make and serve. We have experienced unbelievably great meals made by our friends, Rino, Franco, Alberto, Paolo, Roberto and Giuseppe, to name but a few men, but many people tell us they are legion. We happen to know these people as friends, but are told this is typical. My Sicilian grandfather, Pietro, was a marvelous cook and I have such good memories of sitting at his table for Sunday dinner.

For many people, regardless of ethnic or national background, food memories are important and can be vivid. Thoughts of a special meal in a restaurant or one eaten as a young child at a grandmother's house on a special holiday can linger in the mind and become more real than the one which was actually consumed. Browsing across more than thirty years of my Italian travel journals, I consistently find descriptions of meals enjoyed and chronicled to the last detail. A certain illustration, or aroma, a passage in a book, or even a sleep dream can conjure up these pleasing gustatory memories. Proust was not unique in this respect.

Freshness and high quality of ingredients are of paramount importance to the Italian table. Vegetables or fruits which are out of season are rarely found. Meats, poultry, eggs and milk are raised without antibiotics or growth hormones; wine for consumption within the country is produced without added sulfites. I never tire of looking at shops where food is sold, whether a small greengrocery, a butcher shop, a fish market or a large supermarket. The products are consistently superior, and the displays, especially in the small independent shops, are artistically arranged with obvious pride.

Dining in a restaurant in Italy is the next best thing to having dinner at a dear relative's home who incidentally is also a great cook! I won't be so presumptuous to suggest that every meal eaten out is excellent and better than Grandma used to make, but many small restaurants, especially in small towns and villages are family-run trattorias in which Grandma really does much of the cooking.

Rarely, but occasionally, one can be presented with a meal which is sub-standard by Italian culinary standards. One evening we stopped for dinner at an agriturismo; we have always had excellent meals at these establishments in which the family usually cooks and serves and most of the produce is grown on the family farm. When we finished and returned to our small hotel where we have stayed for many years, the proprietor asked where we had eaten and did we enjoy the meal? We were honest and told him where we had been and that the food was fairly poor by Italian standards. He laughed, congratulated us, shook our hands and then said, "You are really Italian! You can tell the difference! Most tourists would think it was very good, but you are not tourists; you are visitors!"

In Italy one enters a restaurant to eat, and not to have cocktails or to linger unnecessarily before dining. Unlike the northern European or American custom, the cocktail hour does not exist. One goes to eat, not drink. Four hundred years ago in the tragedy OTHELLO, Shakespeare chides the English for their drinking habits when he has Iago, the Venetian, say:

> ". . . in England, where they are most potent in potting. Your Dane, your German, and your swag—bellied Hollander— . . . are nothing to your English . . . he drinks you with facility your Dane dead drunk; he sweats not to overthrow your Almain; he gives your Hollander a vomit ere the next pottle can be filled." II, iii

Of course the playwright was entertaining the English playgoers while giving them a friendly scolding at the same time.

In contrast to this habit, Italians drink wine with dinner as an accompaniment, not as an anesthetic.

At the end of a meal, one is not encouraged to leave; in so many restaurants in other countries it is necessary to turn the tables over several times during the evening for economic returns, but that is not the Italian custom. Just as one might linger at his own dining table, one is not discouraged from doing the same when dining out. Often, it is actually difficult to gain the attention of the waiter in order to get the *"conto"* or check at the end of the meal. No one wants to appear as if he is encouraging a guest to leave.

Homogenization is something which we as Americans take for granted. Hamburger chains, pizza houses, pancake palaces, coffee bars and motel groups offer much of the same fare whether located in Maine or Texas. This is usually not true in Italy, although to a small extent, that is beginning to change as so many countries become more globalized and less individualized in the third millennium. Historically, each district has had its own, distinctive cuisine. Much of what is found on a menu in Tuscany will be absent in Calabria, Sicily or Apulia. There are some items which have now crossed borders, but that is fairly new. Beefsteak is a specialty of Tuscany, and fish and pasta Norma of Sicily, and usually these items remain at "home." Some pasta shapes predominate in certain areas and are not found, or are rarely found in others.

Recent articles in national magazines and newspapers have called attention to the alarming statistics about obesity in America. This is an ever-growing and dangerous health problem. This is not true in Italy; it is extremely rare to see an Italian grossly overweight.

Obese children are at risk for diabetes and heart problems which exacerbate as they grown older. Reasons for this health crisis are varied, but for the most part, two causes are given by experts; first, inactivity as these kids sit in front of television, computer or play video games, and second, the dependence on so much "fast food" filled with fat and carbohydrates as well as the overuse of packaged cookies, crackers and snack foods often made with trans-fatty acids. It is tragic to see so many overweight children, teenagers, and adults, in malls, on sidewalks, or squeezing themselves into airplane seats. This condition is rare in Italy; diet must be a major factor. The Italian diet is heavily swayed in favor of fruits and vegetables; unfortunately we are told that only about twenty-five per cent of Americans can state they eat the minimum five portions of these foods daily.

Fast foods are now making an inroad into Italy's heretofore fabled cuisine, mainly by American hamburger emporiums. School children seem to be the champions of this new trend, but many serious minded adults are concerned about the invasion of unwanted grease and empty calories into their children's diets. A fairly new group called, "Slow Food," is making headlines in Italy by challenging the globalization of food and promoting the culinary specialties, not only from Italy, but from all over the world. A huge fair, held biennially, was held in Turin in October 2000 to allow visitors to taste the best food the world has to offer. The organization wants to promote the preservation of local specialities and to prevent their disappearance or homogenization.

During this period of time, the United States Ambassador to Italy was Thomas Foglietta, a native of Molise. In an article in a September 2000 INTERNATIONAL HERALD TRIBUNE and published in conjunction with the Milan daily, *CORRIERE DELLA SERA,* Mr. Foglietta was attempting to explain to some local leaders in the Marche' that their worries about too much Americanization among Italian teenagers were exaggerated. He made the comparison that if their youngsters wanted to eat take-out hamburgers, wear American blue jeans and listen to pop music from the USA on their headphones, then American teens want to wear Versace and Armani; older Americans want dishes made in Italy, glass from Murano and leather handbags with an Italian label. He stressed that "globalization does not have to mean homogenization." Well, perhaps, but frankly I can't imagine that many teens could afford Versace or Armani!

Between 1880 and 1920, it is estimated that four million Italians emigrated to the United States; the vast majority of these people were from the south of Rome. In Hasia R. Diner's fascinating book, HUNGERING FOR AMERICA, she writes that life for most of these people in rural Italy was unbelievably harsh; living in an almost feudal system maintained by wealthy landowners, the immigrants were constantly hungry. Pasta, meat and olive oil were given to them only three times a year by the wealthy; food and fuel were scavenged daily. Men worked long hours at hard labor; women often worked in the households of the rich while trying to keep their families fed with as little as available to them. The women however, learned to cook as their patrons ate well and they cooked for them. Immigration to America meant that these people had to work at back-breaking jobs for long hours, as they did in Italy, but there was one huge difference. Food was plentiful and inexpensive; the immigrants might be considered to be living in poverty by American standards, but by the standards they left in their homeland, they ate better than they ever could have imagined possible; pasta often everyday; meat, two or three times a week, olive oil, and, most amazing to many, the availability of coffee! The family meal was paramount to their daily lives; all joined together to eat the bounty of the American economy. Many men who came alone to the new world returned after saving money; they regaled their old friends and neighbors with stories of the food availability they experienced.

Some of the descendants of these people from Sicily, Calabria, Abruzzo, Apulia, Campania,—southern Italians, opened restaurants in their adopted country, and this is reflected by what most American people consider Italian food. A perfect example is found in lasagna. In the south of Italy it is a rich concoction; the sheets of pasta are layered with ricotta cheese, mozzarella, Pecorino Romano cheese and quantities of tomato sauce flavored with basil and oregano. Sliced sausages might also be added between pasta layers. On the top, there is a covering of melted mozzarella. However, in the north, lasagna is a very different dish. The pasta tends to be thinner and is always homemade; there is no ricotta, mozzarella or Pecorino Romano, but instead a creamy, cooked white sauce of butter, flour and milk is spread between the layers of pasta, which is then sauced with Bolognese ragu. This sauce is made with meat, vegetables, milk, white wine, a mere hint of tomato and flavored with nutmeg. *Parmigiano reggiano* cheese is added to each layer as well as to the top. A most wonderful creation, but very different from what most Americans think of when they hear the word or order lasagna from a menu.

Food in Italy is tremendously varied in style. I have encountered some American tourists who were disappointed by not finding what they considered to be the only Italian cuisine—the kind they were used to in their small home towns in Ohio, Virginia, upper New York State or Kansas. They were confused by a finely made risotto in Emilia-Romagna, a ragu made with duck, wild boar or hare, raviolini dressed in sage and butter, rabbit, pigeon, or roast pork covered with Tuscan beans. Chicken "parm" does not exist, nor are meatballs served with spaghetti. Meatballs are found on some menus, but only as a meat course which follows the pasta course, and then they are often served with mashed potatoes!

Those people who dwell in the larger cities in the United States are often more receptive to the cooking styles of the north as many restaurants using this style of food presentation have been established in these places during the past twenty years. Food in Italy is not all pizza and red sauce on macaroni, although so many people believe it is. At a dinner party in Florida a well-dressed older gentleman looked pained after Roger announced that we would be spending five months in Italy the following winter. He asked how we could stand to eat spaghetti and red sauce every night for five months? I had to believe that his idea of Italian food comes from a can and a jar. Poor thing.

Many restaurants in the more "touristy" sections of larger Italian cities have menu translations for English readers. I have enjoyed some of the near misses. "Egg apple" was the translation for eggplant; "wire board" for wild boar, "sword squids" for swordfish, and one of the most memorable was, "drowned small polyps" for oysters! Some literal translations from the Italian are fanciful, if not slightly shocking. Would you believe pasta called, "choke a priest" or cookies named, "nun's thighs?"

At dinner in our favorite restaurant in Rome owned by our good friends, our waiter Luigi told us that there was a great treat that evening. Their chef had made *"stinco"* and he strongly recommended that we try it. We knew his English wasn't proficient enough to make a joke, but after our initial surprise we stifled our smiles and ordered it without the slightest idea of what to expect. A tender, roasted shank of veal appeared, perfectly cooked and seasoned, and then sliced at our table; we enjoyed every succulent morsel. The name, pronounced in English was "stink-oh." Without knowing our experience with both the dish as well as its interesting name, our friend Maurizio once suggested that we should try his favorite meat should we ever come across it—*"stinco!"*

During the 1970's we discovered "toast" quite by accident. Walking to a bar for breakfast one morning we ordered *cappucini,* and then decided that we wanted a little something more. We asked the barman for toast. Five minutes later he presented each of us with a sandwich consisting of two slices of toasted bread filled with melted cheese and a slice of ham. At that time we thought he had misunderstood us, but we ate it anyway and found it to be delicious. Later we discovered that in Italy, "toast" means exactly this. A special machine that looks like a regular toaster, but which has two removable containers with grid sides and extended handles, is used to make this sandwich. Two slices of white bread with the cheese and ham between them are put on the removable parts and lowered into the toaster. The heating element toasts the bread and melts the cheese without the use of butter or oil; the result is much like a grilled cheese sandwich with far less fat or grease.

Roger liked this so much we investigated and found this kind of toaster in the States, but the cost was fairly exorbitant. So, on a recent trip, in a huge and wonderful supermarket in Pescara, Abruzzo, he found exactly what he wanted. An Italian "toast" maker! Nothing would do but to buy it at an extremely reasonable price. We used it for the rest of our trip, and typically, tucked it into our suitcases and brought it home to Cape Cod. European electrical voltage is different from the American, but my husband is good at figuring out change, and now we can enjoy authentic Italian toast—well, almost authentic. The ham and cheese we buy is never quite as tasty as what we get in Italy. I had to laugh though, as most people who travel to Italy purchase the famed leather goods, jewelry, shoes, art work, ceramics or alabaster, as well as the usual oil and wine, but our main purchase for this particular trip was a toaster!

I enjoy cooking whether at home or in Italy, and since we tend to remain in that country for months at a time, I cook about half of the time of our stay there. Three meals a day in restaurants, no matter how superb, can get to be less than a treat when lasting many months. We rent apartments or small cottages for most of our stay, so a kitchen is always available. Breakfast is an at-home must; later we always go to a bar for cappuccino. Either lunch or dinner is eaten at "home" or by picnic, depending on that day's planned itinerary. The other meal is usually consumed at a restaurant. Cooking from scratch requires time and patience but often results in excellent meals. Some persons are not willing to do this as they insist they are too busy, which reminds me of Carlo Middione's remark in his cookbook, LA VERA CUCINA, "Americans . . . are always in a hurry to get something done yesterday, whereas the Italian think anything worth doing was already done yesterday!"

I loved reading the INTERNATIONAL HERALD TRIBUNE when we were in Italy and it still existed, and was especially fond of the great small articles in ITALY DAILY published with CORRIERE DELLA SERA which was included in the larger paper. Unfortunately, this part has been eliminated in 2004. A sociologist, Mario Abis, was quoted in the February 11, 2002 edition: "A kitchen is ideal for that third of the population that is reportedly depressed: It is a place in which to be active and interact with the rest of the world through a variety of tasks such as listening to the radio and making sauce." A useful therapy!

When we first began traveling to Italy supermarkets were tiny, if they existed at all. Now, many are truly amazing in size and offerings. This change, similar to that in the United States, has been a curse and a blessing. Many small "Mom and Pop" stores have been forced out of business, while on the more positive side, the large markets have items never before available except in specialty stores in large cities. When one cooks, obviously one must shop and we have found it to be an interesting, enlightening and often delightful experience. At small shops the personal attention is excellent, and the butcher, fishmonger or grocer can make suggestions and offer samples of his wares. However, if one wants to wander and choose from the already packaged meats and other items, the new, vast supermarkets are great fun.

I find I can linger for hours over the enormous array of offerings. One huge market in Abruzzo was such a place; in my journal I labeled it the "supermarket of supermarkets!" At least two hundred varieties of cheese, thirty different kinds of prosciutto, seemingly every fish in the sea, more fresh vegetables than I knew existed, and a meat section superb enough to make a vegetarian question his conversion, filled this huge store. The bakery department had more kinds of freshly baked bread than I could imagine, as well as pastries and cookies by the thousands. In addition, this emporium held a food court where we had individually made pizzas and fresh fruit for lunch. Another section of this capacious market was devoted to selling appliances; approximately one hundred television sets were all tuned in to the same station, refrigerators of all sizes were displayed, as were stoves, and every small appliance one could think of. This area, seemingly as large as a football field, was where Roger found his beloved Italian toaster! Topping even that, we found a supermarket in Sicily so huge it had fifty check-outs !

I admit to being distressed in the parking areas of many supermarkets in the States. Although there are fenced-in places for returning grocery carts, many people either through carelessness or plain laziness, abandon their carts all over, frequently leaving them to roll into other people's cars. Not nice nor attractive! The Italians have developed a simple scheme to alleviate this unpleasant untidiness. The carts are lined up in front of the store; in order to secure one for your use, a coin must be inserted to free the cart. This used to be a 500 lire coin in the old money, and now is either a one or two euro coin, with the value of about two American dollars when I was last there. But, and this is the important fact, upon returning the cart, the money is returned through the device holding the rack of carts. So, the carts cost nothing to use, but without exception, they are properly returned, for who wants to throw two dollars away? Not anyone I've seen, and I've watched all over Italy.

Every small town, and sections of larger ones have weekly markets. Elaborate trucks, looking more like small delicatessens on wheels, bring an array of cheeses; others, like small butcher shops have raw meats, while still others have cured meats such as mortadella and a variety of various *salume* such as prosciuto, boiled ham called prosciuto cotto, and salami. Other sellers offer fresh produce, household plants and beautiful fresh flowers. Still other stalls offer clothing and household goods, but the most fun ones to me are tables which might come from American garage or rummage sales. People from the town as well as many from the surrounding countryside descend into town on market day, to buy, to visit, or simply to be "there" as they have done for years, and just as their parents have done before them.

Among the many specialized vehicles selling food, our favorite is the one offering *porchetta,* or roasted pork. The meat of this speciality is coated with aromatic herbs and salt, and is then roasted to a perfect doneness. The entire animal is displayed and slices can be bought to take away, or made on the spot into mouth-watering sandwiches for a picnic or immediate consumption.

As I have mentioned previously, I am an inveterate and compulsive soup maker, and although I do this frequently at home, it seems much more fun to do in Italy. Perhaps the meats are tastier (I think they are), the vegetables more unique, or simply that I like buying the ingredients and putting them together for interesting lunches, or some late suppers when we have over indulged at the afternoon meal. At the wonderful *agriturismo* we visit in Abruzzo, the lovely lady Olga frequently arrives at our door with fresh vegetables from her enormous garden. These are inevitably a delightful addition to my soup!

In addition she has given me the freshest eggs I've ever had, and, on several occasions, the largest eggs I have ever used! These were from her geese! One can make a large omelette!

How would you react if a waiter asked if you would like "mice" in your salad? I must have looked horrified as he quickly tried to explain that American people usually eat "mice" on the stalk, but here it is separate and often put into salads. I finally realized that he was speaking of what Americans call "corn" and Europeans call "maize." Because the "ai" in Italian is pronouced "aye," the word emerges as "mice!" I then explained to him why I looked so shocked and surprised. I told him the word "mice" was the plural of "mouse"—like Mickey Mouse! He howled with laughter, understanding my initial chagrin; like Coca-Cola, the world knows Disney characters.

Butter in northern Italy is frequently used in cooking but much less often in the South. Although offered at hotel breakfasts in both areas, it is NEVER, EVER put on the table at the noon or night time meals. It is simply not done; to the Italians it would be the equivalent of putting a pork chop on top of a wedding cake. If a newcomer to Italy is unaware of this and asks for butter, it probably will be presented, but the request will be looked upon as if one had asked for drain cleaner. It is better not to, and besides, it is advantageous occasionally to eschew butter for health reasons. The quality of bread is typically so excellent it can best be enjoyed plain, or as my great-aunt Lillian used to say when urging one to eat or drink something without adding anything, "Just have it barefoot!"

I love to read cookbooks, especially Italian cookbooks. There are many fine ones and more are published each year. So far I have thirty-three dealing with Italian food, and although I have cherished recipes in many of them, my favorites are those by Marcella Hazen. My family has teased me for years because when I follow a plan of hers, I try to do it religiously; if I don't have a certain ingredient, I never substitute, but wait until I can find or buy the elusive item. They ask me if I am afraid to deviate from her instructions because I think she will appear at the door and repossess my books. Well, not really, but perhaps; one never knows! She sounds quite strict in the instructions. In addition to great recipes in many books, the history and culture of food is discussed and explained and I never tire of reading about this subject from truffles to tomatoes or pasta to prosciuto.

A mainstay of the Italian cuisine is olive oil. The rest of the world has recently caught on to using this gift of nature and the demand for quality Italian olive oil has dramatically increased, growing at an unprecedented rate. In November of 1998 an article in the INTERNATIONAL HERALD TRIBUNE stated that the amount of this oil exported in 1997 was increased by more than twenty-four per cent from the previous year to two hundred and fifteen metric tons. Forty-five per cent of that, or more than one hundred metric tons went to the United States! Demand continues to grow, not only for its excellent taste, but because health experts speak of its many benefits to one's well-being.

One result of this world-wide thirst is that thousands of new, young, and tiny olive trees have been planted throughout much of Italy, and are being carefully cultivated on oil producing farms, sometimes in newly developed fields, and often between mature trees. On farms in which we have rented houses or apartments, we have seen hundreds of these newly planted trees, as well as constantly observing more of them throughout the countryside.

I never tire of looking at olive trees; they are not only truly glorious, dressed in their graceful, silvery-green leaves, but they don't just stand around looking lovely; they produce what must be the true nectar of the gods. The grape vines and their products might argue that point but it won't be settled here! These trees are evergreens and their leaves last for three years before new ones appear. Not productive until they are at least ten years old, they can live as long as five hundred! Shakespeare was born years after some of these trees were producing olives for oil. On one *podere* or farm, the owner proudly announced that some of his trees were planted during Boccaccio's lifetime; well, that is certainly more than five hundred years ago, but I'll take his word for it. His oil is superb!

These blessed trees which can look almost gossamer in the early morning light vary greatly in size. Most are carefully and expertly pruned so that the fruit laden branches will receive the maximum amount of sunlight. This pruning is usually done in March, and after the cutting, the trees stand over their sheared boughs reminding me of the floors of barber shops, scattered with clippings. For the uninitiated, the bough pruning often looks like the tree is being massacred, but when I asked, I was told that sometimes this needed to be done when the trees had not been well trimmed for several years. During one February when our small rented house stood in the middle of hundreds of olive trees, I was intrigued by the almost constant activity of a large tractor among them. After again asking what was happening, I was told that three times a year, in February, April and late September a tiller plows between every tree. After that is accomplished the tractor pulls a cart filled with fertilizer, and a worker standing in the cart shovels the fertilizer onto the plowed ground. When that phase is completed the tractor continues to pull the tiller behind at right angles to the first plowing which prevents the rain from washing away the soil, an erosion preventative.

Harvesting the olives is knows as *la raccolta* and is a fascinating procedure. This is accomplished in different ways and often on different time schedules depending on the provincial location of the farm. The harvest at the farm in Abruzzo was scheduled to begin on November third at the time we were there. In Tuscany during the same month it was scheduled for the middle of November. I tried to find out how these dates are determined, but my deficiency in Italian language skills made this kind of question difficult. Logically I believe it must depend on the ripeness of the olives as well as the weather; since Tuscany is farther north than Abruzzo, this would seem to make sense. I'm not really positive about that, but perhaps that is yet another thing I love about this land. Not knowing all the answers can be as interesting and more romantic than knowing them. Besides, we always have fun speculating!

In Abruzzo huge nets were spread on the ground beneath the trees. A machine was then attached to a tree which thoroughly shakes it, knocking the olives, both green and black, from the branches onto these nets. The fruit which fails to fall is encouraged to drop by workers with tiny hand-held rake-like instruments; the olives are then gathered in open containers on this particular farm. Many twigs and leaves seemed to be mixed with the fruit; I have no idea how they are separated, but this might be accomplished at the mill where they are pressed. I believe the owner of the grove told us it took about sixteen pounds of olives to produce one liter of oil.

In Tuscany we observed the harvest achieved in a diverse way; it is typical to erect ladders which workers climb and then spend untold hours individually picking the fruit, one at a time. This tremendous job must be completed in only a few days. The weather must be dry before and during the procedure. Both in Abruzzo as well as in Tuscany, farm owners explained to us that a huge problem facing agriculture production is the lack of workers, and this is the reason for the shaking machines which are fairly new, though frowned upon by purists. Many people who work the harvest are older, retired and pressed into service by desperate farmers. In fact, we watched Mario's in-laws and other older people as well, gather the olives; he told us that young people do not want to do this kind of work anymore which has necessitated more mechanization, but even with that, manpower is still required. This hard-working and very well-informed gentleman told us frankly that "Italy is becoming like your California. You have 'guest workers,' legal and illegal who pick crops and accomplish other agricultural duties." This is now happening in Italy as the numbers of immigrants coming to help with the various harvests are expanding at a fast rate.

During one visit to Abruzzo our host took a group of us to see olives pressed into oil. The mill we visited was not his first choice, nor were his olives being pressed at this time, and as he emphasized, not ever at that facility, but it was the only one operating in the vicinity of his farm at that particular time. Burlap and plastic bags filled with newly picked olives were lined up in the small workroom. Whispering to us, Mario explained that truly excellent oil could not be obtained from olives held in such containers. When I asked why this was so, he instructed me to put my hand into a bag. I was amazed at how warm it was; this was precisely the problem, I was told. Superb oil is derived from olives kept in open containers after being picked, so that heat, which destroys taste and therefore quality, is not able to build up. His olives, which were not yet harvested, would be kept in open containers and then pressed at a much more high-tech mill. We have bought his oil as well as having used it while we were guests, and quite obviously he's doing something right! Not only is it delicious, but the many awards adorning his office as well as the entry to the common rooms, such as the National Ercole Olivario, the Gold Medal Award from the Pescara Chamber of Commerce, the Golden Enobby Oriciolo, and the DOP Abruzzo Italia Quality Award, support not only our claims, but those of the experts and judges as well.

At a favorite local restaurant in Loreto Aprutino, Abruzzo, an amiable young waiter brought us a small bowl of olive oil; he insisted that we dip bread into it as an appetizer. He explained that it had been pressed three days before; it was thick and unfiltered. He was right; it was fabulous!

The traveling street markets held one day a week, are often set up on what might be a regular parking or street area during the rest of the week. During the 1980's we parked our rented car in such an area within a small hill town on a Friday afternoon. Unfortunately, we did not attempt to read the numerous signs which were placed at frequent intervals around the site. After breakfast the following morning I looked for the book I had been reading and remembered that I had left it in our car. I walked up the very steep hill to the top of the street to retrieve it and was astonished to see that not only had our car vanished, but that a huge market had been erected in the large parking area where only last evening our rented Fiat had been situated. I met one of the professors assigned to escort a group of American college students who were studying here for the summer. We were well acquainted from previous years and so when I asked, he explained that our car had most likely been towed away. This gentleman, though born in Italy, taught at a university in the United States and was totally versed in the customs of both countries. About to return to the hotel with the bad news for Roger, I spied a large display of olive oil. The professor explained that it was fruity, extra-virgin and specially pressed Umbrian oil when I asked about its quality. I knew I had to have some. The only drawback was that it was being sold only in gallon jugs of glass which were rather large, heavy and fragile. Impulsively, I bought one anyway and was about to return to the hotel with news of the car's disappearance which I had almost forgotten in my olive oil excitement, when Roger appeared. We took the oil back to our hotel room and immediately proceeded to the police station to inquire about the car. A young woman from Tuscany to whom we had recently been introduced, graciously offered to go with us as translator. The bottom line was that we had to pay a fine and then take a taxi about five miles out of town to the garage where towed-away cars were stowed. We retrieved the car just in time, about eleven thirty on Saturday morning; the garage, we discovered, closed at noon on Saturday until Monday morning. This mishap was entirely our fault. Signs in that piazza clearly indicated that no cars were to be parked there after midnight on Friday. Even for English readers, the Italian was quite clear! Incidentally, that was only the second day of our journey that year, so I was obligated to carry that wonderful jug of oil for three more weeks, including hand carrying it on the plane back to the USA. (P.S. The oil was fabulous and worth every bit of discomfort from its heavy weight. Fifteen years later I admit to having any oil I buy shipped and not schlepped by me.)

Late autumn is harvest time for chestnuts. Every night after a late supper, whether we dine at home or at a restaurant, we enjoy these excellent kernels. Washed, pierced, briefly soaked and then cooked over an open fire, a better dessert cannot be found. They appeal to the sense of taste with the woodsy aroma of their origins as well as of their cooking medium. Along the roadsides, they are offered for sale by many vendors with literally full, heaping truck loads of chestnuts, but they are also found in supermarkets and groceries at harvest time. When roasted to perfection, not blackened, and accompanied by a small glass of *vin santo,* they seem even better!

Because we have frequently traveled to Italy in the fall of the year, chestnut season, and like to roast these in the fireplaces of our various rented houses, we have bought at least three chestnut roasting pans on separate trips. Dutifully we carry them home and line them up in front of our fireplace. Our grown children find this quite amusing, but feel it is behavior typical of their parents.

Most people are quite aware of the excellence of Italian wines. A mystery which had intrigued me for a number of years was finally solved. In the United States we had been buying wine called, "Montepulciano D'Abruzzo." I found this to be confusing, knowing that the Italian government strictly regulates the labeling of wine according to district. I had been to the beautiful town of Montepulciano many times and knew it was in Tuscany and known for its excellent wine. Visitors from all over the world come to this place for its history, its charm and its wine. In Abruzzo, I finally found the answer to the puzzle. Grape vines from Tuscany in the area of Montepulciano were brought to Abruzzo; this viticulture has brought much prosperity to a part of Italy where life was somewhat of a struggle for so many years. From the Veneto, other vines were also transplanted to Abruzzo and now its DOC Montepulciano D'Abruzzo and Trebbiano D'Abruzzo have been instrumental in bringing this province economically forward.

As an undergraduate in a class with Professor Vecchio, I learned many things in addition to medieval history, although his lectures on that subject were extraordinary. He told us that wearing a neck scarf would be a method of more easily keeping one warm in the cold weather as important temperature controls, glands, were placed in the neck; he occasionally shouted out the window at a fellow professor that it was better to make love than war. He spoke of a pasta which he said was his all-time favorite; although I had no idea what this was, it apparently remained in my unconscious mind for a number of years until a July day in the

1970's when we were lunching at the Lido in Venice. Appearing on the menu was this pasta dish I had never tasted, but which was the one the professor had described in detail, spaghetti carbonara. I remembered his near ecstasy as he spoke of it and described its deliciousness. I ordered it and immediately found he was correct in every respect. Some time after returning home I was casually looking through a travel magazine and came upon an article by Marcella Hazen about this dish as well as very specific instructions about making it. Immediately it became a permanent part of my cooking repertory and now is one of Roger's favorites as well. Several of our friends in Italy have become aware of this, resulting in two wonderful and separate evenings at two different homes at which we were guests; spaghetti carbonara was the main and delicious attraction of the evening's menu. Thank you Cathy, and sisters Rosalba and Gloria!

Teachers are often not aware of how seriously some students take their advice, not only about the subject being taught, but about life in general. I must thank the professor for his culinary suggestion as he left the school where I was a student and I never saw him again. Incidentally, as soon as the first cold breeze is felt in autumn, Roger is invariably found with a neck scarf. Good advice professor on both counts!

A monument, altar, or impressive public building should be built to honor the wonder of Italian ice cream, *gelato*. Simply, there is none like it in the world! Flavors one would never think possible are typical, and emporiums devoted to it have thrived for years and have become a mecca, not only for tourists, but for legions of ordinary citizens who regularly partake of this heavenly concoction. I immediately think of Vivoli's in Florence and Giolitti's in Rome, but they are only two of so many marvelous ice cream shops in Italy. The chocolate, dark and rich beyond belief, is Roger's favorite, while mine is called "Malaga;" two among nearly countless varieties and flavors. I have read that the Italians invented ice cream; if so, they created an art form with its never equaled perfection. I believe a monument is in order.

Many countries in the world produce cheese; Italy is certainly no exception and excels in this endeavor. Parmigiano reggiano, dozens of different pecorinos, gorgonzola, grana, mozzarella, ricotta, and on and on are only a few of the native cheeses. Some of these are fairly difficult to obtain in the United States unless one lives in fairly close proximity to enclaves of Italian-American people such as the North End of Boston, parts of San Francisco, sections of New York City and a few others. This is slowly changing though, as the demand for these special cheeses increases throughout our country. Most American replicas of these are simply pale imitations, and in my opinion, hardly worth the effort once one has tasted the real item. The comparison would be the taste of freshly squeezed orange juice to that from a can. We always carry Parmigiano cheese home after an Italian journey, and recently have added Grana to that. It is legal to bring these cheeses into the USA after a trip abroad if they are enclosed in vacuumed wrapped plastic.

One evening in a restaurant in Castellina-in-Chianti we found ourselves seated at a table next to a young couple from Bonn, Germany. Conversation followed and we agreed to meet at a different, but nearby restaurant for dinner on the following evening. At the end of a pleasant and satisfying meal, they said their good-byes as they had to return home; their one week holiday in Italy was ending and their employers would be expecting them on Monday morning. They told us that their car was full of Italian cheeses, cured meats, and cases of wine. We asked if they often came to Italy; smiling, they said as often as they could, but at the very least, for one week each year. Again we had a question; "Why Italy?"

In unison they enthusiastically replied, "To eat!"

We Americans do not have the liberty of bringing back many food items or much wine because of our customs and import laws. The European Union partners have the freedom to go across their borders with impunity. Before returning on a flight from Rome to Boston, I had stashed two apples in my pockets as the airline food in coach—or peasant class is often marginal. This is not a complaint to the airlines; getting there and back safely is their major job and that is incredibly effective. I wouldn't care if everyone was told to bring a brown bag lunch and dinner as I have noticed so many passengers are now doing on domestic, "no meal" flights. I consumed one apple on the way and totally forgot the other. After arrival and baggage claim, I got in the customs line. Having purchased very little, far under the allowed amount, I was unconcerned about the typical questioning. Soon I noticed the cutest little brown and white Beagle dog, dressed in a green jacket, go up and down the lines of people, sniffing at suitcases, purses and carry-ons. I wasn't paying an inordinate amount of attention to him as I assumed he was trained to find illegal drugs, and this certainly was not my problem. Suddenly he stopped by me and behaved in a way that indicated I had contraband. Embarrassed, I felt as if everyone in the entire terminal turned to look at me. Customs officers approached and asked me to empty my purse and pockets. What appeared was the other apple I had forgotten, which, along with any other fresh produce is illegal to bring into the United States from abroad. The apple was taken from me, a red-faced returning American. Of course I had known better, but innocently never remembered my forbidden fruit! I felt like Eve in the Garden! That little dog certainly knew his business!

Parenthetically, I have always wondered what happens to those other illegal pieces of fruit or mortadellas which are confiscated; do the agents have a picnic, or are they thrown into infernos to purge them of foreign germs?

I do not care for what is euphemistically called "fast food" whether in my country or Italy or anyplace for that matter. There is a restaurant chain which operates on the autostradas, called Autogrills. Called, "Italian fast food" by some, it could not be more different from the typical eateries found on the superhighways I have been in throughout the USA. From Rome throughout the northern parts of the country, this group makes food on the road a pleasure rather than something to be endured. As someone from New York once said to me, "If this is 'fast food,' then let me always eat fast!" For travelers in this restaurant there are two options; if one is in a great hurry there is a bar on one side which have pre-made, but decent sandwiches and all kinds of beverages. For those with a bit more leisure there is a cafeteria which offers unbelievably excellent meals. Beginning with a well-stocked salad bar and a fresh fruit station, the main line continues with appetizers such as prosciuto and mozzarella, and then proceeding forward, there is an array of many delicious offerings; several kinds of soup, and two or three varieties of pasta. A cook standing behind the counter will grill steaks, chops or other meat to order. A customer will point out the piece of meat he wants, and when it is cooked, he will be summoned to claim the finished product. If the restaurant is located near the sea, many varieties of fish are added to the usual choices, and again, cooked to order. Bottles of good olive oil and vinegar are strategically placed around the dining area for the use of the diners. Traveling on superhighways in our country is nothing like that unless one is willing to leave the main road and journey into a town or city for a regular restaurant. Sticking to the main highways, the fare is very limited. Again, this demonstrates the Italian value of offering food and hospitality as an important part of life. Many of these restaurants in the southern part of Italy are not of the same ilk; the number of travelers does not nearly approach the northern count which is most likely why these restaurants are fewer and offer little compared with the busy, industrialized grills of the north. Each year this changes as traveling and business patterns advance which warrants the expansion of this chain. A few years ago as we drove from Rome to Sicily, we were able to enjoy this fare more often than ever before.

As I read over more of my journals with full descriptions of memorable meals during thirty years, I feel obligated to mention that one cannot always judge the quality of food by the manner of dress worn by the waiter, headwaiter or even owner. I particularly remember a highly recommended restaurant in an historic, but definitely not tourist oriented, northern city; it was a fairly small, unassuming establishment, but so popular with local citizens that reservations were needed on any night in the week. We had been directed there by the managers of the hotel where we were staying. From the outside it was entirely nondescript; we never would have stopped had it not been for the hearty urging of the hotel people. Dinner was superlative; afterward we refused dessert as we were more than satisfied and completely full, but, as has happened to us often, the waiter brought us a few slices of cake anyway. For the most part, Italians are generous and want diners to be contented.

Many of our countrymen might have been upset by the clothing worn by the restaurant employees. Our waiter wore jeans, sneakers, had long hair and wore an earring; the owner wore sandals; the chef came out from time to time and chatted with the guests, the regulars whom he knew; he would sip a glass of wine with them and occasionally smoke a cigarette. There wasn't a tourist in sight; every diner was a local and all seemed to know each other, if only slightly. Our waiter panicked at first because he had no English whatsoever and there were no menus in Italian or in English. He spoke in Italian and told us what was offered that evening; fortunately, we had spent enough time in this country and in its restaurants to recognize the names of almost all of the food, and had no problem ordering. He visibly relaxed and we were on friendly terms throughout the meal. At several restaurants, mainly in the countryside but rarely in the cities, we have observed waiters and often their bosses in various states of what Americans might describe as "dress-down." We have concluded that casualness in attire has no effect on the proffered cuisine. On the other hand we have had meals in very modest places in which the waiters wore dinner jackets and black ties. Each day is a surprise, and rarely a disappointment. Ennui is not an option. Life is being fully lived!

Lovers of seafood have no problem satisfying their desire for fish in all forms. Restaurants specializing in this food are found in all towns near the sea, and since the geography of Italy encompasses much seaside, this cuisine is readily available. We have dined in excellent salt water fish restaurants in Pesaro, Pescara, Civitavecchia, Ponza and all over Sicily. Loreto Aprutino, though not on the water, is not far from it, and we enjoyed a feast of fish at a wonderful restaurant there. Mario took us and he ordered as he was more than familiar with the establishment and the owner. The appetizer alone consisted of twelve different fish dishes. Mussels, shrimp, salmon, oysters, clams, snails, sardines, herring and others I have forgotten. Some hot, some cold, salads and casseroles. Naturally pasta arrived later with more and different kinds of fish; a fantastic repast!

Our favorite sea fish emporium in Pesaro is similar; the fish appetizer alone consisted of fourteen dishes! All fresh and absolutely delicious! In seafood restaurants I always order spaghetti *vongole,* or clam sauce, and I did, but Roger order sole, and four good sized fish were served to him. He managed to finish three; they were perfect in every detail, but he was simply too full to devour the fourth. This we have found is typical; an over-abundance to us, but we have noticed Italians at these places who seem to have little difficulty finishing all. A perfectly cooked meal of fish is treated as a banquet and feast. And it is!

Lake fish from fresh water is the excellent offering of many restaurants bordering Lake Como, Lake Maggiore and the other magnificent lakes of the north. The only disadvantage is that one leaves the table in a near coma from over-eating!

On a beautiful April day, Fabio's parents took us to a magnificent spot overlooking Lake Como where lake fish are the specialty of the house. Four kinds of fish as well as two kinds of fish pate' and roe were served first, followed by pieces of lake fish served on a bed of rice. These, together with salad, bread, strawberries and coffee had us longing for the hour of *riposo,* or rest! A fantastic gastronomic experience, enhanced by the sheer beauty of the immediate lake scene with grandly impressive mountains as backdrop, made us pampered and pleased. In this country where food preparation and presentation are so very important so that client or family will be happily contented, we are rarely disappointed and almost always pleased beyond description.

A note in my 1997 journal states: "Their chicken has more flavor than our chicken. So does Italian milk, butter, eggs, yogurt, cheese and beef. Why?" I do not think I feel this way simply because I am on holiday. We have consumed many excellently prepared meals throughout many states in our country, but although very good, none we can remember have had the elusive and difficult to describe flavors and freshness of those in Italy. This is a mystery and therefore demands more and constant research! Another trip is in order as soon as possible.

I found another note in my journal from a few years earlier than the previous one; we were driving through France, heading toward Italy. "Our judgment is that French food is totally delicious, but we really prefer the simplicity of the Italian cuisine. I miss pasta. So does Roger."

One year we decided to drive north from Italy to visit Switzerland. We went to the resort of St. Moritz; after checking into a luxurious hotel with every amenity, we went to the dining room for dinner. Neither of us commented about the meal while we dined except to notice that it was beautifully prepared and served; the dining room itself was the epitome of style and elegance. We walked through the perfectly arranged gardens after dinner and returned to our room. Almost simultaneously we said, "Let's go back to Italy tomorrow." And so we did!

BUON APPETITO!

URBINO

"On the slopes of the Apennines toward the Adriatic Sea,
almost in the centre of Italy, there lies the little city of
Urbino . . . the country round about is very fertile and rich
in crops; . . . it has been ruled by the best of lords; . . . Duke
Federico, who in his day was (known as) the 'Light of Italy.'
"He built on the rugged site of Urbino a palace regarded . . .
as the most beautiful to be found in all Italy; . . . he collected
a goodly number of most excellent and rare books."

THE BOOK OF THE COURTIER
(IL LIBRO DE CORTEGIANO)
Baldessare Castiglione1528
Translated by Leonard E. Opdycke

Seeing Urbino suddenly appear in the distance is like looking into a drawer full of old mismatched sox and finding the diamond ring you lost two years ago. Amazement and delight come over you; you simply were not expecting that golden-hued community of buildings placed spectacularly on that high hill or sensing its fairy tale quality. This must be a magical place because your pulse quickens and your heart feels happiness. The scene before you is reminiscent of stories that were read to you before you could read yourself; stories of beautiful princesses and brave princes who lived in splendid palaces. This is Urbino.

Driving from Florence through Arezzo and Sansepolcro over the Apennines, the first view of Urbino is simply unforgettable, princesses aside! The amazing sight of this splendid city bursts out after a tortuous and lengthy journey on a series of roads seemingly designed for inducing vertigo. Never have I lost the astounding feeling of wonder I felt the first time I glimpsed the golden Ducal Palace surrounded by the architecture of this special town. That was more than thirty years ago, and though I have returned more than a dozen times, and have approached this rare and beautiful place from the north, south and east, the most dramatic entry, I believe is from the west.

After descending from the mountains but before a glimpse of the town appears, the road passes through the most beautifully manicured agricultural fields. Huge tracts on steep hillsides are perfectly plowed; occasionally there are some sheep and goats or a few head of cattle grazing on a separate hill. In November of 1998 an unusual Siberian cold front swept across Italy causing freezing temperatures and snow to fall as far south as Capri and Naples. In the Marche' the road to Urbino had been cleared as the storm had occurred four days before we traveled there, but the countryside was completely covered with deep snow. This was a very different entry to this enchanting town than we had ever experienced. Hundreds of trees were broken off from the weight of the heavy snow and ice. We spoke to an elderly lady who told us there was a meter of snow on the ground; the following day a resident spoke of the three quarters of a meter that had fallen, and that evening, still another person said one half meter lay on the ground. Depending on where each lived, it was possible all were correct. By any measurement, there was an enormous amount of snow! Staring from our hotel window later in the day, I was awed by the beauty of the white hills and distant mountains. I have looked at this same scene from the same window in the spring, mid-summer, the early autumn and now during the snow in November; the early green of April, with its promise of fruitfulness giving hope for the continuation of life; the heat of summer promising good crops; the harvest season, complacent with the satisfaction of a job completed; the whiteness of winter supplying the necessity of rest at the end of the year's cycle.

The treasure of the unique hill town in the Marche' is the Ducal Palace, built by the illustrious Renaissance prince, Federico di Montefeltro, the Duke of Urbino from 1444 to 1482. So nearly perfect was this man's reputation as he practiced justice and humanity among his subjects, it has been noted by his biographers that he often walked through the city unaccompanied by guards. His palace with its facade of twin towers, designed chiefly by the architect Luciano Laurana, is still today the jewel of this fabled place. When the Duke was alive he filled it with a collection of art that was notable, even for the Renaissance; his library was extensive and it included classic texts in Greek and Latin, as well as tracts and treatises in theology, medicine and contemporary authors. Castiglione and Vespasiano da Bisticci almost fell over themselves with praise for Montefeltro the man, his palace, his library, his collection of art and his lifestyle.

Federico's only son Guidobaldo died without an heir and subsequently much of the library was removed from Urbino to the Vatican while the art was swallowed by the galleries throughout Europe. Sadly, some works have vanished forever. However, great effort has been made in restoration in recent years; the Palace is a more than a worthwhile magnet for students, tourists and all who admire a gentleman as extraordinary as Federico di Montefeltro. An art collection is kept in the palace which is constantly growing and now this wondrous building is the seat of the National Gallery of the Marche'. Each time we return to Urbino we re-visit the Palace and each time it becomes more special. The baths, the wine cellars and the great halls now restored are fascinating, but my absolute favorite room is now as it has been since our first visit in 1975, the Duke's study. Intricate and delightful "pictures" made with inlaid wood make this the place in which I would love to spend hours, reading, writing, or just dreaming. Musical instruments, suits of armor in a closet, and many other figures are all depicted with uncanny attention to perspective and detail. My personal favorite figure is that of a small squirrel with a wonderfully full bushy tail; I have never forgotten this perfect little animal, and recently, I bought a post card featuring this little creature and put it in a frame. I can now enjoy it daily! I hope the Duke enjoyed his private study as much as I think I would.

Raphael, perhaps the perfect embodiment of the Renaissance painter, was born in Urbino. The house in which he lived with his artist father has been restored and makes a most pleasant spot to visit. On one return stay we brought a friend from Florence who had never been to Urbino and again, we visited Raphael's house. She toured the premises while I remained in the reception area and chatted with a young man who sold tickets and the few souvenirs displayed. He explained that this was not going to be his employment forever. Until recently all males in Italy were required to do military service for one year; one could serve this period as a museum worker, and so, there he was in the *"Casa di Rafaello."* Since then I understand that required military service has ended. Many charitable and cultural organizations were concerned about losing their "military assistants," however this will not be final for several years, so those groups dependent on volunteers should have time to make other plans. Thinking of the military, I was rather surprised to read an article in the October 25, 2000 INTERNATIONAL HERALD TRIBUNE, that "Italy is second only to the United States in the number of soldiers it sends on peacekeeping missions."

It so happened that Roger was to have a birthday during one visit to Urbino. I had contacted a friend there and asked her to find a suitable place for a dinner where we could celebrate with all the people we had become close to in the area. She chose a gem!It was an *agriturismo,* or farm which also served meals and frequently rooms to patrons. Located on a small stream in Urbania, a town near Urbino, this complex, run by a husband and wife team, cooked and served a Sunday dinner fit for an emperor, let alone a grandfather having a birthday! Everything was family style and the choices were theirs. To begin we had what I could only describe as a kind of quiche; next there was a frittata made with a barley like grain, which I believe is the now trendy farro, recently "re-discovered" but thought to be a mainstay of the Etruscan diet. These dishes were followed by deep-fried olives in batter, cheese sticks, and a delectable salad covered with finely chopped walnuts. Then the pastas appeared! A risotto, then a lasagne, followed by a penne and then a tiny pasta with a sauce so wonderful I didn't want to stop eating. Next roasted pheasant and rabbit cooked over open fires, baked cubed pieces of potatoes redolent with rosemary and garlic and several vegetables. We ended with two kinds of homemade cookies. The wine, both red and white, was plentiful, and we finished with a small touch of grappa!

There were ten adults and three children present; no one was rushed, no one was stressed. It was the best of an Italian Sunday with family and friends. Roger rose and thanked everyone for coming to his "99th" birthday, and asked if all would return for his "100th" ! He told several stories about how our love of Italy had begun, several of which were quite funny, and everyone applauded at the end. Our delightful guests presented him with a magnificent maiolica plate, made locally in Urbania, which was inscribed on the back with the date and place of this memorable occasion.

We planned on doing this again as soon as possible! At that time we did not know when we could return, but a variety of circumstances found us once again in Urbino only seven months after the March birthday party. Now it was October and the suitable day for all of our friends to be together happened to fall on our forty-fifth wedding anniversary, so we repeated the party with the guests sooner than we had thought possible! Purposely we did not tell anyone that it was a special day for us as we did not want our guests to think a gift was in order. After another different, but equally splendid meal, I rose as it was my turn to speak this time!

After thanking everyone for being with us, I said: "We have been coming to Italy for thirty years. Many people ask us why? Why Italy all the time? I tell them we like the food, the wine, the scenery, the art, the history, the culture; but most of all, we like the people, and you here today are among those on the top of the list. We are so happy to have you share this day with us as it the anniversary of our wedding, forty-five years ago." I held up a paper on which I had written, "45!"

Rosalba, the young woman we had known first when she was a graduate student in the United States, immediately disappeared after I finished and re-appeared soon after with a dried flower arrangement. This versatile establishment specialized in growing and then drying flowers which are then made into stunning bouquets; she had quickly procured one from the owners to present to us. I enjoy looking at it everyday, as it, along with so many other Italian mementoes, reminds me of another treasured experience in a very special place.

The third time we gave a party at this charming *agriturismo* we had grown to fifteen people including four children. After many kisses all around another festival of food began. Beginning at half past noon on Sunday, we finished at five! Of course, not every minute is spent eating; we all had a chance to visit, chat and catch-up on the events of the past eighteen months, for that is how long it had been.

At the risk of being redundant, I must say again, the meal was spectacular. To do otherwise would plague my conscience and embarrass my taste buds. Beginning with platters of sliced strawberries and kiwi, surrounded with balls of ricotta sprinkled with olive oil, we went on to a special salad which included real rose petals! Italian rules for these places insist that all food must come from the farm itself or at the least from the district in which it is located. "*Sformatino misti*" or small biscuits of green and white with pine nuts baked with cheese were next, followed by two pastas! The first was rollatini with garden vegetables; the second, freshly made bow-ties dressed with butter and asparagus. The main meat course was unlike anything I had ever had, but would love to have again! Beef, the most tender I have ever experienced, cooked first almost like a pot roast, then covered with a buttery crust, baked and served with natural juices.

To finish, as if we needed anything more, there were two kinds of wonderful cheeses served with local honey and marmalade, and finally *cantuccini,* a type of cookie and brownies. Throughout the meal, homemade breads were served, and red and white wine. Grappa and limoncello were offered at the end of the meal, but I saw no one partake. Perhaps we were all too full, but for the most part, Italians do not drink very much alcohol unlike some northern Europeans and many Americans tend to. Wine in moderation is simply an accompaniment to dinner.

A pleasant walk from the Urbino town center is the Church of Saint Bernardino. Inside of the building are the sarcophagi of both father and son, Federico and Guidobaldo Montefeltro. Next to this church is the cemetery; I find Italian cemeteries fascinating as they are well-kept, well-attended, and often lavishly adorned with marble statues and tombs as large as small cottages; we often spend an hour or two walking through some, but especially this one in Urbino. Frequently photographs of the deceased are on display, some of the tombs lighted with electric fixtures, and almost all festooned with fresh flowers. November first, All Saints Day, is especially the time when pilgrimages are made to honor one's departed family in respect and fond memory. Stalls selling flowers are invariably just outside of the cemetery gates and are open almost every Sunday throughout the year, but especially for the Day of the Dead as November first is noted.

Urbino is the location of a fine university; founded in 1506, it flourishes today. The old campus is located throughout the town; we had the privilege of attending an economics class having been invited by one of our three close friends who are professors here. Walking through the doors of the building to which we were invited was like entering a time machine. The facade of this particular building was constructed of heavy stone in the manner of serious Renaissance architecture, but once inside, there is a new world. Built mostly of concrete, the interior is modern, stark and very reminiscent of many of the buildings of the State University of New York where I took graduate classes. The auditorium in which the seminar was given was well lighted, had retractable desks and padded seats. The side walls can be opened so that all the auditoria can be used as one. Our friend Cathy told us they were all opened when the university presented Luciano Pavarotti an award!

Not too far outside of the city there is the new campus. Pastel buildings built into the contour of hills make up the newer and expanded university facilities. The Italian students are joined in summer and frequently in semester sessions by many from foreign countries. Both of our daughters studied here in summer programs from American universities which is how we became acquainted with this enchanting hill town in the first place. An added enticement for the young is that buses frequently leave the town for the beach in the city of Pesaro on the Adriatic, and this is often where students can be found after morning classes!

One morning in April as we walked toward the university to meet Giorgio, a professor in the Economics Faculty, the city was bustling; there were many carabinieri and we were told that it was the anniversary of the founding of the university and the head of the Italian Parliament was expected. He was to address the convocation. Giorgio's wife Cathy who also teaches at the university offered to give us a tour of the newly renovated Economics building. This edifice, formerly a monastery, is definitely a classic, retaining much of the style of the original period, but including such modern facets as a glass tower of stairs as fire escape. During the renovation of this building, a Roman wall was discovered as well as many graves of monks; the Italians are very proud of their history and historical sites, and nothing must be damaged, changed or destroyed. In preserving these icons of the past, three years were added to the construction time, but how refreshing to view a society and government honoring its past. I am always saddened when I think of buildings such as Pennsylvania Station in Manhattan and other parts of our architectural history bludgeoned into oblivion.

Roger and I were so taken with this town and its ambiance, that we attended a summer session for six weeks in 1976. Most of the people we knew considered this to be just one step away from insanity, but we didn't listen to them, we just did it. Never have we regretted one minute of that never to be forgotten summer. Roger had recently begun a new business; he left its operation to our eighteen year old daughter and nineteen year old son. This enormous responsibility showed so much trust on both parties; not only were we free for our Italian adventure, but it had to instill super amounts of confidence in these young people. Our sixteen year old son spent that summer commuting to New York City where he was a scholarship student at the American Ballet Theatre and our fourteen year old daughter was safely ensconced in an excellent riding and sailing camp for girls in Vermont near the Canadian border. She was less than delighted at the onset, but in retrospect, she perfected her riding skills and has very fond memories of a now long ago summer.

A few words of respect and gratitude must be mentioned for the professor who made the Urbino summers so special, not only for us and for our daughters, but for the hundreds of people who attended his program during the course of many years. He introduced Italy to us all as a very special place; he stressed the art, the history, the language, and the uniqueness that made this country different from any other. But, more than any other thing, he showed us how to live life and enjoy the world as Italians. On bus trips to Venice, Ravenna, Florence, Rome, Sorrento, Paestum and so many other fabled places, he used his microphone to educate us through entertainment. We sang songs he taught us in Italian, from "Bella Ciao" and "Volare" to the deeply moving and somewhat sentimental ballads of the Neapolitans. He pointed out things we probably would have missed on our own. He taught us about the food, the wine, and the local customs so that we wouldn't embarrass ourselves. He was an educator, an entertainer, a leader in seriousness and in fun. He was a friend.

Driving back to our dormitory in Urbino late one night from a marvelous three day trip to Venice, many of us in the art history class were frantically studying our notes and prints as the art professor had scheduled an important exam for the following morning. The bus was fairly dark making it difficult to read our notes and our leader and friend noticed our anxieties. He questioned us about it, and moving to the front, took the microphone, and solemnly announced that the art history exam scheduled for the next morning would be postponed for a day. This made the art history professor totally ruffled; she was young, new and constantly stressed. When she protested, he calmly announced that he was the boss, and that was "it," which he pronounced as "eat."

Returning to Urbino after another three day field trip to Florence, he announced on the microphone that we should be aware of the "ships." As we were crossing the Apennines at the time, everyone looked quizzically at each other in total confusion. Finally, he exclaimed, "There they are!" Laughter followed throughout the bus; his heavily accented English intended the word, "sheep."

This wonderful man, originally from Modena, was Dr. Gianni Azzi. He is no longer with us, but he remains a vital part of our heart memory. Rest in peace, dear friend, and thank you for the gift you have given to so many of us.

A walk upward through the town of Urbino leads to the Albornoz Fortezza, as well as to the small park where Raphael's statue, palette in hand, serenely gazes forth. The fortress is a gigantic erection built when Urbino came under the rule of the Papal States after the demise of the Montefeltros. Both places offer extensive and magnificent panoramic views, not only of the town, but of the extraordinary countryside. I never tire of these views.

Many day trips can easily be made from Urbino. The city of Pesaro has lovely beaches, very upscale shops, and the House of Rossini filled with much memorabilia of the famed composer. We have always teased Roger, that like an army he travels on his stomach, and therefore, he discovered a wonderful fish restaurant here. We never make a trip to this city without a stop here, not only for the excellence of the food, but for the fun of renewing acquaintance with the owner, his wife, and the headwaiter!

Many day trips near to Urbino are possible. Ravenna is a wonderful place to view early Byzantine Christian art. I stood in awe at the unbelievably stupendous mosaics in the famous churches of Sant' Apollinare and San Vitale.

Near to Urbino is the tiny Republic of San Marino well worth a visit. Claiming to be the world's oldest independent republic still in existence, its entire land area is a little over twenty miles. A main source of income here is issuing stamps to collectors and non-collectors alike. Of course, the many tourists who come to view the castles also keep the economy fluid.

In the late 1980's we visited the small town of Gradara. There were few tourists and shops. How that has changed! People have discovered the castle and its outstanding views of the Marche' countryside, but perhaps, more romantically, the connection between the castle and the sad story of Paolo and Francesca as told so touchingly by Dante in THE INFERNO. In the thirteenth century, the young Francesca da Rimini was married to Giovanni Malatesta for political reasons, a not unusual situation of the period. Lore maintains that she fell in love with his younger brother Paolo, and they began an adulterous relationship. Supposedly surprised together in a compromised position, Giovanni murdered both of them. Dante revealed his feelings for the couple when he placed the murderer in the last circle of Hell reserved for those who were guilty of treachery against their own flesh and blood.

The beloved poet gives Francesca beautiful lines in Canto V, Circle 2: "The Carnal" from THE INFERNO, a verse rendering for the modern reader by John Ciardi. (Mentor Classic, The New American Library, New York and Toronto, 1954)

> "Love, which permits no loved one not to love,
> took me so strongly with delight in him
> that we are one in Hell, as we were above."

Bravely continuing through Gradara as I tried to stop thinking of the lovely Francesca and her Paolo and their sad end, we both remembered that the last time we were here there were mirrors offered for sale in several places. I had wanted one, but the problem of carrying it home was overwhelming, so I did not buy any. But now, I decided that I really wanted a mirror as a Gradara memory. We walked into a shop owned by a man whose personality was the essence of friendliness. I chose a mirror small enough to be easily packed into my small suitcase; I knew exactly where I would place it when I got it home, and that is where it resides now, behind the small bust of Shakespeare so he could be viewed from back as well as front. The shopkeeper told me to take some postcards of Gradara as his gift to me. I chose several showing reproductions of various artists' paintings of the doomed and romantic couple immortalized by Dante Alighieri.

During our first visit to Gradara I was especially interested in taking some pictures of the great portico at the castle entrance which was raised and lowered by pulleys; at that time I was teaching MACBETH to high school students and wanted to show them the need for a "porter" in such medieval buildings to maneuver the huge gate as this character was included in Shakespeare's play. Most modern students think of "porter" only as a person who carries luggage.

We had heard of the town and fortress of Sassocorvaro and set out one morning to visit this place. On the way we traveled through a small village completely adorned in blue and white unbroken strings of flags along the roadside. Bouquets of both real and artificial flowers decorated the roadside as well; both kinds of embellishments were continued for fully five kilometers. Puzzled about what the occasion was, we found out in the evening as our friend and hotel owner Gianfranco told us that it was a local festival honoring Mary, the mother of Jesus. The display was fascinating and totally unexpected as it suddenly appeared along the road, and then just as suddenly, disappeared.

We continued toward Sassocorvaro. This huge fortress was rebuilt by the architect Francesco Martini after Federico Montefeltro defeated the former owner, Sigismondo Malatesta of Rimini in 1463. Having spent so much time in Urbino since 1975, I have been fascinated by the figure of Montefeltro, and in my opinion, he is one of the most compelling figures in Italian history, among so very many intriguing, whether honorable or despicable characters. Montefeltro secured his domain with more than one hundred fortresses, most of which were designed or adapted by Martini. A warrior, and often a mercenary, Montefeltro is better remembered today as an exemplary figure of what a cultured man of the Renaissance should be.

We toured the fortress with a guide; no one is permitted to wander through its vastness alone, and even in the third millennium this huge building remains captivating. Each room is carefully unlocked and then re-locked as one is guided through after having viewed the contents of each successive room. During World War II, 6509 works of art from Venice, Pesaro, Urbino and several other Italian cities were secreted here where they were safely stored and spared the devastations of aerial bombardment and thievery by Nazi armies.

Although added about three hundred years after the era of Montefeltro, I fell in love with a court theatre in the fortress. Built in the eighteenth century after the primary need for a fortress no longer existed, it is richly embellished with painting and decoration. What a perfect place for an intimate Shakespearean production!

The spiral staircase is especially interesting, perhaps mostly to architects and engineers because of its unique design, but what caught my eye was the floor of the courtyard. Built of stone, its pattern is composed of stars and what I saw as primitive sunbursts. I suggested that this would be a lovely pattern for our driveway, but Roger merely looked at me with one of his "fogetaboutit" looks and we walked on.

Planning on continuing toward the town of San Leo, we stopped in a pretty, small village, still showing its medieval heritage. We wanted a cappuccino; touring is really work and we felt the need for a small caffeine dose.

Driving on, we suddenly encountered a thick fog which descended on the narrow, mountainous and extremely curved road, so we decided to turn around and let San Leo wait until tomorrow. As we returned to Urbino, the rain began and intensified into a heavy storm, which explained the heavy fog curtain we had experienced earlier.

The following day, bright and sunny, we once again set out for San Leo. Named for its patron saint, its origins go back to the time of the Romans, and like Sassocorvaro, its fortress was rebuilt under the auspices of Martini at the behest of Montefeltro. As we neared the town, the imposing fortress stood out against the background of the vividly blue sky. Gradually we became aware of the sound and then the constant motion of a helicopter. Truly, this was the twenty-first century converging on the fifteenth! As we drew nearer we could see the efficiency of what was happening. The fortress was being repaired and the helicopter was constantly engaged bringing materials from the ground level to the high position of the fortress. Driving these items to the top by truck would have taken infinitely longer, especially considering the extreme narrowness of the road which wound around the mountain on which the fortress was placed. The activity and noise were incessant.

When we finally arrived we discovered an attractive town with perfectly aligned stone streets, palaces along the main piazza, an impressive church, a twelfth century tower and an overlook which encompassed a gorgeous expanse of the Marche' countryside. We got a tourist brochure which stated that, "A day discovering San Leo is not a day wasted." True.

This was May and the green of nature so vivid, the mountainsides and valleys so completely picturesque as to make one think this must be a painted unreality, but happily, the panorama was truly real.

Few Americans except for students travel to Urbino. The Marche' location is off the usual tour group track for people from the United States, but European tourists have known of this city and have come here for years. A motorway is being constructed, so I assume in time, the tour busses will be arriving in droves.

Urbino, known for almost six hundred years as the "Ideal City," has always been a special place to us; we never go to Italy without spending some time here. One can only imagine our shock when in 1996 we arrived and walked into the main piazza. There was a fountain, obviously old and weathered, placed directly in the middle of this square. Roger and I looked at each other; I did not remember ever seeing it and neither did he. Were we losing it? Prematurely senile? We had been at this site at least a hundred times, yet we couldn't remember this old, but stately fountain. Later, a friend explained the situation to us. The town had acquired this fountain from another place and it was "new" to Urbino. We felt much better, and marveled yet again at its ability to enchant with romance and magic. This is Urbino.

URBINO

Renaissance *palazzi*, (some with video game parlors inside)
Open to arcaded walkways often filled with bearded students
Strolling; cell 'phones seemingly welded onto their ears.
This is Urbino.

Perfectly aligned stone paved streets—that is the stone and not
    the streets,
Penetrate into the famed *Piazza della Repubblica*
Crowded with tables filled with *caffè*, *gelato*, or Campari.
This is Urbino.

The spirit of Federico Montefeltro presides gently
Over this city, much as he did in his active residence.
A perfect palace, art, and books reflect the values of this man.
This is Urbino.

"Light of Italy," bestowing grace and love through liberal arts,
Inspire all citizens, civil, artistic and academic
To honor your perfect ideals, stated by Castiglione
And given life through the painting of the Divine Rafaello.

INCONSISTENT CONSISTENCIES, CERTAIN UNCERTAINTIES AND CONFLICTING CONUNDRUMS

"There are those who would misteach us that to stick in a rut is consistency—and a virtue, and that to climb out of the rut is inconsistency—and a vice."

Mark Twain, "Consistency"

"Lump the whole thing! Say that the Creator made Italy from designs by Michael Angelo!"

Mark Twain, from INNOCENTS ABROAD, Ch. 27

"They spell it Vinci and pronounce it Vinchy; foreigners always spell better than they pronounce."

Mark Twain, from INNOCENTS ABROAD, Ch. 19

Italy is inconsistent. Consistently. This keeps one off balance just enough to be keen about receiving life's signals, antennae up. It is rather like a marriage that's not dull because it is not predictably programmed.

I treasure a photograph I shot in a cobbler's shop in Florence. The decor of the wall behind the counter is the subject. It displays:

1. A colored picture of Pope John, XXIII
2. A reproduction of The Virgin Mary from a Renaissance fresco
3. A sign forbidding smoking—"*Vietato Fumare*"
4. A photograph of a modern naval ship
5. A large colored picture from a calendar showing a sexy young woman emerging from a lake, still dripping wet, whose see-through blouse would be the envy of any entrant in a wet tee shirt contest.

The proprietor obviously sees no contradiction in his decorating scheme. Inconsistent.

I bought an apron at a souvenir shop to give to a son who likes to cook. Printed on it were the following words:

In Heaven:

> The English are the police
> The French are the cooks
> The Belgians are the bankers
> The Spanish are the dancers
> The Italians are the lovers
> And, it's all organized by the Germans.

However, in Hell:

> The English are the cooks
> The French are the police
> The Belgians are the dancers

The Spanish are the bankers
The Germans are the lovers
And, it's all organized by the Italians.

True? Well, perhaps a bit; even the Italians might be the first to agree, especially if the subject is their governmental bureaucratic organization. At first glance many things seems to be chaotic here, but a closer look suggests an ordered disorder, and to a foreigner, what appears to be without order, is often simply a cultural misunderstanding. I think of Polonius' line from HAMLET, "Though this be madness, yet there is method in't," while remembering Claudius the King's answer: "Madness in great ones must not unwatch'd go."

Just as Hamlet was not crazy, only pretending, neither is Italy; its method and style are always watched by the rest of the world, in wonder, and somewhat in envy. An uncertain consistency?

Having mentioned my favorite author, William Shakespeare, have you wondered why he used Italy as setting for so many of his plays? I have, and I used to imagine that he visited that country, although I never have read anything scholarly that suggested such an idea. Of course we know Chaucer was in Italy almost two hundred years before Will took quill pen to paper, and Anglo-Saxons have been drawn to this mystical, spiritual and sensual land for centuries, but most likely the world's most famous dramatist took most of his pertinent information from travelers or books. The comedies, set in various parts of Italy, are THE TAMING OF THE SHREW, TWO GENTLEMEN OF VERONA, THE MERCHANT OF VENICE and MUCH ADO ABOUT NOTHING; the tragedies, ROMEO AND JULIET, OTHELLO, and CYMBELINE; THE WINTER'S TALE is partially set in Sicily, and although THE TEMPEST takes place on an uninhabited isle, two of the characters are the

King of Naples and the Duke of Milan as well as others who are native to what is now Italy. The four Roman plays naturally are set in this land: CORIOLANUS, JULIUS CAESAR, ANTONY AND CLEOPATRA, and TITUS ANDRONICUS. A consistent certainty.

It was no literary sin during Shakespeare's era to "borrow" from other authors, and he used many Italian novellas and plays for beginning ideas; it was his genius however to reconstruct situations and characters to satisfy the English audience he was pleasing and to make the plots and characters ever more fascinating. In the English history play, RICHARD II, the Duke of York says to John of Gaunt:

> Report of fashions in proud Italy
> Whose manners still our tardy apish nation
> Limps after in base imitation.
> (II, i, lines 21-23)

This would seem to be a foreshadowing of the excellence and universal acclaim accorded to Italian design, whether in leather goods, clothing, furniture, jewelry, ceramics or racing cars. Apparently it was true in the seventeenth century as well. A certain consistency.

The magnetism which has drawn northern Europeans and more recently droves of Americans to Italy, has been the subject of many books, essays and discussions. More than thirty-five years ago Luigi Barzini noted this in his book, THE ITALIANS. He described the masses of tourists descending on Italy each year as a group, searching for an undefinable experience, unknown, unavailable, or beyond the bounds of what their own cultures offer or approve. He was discussing tourists as well as the numbers of ex-pats who were living in Italy in the 1950's and 60's and who often arrived like lemmings, with the fervor of those questing after the Grail; recent tourists for the most part are more sophisticated and understated. However, their purposes are very similar, if slightly camouflaged in less flamboyant traveling attire, with more information about culture differences, and a quieter attitude about trying to imitate the people, attitudes, customs, and even gestures of the Italian people. But deep down, silently, secretly and often unconsciously, many want to be Italian as they so sincerely admire the methods Italians use in dealing with life.

In April 2002 the Italian news section in English, of the INTERNATIONAL HERALD TRIBUNE, "Italy Daily" headlined:

"For U.S. undergraduates, Italy is still a Grand Tour." The number of one year or semester university programs offered through American schools number more than three hundred! While the number of students from the U.S. studying abroad has increased dramatically over the past fifteen years, the number studying in Italy has jumped from 3,782 in 1985 to 12,930 in 2000, a larger per cent of increase than in any other part of Europe. As the study abroad advisor at Bates College in Maine states: "Italy is the place you need to go if you're interested in Western culture." A huge number of American college programs are centered in Florence, which has upset some students as they feel being among so many students from their country has detracted from the Italian experience, but Stefano Albertini, a director of the NYU summer program in Florence states that it is an extension of "a centuries-old tradition of Anglophone intellectual attractions to Florence."

Any student who has been in an English or American literature class can name the many writers from England or the United States who have lived in Italy at one time. Byron, Keats,

Shelley, the Brownings, Mark Twain, Bernard Berenson, James Joyce, D. H. Lawrence, Ezra Pound and so many more. In 1818, Byron was said to have remarked that Rome was "pestilent with them;" to him, the "them" were the English! The recent film, TEA WITH MUSSOLINI, a somewhat autobiographical picture of the young life of the Italian film and stage director, Franco Zeffirelli, shows there were many English people living in Florence prior to the Second World War. Several of these women took an interest in the young boy and introduced him to English literature, especially to Shakespeare. Until this time I had always been curious about why a noted man in the Italian film industry had made films of Shakespearean drama—and in English! When I taught a high school elective in Shakespeare I always included showing the films ROMEO AND JULIET and THE TAMING OF THE SHREW after we had read and studied the plays as a class. TEA WITH MUSSOLINI solved the mystery for me. Even today, there are many English speakers living in Italy, including many literati and "wannabes" as well. Off the record, at least officially, much of Tuscany is known as "Chianti-shire" due to the numbers of British and Americans now living there. A consistent certainty.

I completely understand how these people feel about living and working in Italy, as well as what impelled others in the past to remain; I empathize with their great fondness for the ambiance of the Italian culture, emphasizing the importance of family, the goodness of food shared with others, and the noteworthiness of living and enjoying life to the fullest. I think of the character in Robert Frost's poem, "Stopping by Woods on a Snowy Evening," who would like to remain deep in the wood, but is drawn away as he remembers, "But I have promises to keep / And miles to go before I sleep;" I sympathize with the desire to stay forever, but, for now, I satisfy myself with annual trips of longer and longer duration. A conflicting conundrum.

So much in Italy is changing, being modernized, and adhering to the standards of the European Union. I chuckle though about several experiences I have had at the post office. In a small town in Tuscany I was a part of a scene which could have been in "I Love Lucy." We were long-time renters and therefore I frequently went to the post office to buy stamps and send mail. A gentleman usually waited on me, but on this one day he must have been on holiday and an attractive blonde woman was at the window. I showed her a postcard addressed to the USA, labeled "priority mail" and asked for "*venti francobolli*" or twenty stamps. Previously when I bought them they were stamped "1500 lire" for each. She then brought out forty "800 lire" stamps and said to me, "Put '*due*'—or two on each card." I looked surprised and said that last week they were "*quindici*"—or fifteen for each, not sixteen. Not understanding me, she immediately took ten away so that I would have enough stamps for only fifteen cards rather than twenty. I must have looked extremely puzzled, but a man next to me who had some English told me that the post office was out of 1500 lire stamps, but she'll give you two 800 ones for each card, but only charge you for 1500 ones. I thanked him, and smiled. When I got into the car I laughed hysterically; I cannot imagine a country of this size with its enormous GNP having post offices run out of stamps! From experience I know it has happened here before, but now with the EU I felt the rules would be more strict! I was wrong! Another oddity was apparent; although the stamps were printed in lire, the only acceptable national currency is the Euro! This reminded me of a situation of five years before. We were in Sicily and again, I wanted stamps for my post cards. They are sold in small shops called, "*tabacchi*" or tobacco shops. Since we had been in the north of Italy before going to Sicily I knew that the then going rate was 1300 lire for each card. I asked the young lady at the shop for twenty 1300 lire stamps and showed her my cards. She was horrified, pulled out an official looking book and pointed to the number she said was enough for the cards,

900 lire. I tried to disagree but she wouldn't hear of it, and so I bought twenty 900 lire stamps. After I wrote and put the stamps on the cards, I went to the post office in the town of Terrasini and presented them at the window. The postmistress said, "No, no! Not enough!" She told me I needed 1000 lire on each, and so I bought these extra stamps, put them on the cards, and gave them back to her to make sure they were now correct. She said, "*Bene*" and flourished her stamp as she smacked the official seal down twice on each card. She said all was fine.

Our next stop was Amalfi where we had rented a water front apartment for one week. I needed a few more stamps and went to another tobacco shop; I asked the proprietor how much postage was required for a priority mail post card to the USA. 1300 lire was his reply!I checked with the very fluent manager at our apartment complex and he said, 1300 lire. I wondered if Sicily had an independent post office system and hoped that my post cards would arrive before we returned home. Three weeks later we were home; the cards from Sicily had not yet arrived, but within two more weeks, they were. We finally figured out what the confusion was. 1300 lire paid for airmail; for 1000 lire our cards had a long sea voyage from Sicily to the United States! Conflicting conundrums!

Eight months after 9/11 we went to the American Express office in Florence; there was a guard at the door with a hand-held metal detecting device. I sat on a chair provided for those who didn't want to go through the device while they waited for someone else. I held Roger's spare change and Swiss army knife in my purse and he went in to cash a check. Having nothing to do but observe, I watched a scene somewhat akin to Abbot and Costello or The Three Stooges!

A friend of the guard came in and they went to the back of the office and laughed and joked. Meanwhile two women entered;

no examination. Then the guard and his buddy went across the street for coffee. No one was guarding the door. A man entered with a very large briefcase held by an over the shoulder strap. He could have had a tommy gun or a small nuclear device in it. No problem; he just walked in. A certain uncertainty.

We have traveled by car from the Lake District in the north to the far south, staying variously in hotels, apartments, and in *agriturismo,* farm accommodations. In three of them the owners or managers never asked for our passports; in two hotels only one passport was required, either mine or my husband's; it did not matter to the clerk. In three other places, both of our passports were required without exception. When I inquired about this inconsistency, one gentleman told us it was decided by the local provincial office and not the hotel or apartment landlord. Well, perhaps. A consistent inconsistency.

Many years ago we once spent five weeks in a small hill town. Each morning we went to the same bar for a light breakfast, often only a cup of tea. Each morning the same young man behind the counter waited on us. And, each morning after his *"Prego?"* (Please?) we replied, *"Vorrei due the' con latte'."* (I would like two teas with milk.) He would then ask, *"Limone?"* (Lemon?) We would reassure him that it was milk and not lemon we wanted. It became a ritual; we almost began to fear he wouldn't question our desire for milk rather than lemon. To be fair, this was a very provincial town thirty years ago; the lad, though good-natured was not a rocket scientist, but then, most of us aren't either. An uncertain certainty.

In large cities many bars have three prices for coffee or for anything else for that matter. The least expensive is for those who stand at the bar to drink whatever it is they have ordered; the next level up is for those who choose to sit at a table within the bar; the most expensive is for those who decide to sit at an outside table in the good weather. In Venice, years ago, we noted a fourth. Occasionally a full, formally dressed orchestra will perform in the Piazza San Marco; when the music is playing the prices once again can rise. Although this is a reasonable element, many first time tourists do not understand and can become irritable because they believe they are being cheated. Unfortunately many of us do become annoyed at that which we do not understand. A conflicting conundrum.

Having stated the rules about bar prices, I must add that outside of the large cities, this is not always true. Most of the time if we are unfamiliar with the bar, we stand and drink our coffee or cappuccino as do the vast majority of the Italian people. But it is often different in a small town, especially if one is a "regular." Our favorite bar in a small town in Tuscany, family run and most comfortable, does not adhere to these standards. When we are in town we go there every day but Wednesday; they are closed on Wednesday. The Signora is always urging us to sit. We've noticed that some of her regular patrons do come in and sit and read the available newspapers at a table, so occasionally, we also sit. The prices for tea or coffee do not change. She seems pleased when we do take our time to read or when I write in my journal. Perhaps she is content with the fact that these Americans return to her country, and especially to her town, year after year, preferring her bar to the others just as most Italian patronize a favorite bar. It is so pleasant to recognize the same faces who are there day after day, as you are, feeling as if you belong to a special club; you are greeted with warmth as if you haven't been seen for months despite the fact that only yesterday you stopped by for a coffee and small pastry. That is a certain consistency!

Many years ago we stayed in an outstanding hotel in Milan filled with exquisite antiques, ancient statues and gorgeous

Oriental rugs. Mounted on the back of each bedroom door there was a sign written in four languages. As most hotels in all parts of the world do, the notice advises guests when they must vacate their rooms or be charged for another day. A compulsive reader, I almost shouted with laughter when I read the instruction given in this most beautiful, yet intimate hostelry.

(In Italian)
LA CAMERA DEVE ESSERE DISDETTA E LASCIATA LIBERA ENTRO LE ORE 11, ALTRIMENTI SI INTENDE TACITAMENTE CONFERMATA FINO AL GIORNO SUCCESSIVE.

(In French)
MESSIEURS LES CLIENTS SONT PRIES D'ANNOUNCER LEUR DEPART AVANT MIDI, ENCAS CONTRAIRE ILS SERONT TENUS DEPAYER UNE AUTRE JOURNEE.

(In English)
GUESTS ARE KINDLY REQUESTED TO ADVISE THE MANAGEMENT OF THEIR DEPARTURE BEFORE NOON. AFTER THAT THEY WILL BE CHARGED WITH THE COST OF THE ROOM FOR ANOTHER DAY.

(In German)
UNSERE VEHEHRTEN GASTE WERDEN GOBETEN, IHRE ABREISE VOR 12 UHR, DA SIE SONST DEN PREIS FUR EINEN WAIRTEREN TAG FUR DAS HAUS HAFTET NICHT FUR WERTGEGENSTANDE, DIE NICHT BEI DER DIREKTION ABGEGEBEN WORDEN SIND.

Do you see the humor? In French, English and German, hotel guests are advised that they must leave their rooms by noon. In Italian, the time is 11 A.M. Inconsistent, but by design a consistency. I can only assume that the management can hope that by advising their Italian guests they must vacate by eleven, that it will probably happen by noon. Obviously the French, English and German speakers feel much more obligated not only to obey directions, but to regulate their lives by designated hours and minutes. The charm, and I suppose the exasperation some feel about the Italians is that they feel no such constraints about time, and often move with the flow of their inner feelings. Obviously this is changing more and more each year as the pressure of business increases in keeping with the economic drive to keep Italy in tune with the European community. Old habits can change and do, but often slowly. A certainty.

Inconsistent patterns are exasperating, more so to Italian people than to tourists, who do not have to deal with the more bureaucratic stumbling blocks that the people who live there do with annoying regularity. A friend who owns a hotel is continually frustrated in dealing with the vast government system; it took him twelve years to finally procure the permits to add additional rooms to his lovely hotel! Another friend who owns and operates an estate in Tuscany on which he grows olives and grapes, spent several years getting permission to build a garage on his seventy acres to store his tractors and other farm equipment. Both of these gentlemen laughed at my husband's complaint that in our country it took two years and a goodly sum of money to receive permission to build a dock on our own waterfront property. A conflicting conundrum.

This Orwellian mumbo—jumbo may be the reason that throughout so much of Southern Italy, especially in Sicily, Calabria, Basilicata, Apulia and other parts of some provinces, there are literally thousands of buildings, begun but unfinished and abandoned. These homes, apartment houses, hotels and offices stand with gaping holes in their structures, like missing eyes, intended to have been windows. Some have remained that way for so long that weeds and occasionally flowers, protrude from the masonry. Vast amounts of money are represented in partially built structures which stand unused and unusable throughout these areas. Repeatedly we have asked many people why this is so. Some have answered that the permits were not done correctly or were never issued, and that they were stopped by law enforcement. Still others maintain the buildings failed safety codes, or that financing went awry. With a shrug and a knowing look, a few declare it was the influence, or lack of influence of the Mafia. Another mysterious uncertain inconsistency.

How do you get into a taxi? After calling for a taxi one evening in Florence and entering it, the smiling, very friendly taxi driver greeted us and said we were Americans. We had not spoken to him as the waiter at the restaurant had called for us so he did not hear our voices. We asked him how he knew. Laughing, he told us it was the way we entered his vehicle. Americans go into cabs with head and hands first; he jumped out and demonstrated the way Italians enter—feet first!A consistent certainty?

When our daughter and her husband visited us in Tuscany during her Easter vacation we visited Elena's ceramic shop. We both, Leslie and I, have patronized this delightful woman's perfect small shop for years and have become a friend of hers and her husband and children. Both of our houses display wares bought here.

Our Italian fluent daughter spied a large terra cotta bust of Dante Alighieri on a high shelf; we could tell she liked it very much, but because it was fairly large and extremely heavy and consequently would cost more to ship than the original price of the sculpture, her husband discouraged her from purchasing it.

Well, what are parents for? After the young couple returned to New York, we went back to Elena's and bought Dante! I decided that he would fit—just—into my carry-on bag and that I would personally transport him back to the United States when we returned. Thus began an interesting yarn.

In the Malpensa airport in Milan we were going through the check point in which anything one is carrying is x-rayed. The young woman operating the security device suddenly gasped, halted the conveyer belt and summoned the manager. We peeked over the rail to see what was in our bag that halted the process and upset the operator. We almost gasped ourselves, because through all the Styrofoam and paper protecting our terra cotta Dante, the x-ray image looked precisely like a decapitation. When the manager arrived he peered at the projected image, frowned slightly, then looked at Roger. Again he stared at the image for a few seconds, then looked at me. Smiling, he nodded at the operator of the security device and said, "OK, OK, *Americani!* (Americans!)" I guess our innocent faces, together with the demeanor of grandparents, erased any thoughts he might have had about our strange carry-on content.

I said, "That's Dante Alighieri." He again smiled and ushered us through to the boarding area. That story has continued to amuse us, our family and friends, and greatly embellished our Christmas gift to Leslie when she received her surprise head of the most famous Italian poet.

In the weekly street markets, whether in sizable cities like Siena, or very small towns such as Panzano, there is always at least one vendor for women's underwear. The amount and the variety of items on display at these open markets are amazing. There are many shops in the cities specializing in these interesting articles of under apparel, often shown in their windows in an almost salacious manner, but the vast quantity in street markets is overwhelming. Lace is the material most in vogue in bikinis and thongs; found in many colors, they hang from the awning tops of the mobile trucks.

What is truly puzzling to me is the dearth of women I have observed purchasing these items. Most likely I simply missed the transactions; they must make sales or obviously they would not continue to be in business, and these stalls are so ubiquitous business must be booming. In all fairness to the patrons of these kinds of markets, most shoppers are serious, mature types, often grandmothers in charge of small grandchildren or women seemingly in pursuit of vegetables for dinner or a new tablecloth, and not the teen or young twenty types whom we think are purchasers of these sexy and often beautiful items. But, perhaps again, I have it all wrong. Could it be that all Italian woman of all ages wear fantastic and provocative underwear? If so, good for them! Brava to each! An uncertain certainty!

Italians seem so much less uptight about the human body or mentioning its various functions. The Creator made human beings in only two forms they seem to suggest, so what's new? Perhaps being raised with the sculptures from the Greeks and Romans, as well as with the magnificence of the statues and paintings of the Renaissance, have made these people much less uptight about the human body; as I mentioned, there are only two possibilities.

Being raised from early childhood without the prejudice of being afraid of the undressed creates a much more normal person. One of my daughters has a reproduction of Michelangelo's "David" on her piano; another daughter has the statue on the dining room china closet; after a trip to Italy the older one returned with a statue copied after Botticelli's "Venus." As she placed it next to "David" her then three year old son exclaimed, "David's wife!" Neither statue is obviously adorned.

I do not mean to imply that erotic magazines and calendars are strewn through households, but advertisements for legitimate products often display the human body or parts of it in context. A pharmacy window showed an ad for a baby bottle nipple. Next to this rubber nipple there was a photo of the human female breast. The gist of the message was that it was better to nurse your infant naturally, but if you could not, our brand of nipples most closely resembles the human one. I know I would never find this in the window of my pharmacy.

A TV ad showed a small boy sitting on the toilet. He was holding his nose and making a face; suddenly he squeezed an air freshener next to him and he became all smiles! Suggesting this universal body function would not play out I think on American television.

One of my grandchildren, then a third grader, went to the library with his class. He found a book about someone he recognized and was excited. Too large to put in his back pack, he carried it onto the after school bus. Sitting next to a friend, he began to show and explain some of the pictures of the objects in the book. Suddenly, a fifth grade girl began screaming at him; "That's dirty! You are bad! I'm reporting you!" Frightened, he closed the book and became very quiet for the rest of the ride home.

The following day he came home from school and sat at the kitchen table for a snack and homework. His mother was standing by organizing the kitchen in preparation for dinner. He spoke, somewhat lawyerly, saying, "How many times do you think I've been sent to the principal's office?"

His mother cooly answered that she had no idea—perhaps twice, four times, five? Just as cooly, he said, "Just once, and it was today."

He explained about the book and the incident with the girl on the bus; apparently when she got home she told her mother who then telephoned the school principal to complain about the reading material of this child she named, and that he had gotten it from the school library. The principal went to the library the following morning and asked what book had been taken out by my grandson. The librarian teased her for a minute we later found out, as she said that she couldn't reveal the title as it would be a violation of the first amendment! Of course she looked in the computer and they both saw the name and subject of the book in question. After returning to her office she summoned the young lad to her office and asked him about the bus incident. He told the principal that his mother was an Italian teacher, and that they had many sculptures in their house. He then added that he saw a book about Michelangelo and that he was trying to explain what he knew about him and his work to his friend. He told her that this boy didn't know about "David." Then he added in all confidentiality to the principal, "But, Michelangelo was not the first sculptor to do 'David;' Donatello was." Rather impressive for an eight year old!

This very competent woman then told this precocious youngster that he was permitted to take any book he wished from their school library. Later that evening she met with my daughter as it was parents' night, and assured her that all was well, and that her son was polite, well-behaved, and very bright. This incident would never have happened in Italy. A certain certainty!

Italians are full of opinions and contradictions. Religion has always had a most important place in the lives of most people, and yet certain situations provoke unexpected answers. During the period when the United States President Bill Clinton was being vilified in the media almost daily, we had dinner with a retired carabinieri officer, a man best described as politically conservative. He asked us with great consternation, "Who is this terrible man, Starr? Why is he bothering President Clinton? This man is leader of the free world and he is being annoyed by questions that do not concern the world."

We were constantly bombarded by these kinds of accusations, not only in Italy, but in England where we had stopped for a week on our way to the continent; we were at a loss to explain why some people in our country were having such glee on a witch hunt. In Italy, whenever we met French, German, British or other Europeans who spoke English, or Italian nationals who did, we were repeatedly asked why many of our politicians were pursuing this situation with the zeal of the Inquisition. They were totally mystified; one woman said they would worry more about their leaders if they didn't have a small scent of scandal about them as that would probably mean they were martinets, or worst, tyrants. A certain consistency.

About twenty five years ago, an eighteen year old exchange student from Parma stayed with our family for three months. Our younger son was also eighteen and they both attended senior classes in the high school in our town. When he first arrived on Saturday evening, I asked him if he would like to attend Mass the following morning as we would see that he got there. He frowned, and said, that no, he never went to church. I asked him if he were a Roman Catholic; he replied that he wasn't. I then asked him if his parents were Catholics; again, he answered negatively. I said, "But when your parents were married, did they marry in the Church?"

His reply, "Of course." Inconsistent!

A professor from Italy who was teaching at a university in the United States and with whom we had become friends, was terribly disturbed by much of the negative rhetoric in our country about birth control. He considered himself a Catholic, though I suspect somewhat lapsed, and as he scratched his chin and furrowed his brow, he referred to the men of the Church and stated that if they didn't play the game, they shouldn't make the rules! I was surprised and somewhat taken back by his frankness, but after becoming more and more acquainted with Italian people and the way in which they approach life, I was no longer startled by his pronouncement. Incidentally, since the 1960's, Italy has had the lowest birth rate of any industrialized country in the world; single child families are prevalent, although as the economy continues to accelerate, we are told that many couples are now having a second child. A consistent inconsistency. The February 21, 2002 edition of "Italy Daily" published with CORRIERE DELLA SERA, states that," Italians top world rankings for having sex; . . . the study examined the sexual health of more than 26,000 men and women between the ages of 40 and 80 in 29 countries." The downside was that in Italy only "44 per cent of men and 32 per cent of women said that they were fully happy with their sex lives." An interesting conundrum!

Some incidents which captured much media space a few years ago indicate that there is yet much division in attitudes about alternative sexual practices. A priest from Piedmont was defrocked as he defied his bishop and married many gay couples despite being reproved for thirty years. Transvestites devoted to Mary, the mother of Jesus, have traditionally participated in The Candelora, a celebration at the twelfth century sanctuary of Montevergine, near Naples. Last year they were prevented from doing so by the local abbot. An uncertain conundrum.

Italian children do not have to learn how to spell. The words in their language are spelled precisely as they are pronounced. I once asked a highly educated Italian woman how to spell a word I was trying to write in her language and she looked at me quizzically, as if I had asked her to define relativity. School children do not realize how fortunate they are in never having to learn the unruly letters that English speakers and writers must. If you have ever helped a child who has a spelling test learn the words, "rough," "bough," "though," "through," and "thorough" or have tried to help a non-English speaker with the pronunciation of "knife" or "gnaw," you can appreciate the beauty of the Italian language. This is a certain consistency, but it reminds me of an experience I once had. I was dozing in a comfortable bed in a hotel in Rome when I heard my husband speaking fairly quietly on the telephone. I thought at first he was trying to speak in tongues, or that possibly he had gone round the bend. Deliberately and somewhat slowly he said: "PALERMO, EMPOLI, TORINO, EMPOLI, ROMA, KAPPA, IMPERIA, NAPOLI." Was this a quiz on Italian cities? A joke? Was he being weird? Then in a few more seconds I realized he was making a dinner reservation by spelling our last name; one spells foreign names or places by using Italian cities, as ordinary letters are pronounced differently in English. He spelled PETERKIN ! That's just how it's done here. Neat! Its inconsistencies are often interestingly consistent!

Mark Twain's philosophy about inconsistency not necessarily being a vice, nor consistency a virtue, made me recall a statement made by another professor in grad school. She was a brilliant woman whose lectures held me in rapt attention. Several times during the semester, she emphatically stated: "There is a queer beauty in consistency," if she were pointing out an inconsistency of point of view in a student's essay. During one lecture on a British drama from the 1920's, she declared that the behavior of a major character was predicated by his need to compromise. This class took place during the late 1960's; there were many intelligent, fervent, and sometimes misguided young people, who for the most part wanted to change the world for the better as they interpreted it. One of these determined souls was in our class. As soon as the word "compromise" left the professor's lips, Robert's hand shot up dramatically and he nearly shouted, "I believe all forms of compromise to be immoral!"

Our very bright and attractive teacher merely sat still for about thirty seconds. Then, with a knowing look, she stared directly at him, and firmly, but not unkindly, said, "Baby boy, you've never been married." Robert had little to say for the final two weeks of the course after having made continual comments for the prior three months. Consistent inconsistency, even in New York!

People in Italy are extremely hard working. No matter where we are we see labor in action. Simply watching the physicality of men artfully construct a wall, or replace stones in a street in the perfect pattern in which they were removed, so that even after new gas lines or water pipes were placed under the street, the intricate surface design will be so perfect no one could ever know they were disturbed, is totally intriguing. Making this work even more difficult is that often, the streets used since the medieval period in some instances, are so narrow and filled with pedestrians there is an acute lack of room for the workers and their equipment. But, they manage.

We have observed people in the fields pruning olive trees and grape vines from early morning until dark; both men and women harvest kiwis; and again, both men and women cook for crowds, clean houses and hotel rooms; the almost balletic non-stop movement of pizza makers, and what appears to me as the carefully choreographed movement of restaurant waiters are exciting to watch; these are only some of the constant displays of labor. I especially recall a small restaurant in Fonterutoli. In addition to the six tables, each holding between two and four diners, there was a large party of sixteen men and women. The owner was alone that evening in the dining room. He took every order separately, served wine and water, and took a minimum of three different courses to each person. He was never flustered or appeared rushed; it was a joy to watch him. No one at any other table was ignored either, and after everyone finished he made espresso individually for any who wanted it as well as serving many different desserts.

Though these are employments with a great deal of physical movement, we have observed the same untiring work ethic from office workers in hotels, banks, offices, postal offices, airports, and so many other places in Italy.

Americans from all parts of our country, from all economic groups and ethnic groups are very hard workers as well, however, there seems to be one noticeable difference. This was pointed out to us many times, not by Italians and not by American tourists, but by Americans working for Italian companies or American companies with branches in Italy. These people were living in Italy after having worked many years in the United States. They all said: "Americans live to work. Italians work to live." Life is a priority to the Italians; spending time with family is more than important, it is necessary for a good life and a good family. That is what life is about.

Our British friend who has lived in Italy for so many years has had many American guests stay in his rental apartments. He, though a most energetic and diligent man who seemed to be constantly directing, organizing and working with his employees on his estate, reiterated the same theme we had heard from the temporary ex-pats. "I am amazed and a bit horrified at the stories I hear from so many Americans about the hours they work, including nights and weekends. Their families must suffer from this; money isn't everything." A conflicting conundrum.

When the American Express Company first offered travelers checks on which two signature could be written so that either person could use them without the other's presence, we opted for this convenience. There was no problem doing this in Rome, Florence, Urbino or many other places, but in Pescara at the Bank of Napoli, we found an obstacle. Before we knew this I sat in the car reading while Roger went into the bank to cash a check. He said he'd be back in ten minutes. After twenty minutes had elapsed he returned and said they refused to cash the checks unless I signed them as well as he. The news about two signature checks had obviously not reached this particular bank.

I then accompanied Roger to the bank. The teller and the manager both said they had never seen these checks and were reluctant to cash them even if we both signed! Suddenly, two other bank employees materialized and the four men consulted, discussed and argued for at least fifteen minutes about the correct way to handle this new situation. One man seemed very informed and strove mightily to convince the others. Finally he prevailed, although the others were reluctant and suspicious. We tried to ask them to telephone the American Express office, but the language difficulty hampered this. First, both of our passports had to be examined and then xeroxed; we then had to sign the copies of the passports as well as three or four other sheets of paper relating to the check cashing. The total amount we were cashing was only two hundred dollars, but I believe the drill would have been the same for a check of a ten dollar denomination. Finally we did get the lire we needed, which was used prior to 2002. Incidentally, I had to leave my handbag with the guard at the door in order to enter the bank; Roger had to leave his keys and camera. This was done so that we could get through the sensitive electric doors. Another adventure! Definitely inconsistent with respect to many other bank visits we have made.

Energy is extremely expensive in Italy whether it is electricity, gas for the home, or gasoline for cars. We had read that nuclear power plants were rejected by the Italian people by national referendum years ago, and as a result the country must buy much electricity from other countries. Many hotels and rental units have low wattage lamps, lights operated by timers in halls and on stairways, lights which automatically turn off when the door to a hotel room is locked from the outside, and I know of only one family who has an automatic clothes dryer. Laundry is hung on lines outside, or in unused rooms inside in inclement weather. Italian clothes washing machines tend to be much slower than American ones, but save great amounts of water, and actually seem to do a better job.

By standards in the United States, gas for the car is horrendously expensive as it is throughout most of Europe, which is why Europeans feel Americans are terribly spoiled when we scream about the price of gasoline if it is raised a few cents. Their prices are often much higher than what it costs us per gallon. Being in Italy always makes me aware of being more conservative about energy of all kinds. We Americans tend to waste so much needlessly. Someone once told me that we make up six per cent of the world's population and use twenty-five per cent of the world's energy. A consistent, if somewhat embarrassing certainty.

The old adage about not judging a book by its cover could apply to Italy very well. Many years ago we drove a young man to a small city near Naples; an American college student, he had been studying at an Italian university for the summer and before he returned to his home in New York, he was going to visit relatives. We were more or less going in that direction and offered him a ride. After we parked we accompanied him to the residence where he would be visiting as he wanted us to meet his aunt and cousin. We proceeded down a dreary alley and approached what appeared to be a run-down, paint-chipped building, complete with a door I can describe only as being similar to those I've seen on dilapidated barns. When we were enthusiastically greeted and entered the house, I thought I must be having delusions. Lush Oriental carpets covered every floor; well-made mahogany furniture filled the rooms; a sideboard was filled with exquisite pieces of silver, crystal and china. From the outside, this house looked as if poverty reigned; inside it reminded me of what I thought of in the word, "palatial." This type of experience has been observed by us many times in many different ways. Don't judge that book! A consistent certainty!

Our good friend Bill, an American employed as an executive with a world famous Italian fashion empire, lived in Florence for many years. We visited him each time we were in Italy which was always enjoyable. Our relationship went back more than twenty years from the time one of our daughters was employed by the same company in Manhattan. They both began there in the fashion business, and though their career paths have widely diverged, they have continued their friendship; she and her husband always visited Bill when in Italy.

One year we were in Italy in October; Bill had decided to have a Hallowe'en party and he invited us. There was no way we wanted to miss this affair knowing his impeccable taste and style, as well as the array of fascinating international guests he would have from the fashion world, the art community, the merchandising business, some Americans who lived in Florence, and simply, some friends such as we were. We'd be there! That was a consistent certainty.

Hallowe'en, as Americans celebrate the day, is a fairly new concept to Italians. Generations have held November first, the day following Hallowe'en, All Saints Day, as a time for a serious tribute to the departed. It is a national holiday and one is obligated to visit the cemeteries to honor the family members who have died.

Globalization and marketing are making inroads on this seriously thought of day in Italy; jack-o'lanterns, black hats adorned with witches or cats, costumes and party favors with a Hallowe'en theme are beginning to appear in many department and specialty stores. Many Italians, especially those who are older, are very offended by this movement which they feel is not Italian, but an unattractive American import which detracts from a day of serious reflection and obligation.

Be that as it may, Bill, an American from Pennsylvania, was having a party! His friends, mostly young and internationally minded, were enthused. The problem for us was simple; we were expected to wear costumes, and although typically we had packed more clothes than we really needed, Hallowe'en costumes were not among our traveling possessions. What to do without spending a fortune?

There are many vendors throughout Florence, as well as in most other major Italian cities, who offer tourist oriented tee shirts, calendars, post cards, dish towels and many other items; most of these have the names of the particular city, or "Italy" or sports stars imprinted on them. Aprons are a popular feature; some show pictures and names of Italian cheeses, others Italian wines, desserts, Pinocchios, or maps to catch the eye of the traveler.

I remembered seeing one apron which pictured Michelangelo's sculpture of "David" reproduced from the neck to the thighs in all his robust and accurately portrayed nakedness. Another one was of a gorgeous female body, perhaps inspired by Botticelli's "Birth of Venus," but decorously covered with two slices of tomato and a bunch of basil in appropriate places! We bought one of each!

We found two Hallowe'en bowler style hats, but could find no masks. Remembering that we had saved the sleep masks provided by the airline for night flights, Roger cut out eye holes so we could see, and we were ready!

Attempting to accentuate the surprise, if not the hoped—for shock of our pornographic apron costumes, we decided that over our aprons we would wear the terry cloth bathrobes provided in our cottage for use at the pool during the summer. On cue, we would pull open our robes as the "Chianti Flashers!" Needless to add that beneath our salacious aprons, we were fully dressed.

After parking our car near the Porta Romana and then walking to Bill's apartment about ten blocks away, I was certain we would be arrested if not for vagrancy, at least for weirdness as we proceeded down the street in bathrobes and hats. Fortunately it was dark and no one noticed, or pretended not to. I recalled hearing that people, including vandals and criminals of all kinds, avoid lunatics; thinking about how we must appear to strangers, this thought ran through my mind and comforted me.

Bill's apartment was large and attractive. A huge terrace opened from his living room and on this warm October evening in Florence, many people were outside. The caterers had provided many varieties of wonderful food; wine flowed, music played and we arrived. Although many guests had very elaborate and expensive costumes, no one got as much attention or more laughs than we did with our flash act. This was definitely a very different evening from any we have ever had in Italy, but it will remain one we shall never forget! A consistent certainty!

Two years later, at a special birthday party for Bill, many of his Italian friends remembered us and mentioned our very "interesting costumes!"

Among the many successful, interesting, intellectual and artistic people we met at the Hallowe'en fete, I was impressed with a young woman who at the time was an executive assistant to Bill. I assumed she was American as her English was totally without accent and included the typical idioms of younger people. She laughed when I asked her what part of the States she was from; she replied that she was born and raised in Florence. Her English, she explained, was from the situation her very bright parents had created for their children. Knowing that a fluency in that tongue would be an asset to them, they had American exchange students live with them every year from the time their own children were babies. As linguists have stated, if a child hears and learns another language by the age of ten, he will speak that language without accent. An obvious consistency!

Just as many Americans who have not traveled have misconceptions about other countries, so do many Italians who have not crossed their national borders, or especially the Atlantic Ocean. Many people feel that violence is so common and typical in the United States that it would be foolhardy and dangerous to visit here. One gentleman, a successful businessman in a rather provincial, but nevertheless a university town, solemnly asked us with great concern why every American child carried a gun to school. All our protestations did not truly convince him otherwise. Another person said he would love to visit California, the photographs he had seen of its mountains and beaches were so beautiful, but that too many people were killed by drive-by shootings; a young German business man living in Italy said he would like to see New York City very much, but he was afraid that he and his wife would be mugged and even killed in the Bronx! Another bright young couple we have become close to would like to visit us on Cape Cod, but are afraid of all the possible terrorism reports they hear about. These fears, engendered by irresponsible and some trash media and given seeming veracity by the violence in American movies and on exported television shows, are similar to what many American people, even those who are educated, feel about Italy.

I was amazed when one person whom we know well suggested that the reason my husband liked Sicily so much was that he liked to watch the Mafia?????? Hello?? Another American we also know well was constantly afraid of being cheated; we didn't think he understood the money and exchange rate; another man would not rent a car because he was certain it would be stolen. These misunderstandings, both in America and in Italy, are not only unfortunate, but sad, as they preclude so much enjoyment which might have been derived on both sides. But, again, these attitudes and situations are changing daily, and one hopes, positively and consistently.

After more than thirty years of visiting this country of which I am so enamored, when I think I've finally figured out the correct system for: checking into a hotel, parking the car, surrendering my passport, entering a museum, including a tip, getting a taxi, cashing a check, knowing exactly what "ragu" is, choosing fruit from a tiny greengrocery, embarking on a ferry, taking a bus, or buying a stamp in the correct denomination, I'm often wrong! After being refused entry to one of the Olympic sized pools in a hotel in Civitavecchia because I wasn't a long-term renter, why are we the only pool users in the lovely, fully booked hotel on the island of Ponza? Some of the most intricate and beautiful tile work found anywhere in the world can be seen in Italy. Why is it then in many bathrooms there are no barriers on the floor of the shower to keep the water from sloshing all over the floor? Does it never leak to rooms below? The juxtaposition of fabulous plantings and flowers which abut weed choked patches, especially in some areas of the south confuses. Million dollar sailing yachts occasionally float among a plethora of plastic flotsam. These inconsistencies are an enigma.

Consistent inconsistencies, certain uncertainties, conflicting conundrums can all apply to Italy at various times. Being there is always an adventure and almost always a pleasant surprise; it is a land we have come to know, admire and love, full of *baci e abbracci* (kisses and hugs). We have pondered its mysteries and magnetism and have been baffled by its reasonable confusion and yet, in spite of those oddities or because of the wonder of it all, we love the country and its people more each time we are there. A certain, consistent certainty!

ROME

"O Rome! my country! city of the soul!"
CHILDE HAROLD'S PILGRIMAGE

Canto IV, st. 78

"While stands the Coliseum, Rome shall stand;
When falls the Coliseum, Rome shall fall;
And when Rome falls—the World."

CHILDE HAROLD'S PILGRIMAGE
Canto IV, st. 145
George Gordon, Lord Byron

"Not that I loved Caesar less, but that I loved
Rome more."

Brutus: JULIUS CAESAR, ACT III, ii
William Shakespeare

Rome was the first place we touched in Italy; it was love at first feel, or step actually, which soon became love at first sight, and then at first taste, and on and on until all our senses were totally engulfed by this magical city. These first impressions have never stopped and we are as enamored of Rome now as we were more than thirty years ago on that memorable first touch.

After we left the plane on that never to be forgotten first day and found our rented Fiat with the license plate whose letters I still remember, "MIMO," we drove from the airport Leonardo da Vinci at Fiumicino into the city of Rome. Roger, an intrepid and superb driver, was never intimidated by the rumors about the perils of using a car here, and thus began an adventure we have shared for a very long, interesting and joyful time.

As we got to the *"centro"* or center, I shall never forget my total amazement on that unbelievable morning as I spotted the Forum! Immediate recollection of my beloved fourth grade geography book with its pictures of the Forum and the Coliseum first came to me, quickly followed by similar memories from the illustrations in the Latin I textbook from ninth grade. I had always dreamed of seeing these places, and now the reality was overwhelming.

I literally yelled with excitement at what I was seeing, and Roger immediately pulled over; we gawked. There was the Forum, and totally thrilled, we took the first of what would eventually become thousands of Italian photographs.

After finding our hotel near the Piazza Euclide, we took a brief rest, showered and met a friend who was also visiting Italy for the first time. She was staying with her cousin Vincent, an art history professor who spent each summer in Italy. We four met for dinner and the two of us had the first and totally genuine lesson in appropriate Italian behavior.

Lesson number one was for Roger; Vincent told him to follow his car through Rome and we did in our tiny one, at times at what I thought was breakneck speed, but of course was not. He displayed the verve and skill of driving in Rome and later explained the difference between a *"bella figura"*, or a good image, and a *"brutta figura"*, a bad one. A safe, but courageous driver has a good image of himself, but one who is always lagging behind has a bad self-image. It was important, the professor emphasized, to sustain the good image. Rog caught on immediately and exhibited the correct *"bella figura!"*

The second lesson occurred at dinner; how and what to choose from the menu, and in what order, what to expect and what never to do. We dined at a legendary restaurant I had heard of for years, located near to the Piazza Navona; I couldn't believe my good fortune at living a reality I had dreamed of for so long. Surprisingly I do not remember what we had for dinner that night, but I believe it might have been fish. I think I was so awe-struck by the entirety of the first day's events I probably paid infinitely more attention to the happenings around me than to what I was swallowing.

The next lesson was how to go to a bar for coffee; first, one pays the cashier, receives a receipt which he hands to the barman, and then gives his order. This is the routine for having coffee while standing. If table service is required, one sits, the waiter takes the order, serves it and collects the money; this procedure is naturally more expensive. This particular bar in the Piazza Navona, noted especially for its ice cream specialties, was yet another place I had read about for so long, and perhaps because of the romance of the experience, I enjoyed the coffee much more than I might have at another time.

After our espresso we walked around this magnificent piazza for the first time. Since that time, I do not believe we have ever come to Rome without repeating this walk. Three famous fountains are placed here; the fountain of the Moors, Neptune Wrestling with a Marine Monster, and the most famous and considered the best, in the center, the Fountain of the Rivers by the master, Bernini; four huge statues which represent the four corners of the world stand at the sides of a huge rock.

Following the leader again, for the last lesson of the evening, we set off on foot for ice cream at the famous *"gelateria,"* or ice cream emporium near to the Pantheon. Soon afterward, fatigued by travel and the excitement of the wondrous first day in Italy, we had to sleep. We were so fortunate to have had lessons in proper dining, as well as coffee and ice cream purchasing by a gentleman who had been living in Italy for several months every year for a long time.

This amiable professor had one more lesson to give us. At dinner on the following evening we were at the sea side; I ordered a pasta with red clam sauce and when the waiter brought it, I asked him for cheese. He looked slightly troubled; we were far off the beaten tourist path and he was mostly used to waiting on Italian nationals. Vincent immediately explained that pasta with any kind of fish sauce was NEVER, EVER served with cheese in Italy. I have never forgotten this and have adapted it in my own home. Pasta plus fish equals no cheese!

We have dear friends who travel all over the world for business; they do this with great frequency and they have done so for forty years. Never have they had an airline misplace one piece of their luggage. We must be the bad luck guys because it doesn't matter where we fly, domestically or internationally, many of our flights have ended with one piece of our luggage missing. This has happened most often in Florida, but also in California, Aruba, New York, Massachusetts and on three separate occasions it has occurred on arrival in Italy. It doesn't matter what airline we have been on; with us they all seem to misplace luggage with equal opportunity. Temporarily lost has never been a serious threat as all has always been found and delivered to our hotel within forty-eight hours at the latest; nevertheless, the lesson I have learned from these experiences is always to "carry on" what I immediately need for a day or so. This was imperative when we were on our way for a wedding in Italy. I carried my dress and shoes for the festivities in my hand baggage, and therefore was perfectly able to dress and enjoy the wedding while my suitcase traveled from Milan to Urbino the following day.

I mention this type of small, if bothersome event because it precipitated an interesting situation one afternoon in Rome. Usually it has happened that my suitcase is the one delayed, but on one occasion, it was Roger's. He had nothing but paper work in his small carry-on; no clothes, toothbrush, shaving items, nothing except what he was wearing. It was summertime and as soon as we got to our hotel and had a brief snooze, we went to one of the large Roman department stores. Roger picked out a few golf type shirts, underwear and sox; signed his American Express card and together we left, or I should say, we attempted to leave the store. Alarms and bells went off and two security guards immediately materialized as we went through the door to the street. Voluntarily we stopped, more from curiosity than fear, to see who the "idiot" was who was trying to shoplift. Shocked and embarrassed, we soon found out that it was we who were being stopped and it was our packages to be inspected! The one I was carrying passed; I was told that I could leave. Roger, on the other hand, was escorted upstairs to the men's department. Thankfully, the same clerk who had waited on him was there and looked askance when he saw Roger being conducted toward him. He examined the shirt in question; he had forgotten to remove the gadget or bar attached to the shirt which prevents shoplifting and must be removed by a special device. After he removed it, the security guard presented another problem. The price marked on the shirt ticket did not coincide with the amount on the credit card receipt. The employee in the men's department explained to the security men that the shirt was on sale, and that the price on the ticket was not the sale price which had be to written by hand and that all was legal! It does rattle one, especially in a foreign country in which one does not speak the language to be even temporarily accused. All worked out, but I must say, Rog was a bit unnerved for awhile. He was extremely careful as we went to the next shop to buy shaving things and a toothbrush. No alarms please!

A person could spend months in this fascinating city and not yet see all its treasures; as vital as those museums, monuments, fountains, piazzas, churches and architectural gems are, a living city is much more than the sum of these things no matter how historically or artistically important. A city is people, stores, restaurants, public transportation, theatres, and so much more. A city is alive, moving, frequently noisy, often annoying, more often delightfully pleasant. I stated in the beginning that this was not to be a guide book nor historical treatise; I can share only some experiences and descriptions of places we have visited in Rome. Words, scholarly, critically and occasionally bombastically have been written about this ancient and yet modern city; works that describe its grandeur, history, wars, insurrections, glories and depravities. I have nothing to add to this mountain of information and occasionally misinformation. My words are more of a personal experience taken from the extensive journals I write as we travel. Therefore, I shall talk of places we have enjoyed here, while emphasizing that these destinations have been visited in a haphazard if happy order, and only several on each visit. As I search through my diaries of these many years, I find I spend infinitely more words describing interesting people, wonderful food and fascinating experiences more than the various monuments and museums. Many guide books are available for one who wishes to know more about a particular destination and frequently are an invaluable help for touring. Organized half or all day tours by bus can also give a newcomer a feel for a city's layout as well as highlighting the most visited spots.

One of my favorite visits in Rome is to the Villa Borghese; the museum is the showcase of some of the best sculptures of Bernini. This exquisite seventeenth century building, which was the opulent home of Cardinal Scipione Borghese, nephew of Pope Paul V, is set in public gardens; closed for thirteen years for extensive restoration, it was grandly re-opened to the public in the summer of 1997.

The Cardinal, patron of the arts and most famously patron to the young Bernini, amassed a collection which is not only outstanding, but is displayed in an atmosphere to its best advantage. History informs one that the young cardinal was not very interested in politics or in the Church, and that his efforts were almost totally concentrated on the single minded idea of gathering works of art, which he masterfully achieved in diverse ways, including some that have been best described as rather devious. Many of the ancient sculptures collected by Cardinal Borghese were long ago sold, looted, or removed by other methods, but if only some of the Bernini sculptures are there, the Villa would still be well worth visiting. I love his works! Dynamic, athletic, and vivacious with human emotions shown on each face, I find it difficult, almost impossible to believe that these works, with seemingly high velocity motion, could be hewn from the hard rock of marble. "Daphne and Apollo" shows Daphne's fingers believably turning into leaves as she is transformed into a tree; David's face is contorted with effort as his body is twisted to throw the rock in his sling at the giant, Goliath; Pluto's fingers are so realistically pressing Persephone's thighs one can imagine and almost feel the erotic pressure at the indentations of the flesh.

One American art critic rather cynically I thought, questions the achievement of much of Bernini's work because of its position in the Baroque period, so characterized by the Protestant distaste for the excesses of the Roman Catholic Church. No expert I, but simply one who is ever impressed and happy to look at the exciting life-like figures he created; faces showing energy and fright. I like Bernini and never tire of seeing his works in all parts of Rome.

The Gallery Borghese contains much more than these sculptures. They just happen to be my favorites! Paintings by Caravaggio, Titian, Raphael and other masters can be viewed here. The gardens are beautifully planted and a welcome respite from the Roman heat in the midst of summer.

Another sculpture by Canova in this gallery done in the early nineteenth century draws a great deal of attention. Pauline Borghese, the sister of Napoleon posed for what has been described as a "naughty" work of art. She imitates Venus in a state of lovely, if almost total nudity. After completion, so the story goes, her husband took the perfect white marble work of art, with the lady so realistically portrayed as she reclined, and locked it away from view. However, now in the Borghese, bold Pauline is once again displayed on the classic couch in her total state of marble hard nakedness.

A photograph, forty inches high and thirteen across, of the Trevi Fountain hangs in the entranceway of our house. Considered by many to be the most beautiful of all the many attractive fountains in Rome, its drama is shown by Neptune's chariot drawn by Tritons, while gallons of real water pour continuously over its surface. The old well-known tradition that anyone who throws a coin into the basin will return to Rome has produced an endless supply of money. This money is supposed to go to charity, but in the August 7, 2002 edition of the NEW YORK TIMES, it was discovered that most of the money was being scooped up by a mentally unstable man who had been "fishing" for money in the fountain for thirty years. The police were amazed at the amounts he was able to harvest. This fountain, as most of the others in Rome, was ordered by a pope and completed in 1762. Interestingly, almost all of these fountains depict pagan deities and not religious figures.

Although we had looked up from the street as we walked, driven close by and had marveled at Hadrian's Tomb, or as it is now better known, the Castel Sant' Angelo, we had never gone into it. Finally, after twenty-five years, we did! If for no other reason, the views of Rome from on high are so well worth the effort. Built as a fortress, this edifice has had many uses in its almost two thousand year history from tomb to prison to residence of several popes. Its current name is for the huge statue of Michael, the Archangel, on the very top of the structure; this was sculpted in the eighteenth century.

We first went there in February; it was a windy, though sunny day and the temperature was about 55 degrees, Fahrenheit. With the Tiber below and many flags flying in the breeze, it was a great day for photographs. We enjoyed the view so much we returned the following November for another glorious look around this incredible city. A museum located within demonstrates the history of the building, but personally, the best part for us is looking at the panorama below. One of the popes who related to this castle, Paul III, a Farnese, used as his motto, *"Festina Lente,"* or "Make Haste Slowly." Fine advice, then and now; seek the view slowly as its drama is hastily, but perhaps permanently, imprinted on the memory.

A comparatively new building, 1911, which celebrated the fiftieth year of the Kingdom of Italy and is a monument to King Vittorio Emmanuel II, is often referred to by the Italian people as the "Wedding Cake." Built of white marble, they consider it overdone with its fountains and statues and not blending in well with the architecture of the rest of Rome, but located in the city center, it's hard to miss and really shouldn't be. At the very least, it can be useful as a landmark when one is learning his way around the city.

Summer heat in Rome can be overwhelming, especially during the day. Usually by nightfall when the sun has set, the evenings can be delightful. Outdoor cafés and restaurants fill with people enjoying the ambiance along with the cooler temperatures. On such an evening we had a new experience. Formerly when I was teaching, our Italian journeys occurred only during the summer vacation period; now we are free to pick and choose from among the other three seasons. I vividly remember a wonderful and unusual summer evening during the 1970's. We attended Verdi's opera AIDA at an outdoor performance in the Baths of Caracalla. The production was unlike anything we had ever seen before; the music, the singers and the sets were outstanding, but the amazing part to us was the use of live camels on the huge stage and a chariot drawn by real galloping horses! An incredible and delightful memory!

Volumes have been, are, and will be written about St. Peter's, the Vatican Museums and the Sistine Chapel. They could be visited and re-visited from now until forever, and each time, something will be seen and noticed which had not been noticed before. We never go to Rome without going into St. Peter's Basilica. Beyond my powers of description, it simply overwhelms the reality of being a mere human being. Huge beyond huge, it tricks the eye into believing it is not that large as the proportions are so perfect. I have a photograph of Roger standing next to a statue of a cherub whose foot equals the length of this man's hand to elbow. On the floor there are lines and inscriptions which show the size of many other well-known major cathedrals throughout the world, all smaller than this one.

Underneath the magnificent *"Baldacchino"* or bronze covering designed by Bernini, there is a marble altar at which only a pope may say Mass. One of the first times we were there we were fortunate to be with an art historian who pointed out one of the most fascinating and yet human designs found there, and one which would not be readily noticeable to most amateur viewers. At the base of each of the four columns, there is a marble square; two sides of each of the four squares are visible. Seven of them depict a beautiful young woman in the various stages of the labor of childbirth. Several are fairly relaxed portraits, while others reflect a woman in the extreme agony of intense pain. The eighth and final one is of a beautiful baby. We were told that the reigning pope at the time had a niece who was expecting a child, and this is supposedly representative of her. Whoever it is, the sculptures depict a very human reality with a most positive ending.

When we first visited St. Peter's, Michelangelo's most famous *Pieta* was located in an open side chapel. This famous sculpture, carved by the artist when he was twenty-five years old, was accessible to all tourists and pilgrims. Unfortunately, in 1972 a deranged person attacked this precious work and since then it is protected behind glass. Nonetheless, it is worth a long, long look.

Below the main floor there are tombs; Pope John XXIII is buried here and unfailingly, his area is filled with more flowers and with more people paying homage to him than there are to any others entombed in this place. Years after his death, there are outpourings of love to this holy and humble man. Many streets throughout Italy are named for him and his picture is constantly seen in all parts of the country as well.

The Sistine Chapel is all and more every art historian has said of it. Michelangelo's ceiling is beyond human description, and when one thinks of the years he spent on uncomfortable scaffolding creating these paintings, the mind is overwhelmed; one's own existence and achievements disappear in the company of this majestic talent. These monumental frescoes are all the more impressive as the artist himself did not consider himself a painter, but first of all, a sculptor. He was so much more though, even designing the dome of St. Peter's when he was eighty-one.

After having been closed for years for restoration, the renewed interest by tourists has generated throngs of visitors. This is true of the Vatican Museums as well. I have memories of standing in line with crowds and then being hurried through, but now, as we are able to travel in the more non-touristy months, this is much less a problem.

On the day of the American Bi-Centennial, July 4, 1976, Roger and I were in Rome; we were a part of a group of students who were spending six weeks of the summer in Italy at a university program sponsored by the University of the State of New York. Before we left for Urbino where we would all go to school, we were spending several days in the Italian capital. Many of us decided to go to St. Peter's Piazza that morning; the Pope, Paul VI, was giving his blessing to the huge crowd assembled in the square. After a blessing spoken in Italian, the Holy Father suddenly began speaking in English, directly addressing the vast numbers of Americans present on that morning. He wished us well and congratulated our country on its two hundredth anniversary. Then, without preamble, he recited the Pledge of Allegiance; I did not see a dry American eye.

There were many American bishops and cardinals in the Basilica that day, as well as a symphony orchestra from our country. We didn't have tickets for the Mass, but it was a grand beginning to a day of which we were all proud. At noon, our professor leader took us all to the town of Tivoli, about fifteen miles from Rome. We first visited the gardens of the Villa d'Este, home to Cardinal Ippolito d'Este, son of Lucrezia Borgia and grandson of Pope Alexander VI, in the mid 16th century. As with the Villa Borghese, one surmises that `the princes of the Church understood the pursuit of the "good life" and attained it. An extremely wealthy man, his career in the Church bloomed early; he was made Archbishop of Milan at age ten. Sadly, he died expelled from the Church after being convicted of selling church offices for money.

Although much of the estate has been neglected in past years, the grounds are known primarily for the wonderful fountains. The Terrace of One Hundred Fountains is breath-taking in its one hundred meter length and the constant play of water, but most critics feel that its majesty is long gone and the demons of corrosion and decay have stolen most of its beauty. However, we have a framed photograph taken on that hot July day which we still enjoy. The fountain I remember most is The Ovato. As the middle of the July day grew ever warmer, the students with us walked and ran under the oval shape and enjoyed the refreshing splashes of the cooling water. We did not go into the Villa itself although I have read that it has been totally restored.

Our next stop was to the area around Hadrian's Villa, not far away. One can only imagine what must have been here during his lifetime; this enormous estate was built about nineteen hundred years ago in Tivoli by an emperor history has described as a cultured man, a military leader, a builder and a clever politician. The vastness of the grounds has been depleted; the remains of the buildings barely suggested by the columns and pieces of marble ruins. Time alone has not done this kind of severe damage; armies of the Goths and Byzantines used the area as a camp and used much of the marble which they burned to make lime for cement. And sadly, as with the situation of the Coliseum, many people who ought to have known better, used these ancient buildings as quarries for their own mansions.

Art historians tell of the literally countless works of art that were contained within the buildings, and of the statuary and architectural treasures throughout the three hundred acres. In addition the emperor is said to have had replicas built of his favorite buildings from the ancient world. Most of the works of art have disappeared either from plunder or greed into private collections, to museums throughout Europe, to the Vatican museums, and according to some historians, by Constantine who appropriated many of the art works from Hadrian's villa when he moved the capital to Constantinople.

Since that day in July 1976 was our first visit to Hadrian's Villa, we decided last year that it was time to return. We did and found that it was much more organized, restoration is continuing, a museum and bookstore have been opened, and over all a most pleasant excursion. This return was more pleasant than we had hoped.

We ended that long ago 4th of July celebration with a joyous dinner party arranged by our professor. A sumptuous meal was accompanied by live music and dancing. The evening was a very special one for all the American students, and I must mention that the age of the people in our group ranged from seventeen to a few people in their early seventies who were interested in Italian culture and who bravely joined the majority who were of traditional college age. Our ages fell between the senior citizens and the college students which made it really neat to relate to all ages and all people. Although we were not in the United States to celebrate this auspicious anniversary in American history, I think we probably were more in the spirit of celebration being away from home. Our thoughtful and wonderful professor had provided American flags for all and from morning to late at night we thoroughly enjoyed a very special day.

Raffaello Sanzio, or Raphael, is buried in the ancient Roman building, the Pantheon; numbered among the world's greatest artists, he is a native of one of our favorite towns in Italy, Urbino. We make a pilgrimage to his final resting place each time we are in Rome. An additional attraction I must confess is the Pantheon's proximity to the hundred plus year old fabled Café' Giolitti and its legendary ice creams.

The Pantheon is a most unusual edifice. Originally built by Agrippa, a general serving Augustus in 27 B.C.E., it was restored by the person so interested in architecture, the Emperor Hadrian, during the second century C.E. whose other works included walls, temples and villas which stretched across the Empire. This building was intended as a temple. During the 7th century it was consecrated as a Christian church and now it houses the tombs of not only Rafael, but since the Unification of Italy in the 19th century, those of the kings of Italy as well.

The building's dome is coffered to reduce its weight; as a seventeen year old college freshman in a very large art history class, I vividly remember the professor explaining this phenomenon. She was effusive as she described the ceiling and as excited as I might have been if I had found a sack of money! Mostly interested in the architectural details, she never mentioned it as Raphael's burial place. Not until seventeen years later when I first arrived in Rome and got to view this magnificent structure did her remembered words return to me. I was amazed that I recalled as much as I did however, considering that at age seventeen, I was far more interested in meeting my boyfriend on Saturday afternoon than I was in the dynamics of decreasing the weight load of the ancient dome.

An interesting relation between the Pantheon and Saint Peter's Basilica was arranged by Pope Urban VIII, though the association between the two buildings was separated by about fifteen hundred years. When Bernini was building the Baldacchino over the Papal Altar, perhaps his greatest work, there was a shortage of bronze. The Pontiff, whose family name was Barberini, ordered the bronze beams from the Pantheon to be removed so that the artist could use them in the Baroque canopy. This act, which angered many Romans, resulted in the saying, "What the barbarians did not do, the Barberini did."

Our very dear friends, Tiziana and Fabio suggested that on the day their restaurant is closed, the four of us drive out of Rome to the small village of Trevignano on Lake Bracciano. We met Fabio's parents there and had lunch at a lovely restaurant overlooking the lake. Although it was the thirteenth of March, the day was magnificent and we were able to dine on the terrace under the welcoming sun.

After finishing our meal the owner of this restaurant and his wife took us aside and presented us with a lovely ceramic plate of their establishment made by the famous ceramists of Deruta. After we returned home and hung it on the kitchen wall, I photographed it and with a sincere thank you note, sent it to the kind people who had given it to us.

We took a long walk by the promenade by the lake, and then through parts of this medieval town. Later we drove to the really old town of Sutri. Legend maintains that Pontius Pilate was born here, but the local people emphatically deny this and give the dubious distinction to a neighboring village. Naturally, the inhabitants of that village strongly refute such a myth and return the rumor to Sutri.

Another less stressful legend is that Julius Caesar stopped here on his way to conquer Gaul so that he could have special shoes made for his long journey. Who knows for sure? After having enjoyed a marvelous lunch by the lake, my theory is that Caesar stopped here for a meal of excellent lake fish. Armies do travel on their stomachs I've been told!

One afternoon in Rome we decided to go to a laundromat; at many of our rented apartments or cottages we have had washing machines, but we were staying in a hotel at this time. After washing and drying our clothing, Roger and I were walking back when we passed a large store specializing in various kinds of accouterments for bedroom and bath. Simultaneously we spied an attractive shower curtain in the large window of the shop. The curtain looked like a mosaic from a two thousand year old Roman villa with its tesserae defining various kinds of fish and ocean creatures in a sea of aquamarine. Roger said, "Let's get it! An Italian shower curtain!" We entered the shop and told the clerk what we saw and that we wanted to buy it. She took one from the shelf, we paid for it and continued on our way back to our hotel, pleased with our unusual find. Roger added that we really should have bought two in case one wore out, and furthermore it wasn't expensive, but I convinced him that if that were the case we could get another on our next trip.

When we got to our room I excitedly unwrapped our package to gaze with pleasure at its ingenious design. After a moment I suddenly began roaring with laughter; my dear husband quizzically looked at me with slight suspicion at my nearly hysterical laughing and asked what was so funny?Barely able to speak through paroxysms of giggles, I read directly from the package: "Made in Los Angeles, California, USA." Our prized Italian find was neither!

Il Museo di Roma, the Museum of Rome, re-opened in May, 2002 after fifteen years. Located in the eighteenth century Palazzo

Braschi between the Piazza Navona and the Campo di Fiori, the exhibition depicts the history of Rome between the seventeenth and nineteenth centuries. This exquisite palace was built at the request of Pope Pius VI. According to a newspaper article covering the opening, this museum has thousands of articles in its archives from this period including paintings, photographs, furniture and clothing. The hundreds on display show a rich retrospective of the period.

The central staircase in the palace is made of marble and for stunning beauty, I thought it alone was worth the price of admission. The panoramic paintings depicting events in the Roman Catholic Church of the period are extremely detailed showing the riches and splendor of ceremonies such as the investiture of silk clad cardinals, or the visit of Queen Christiana of Sweden with a procession of hundreds of prelates. I could not help but think of how all this pageantry evolved and what the sandaled carpenter from Nazareth in whose honor these events were supposedly held, would think of it. The museum is well worth a visit; we enjoyed it so much.

We were invited to spend a few days at our friends' wonderful home in the Parioli district of Rome. One evening we dined at a restaurant with friends of theirs, whose eighteen year old son accompanied us. He was an absolutely delightful young man, witty to the point where he had us laughing continuously. I was showing him photos of our home and family and suddenly he looked at one of our then sixteen year old granddaughter. His eyes grew large and he gasped out, "She's beautiful! How old is she?" When he was told her age, he said, "Oh! She's too young! I'll go to prison!" I told him we would introduce him after he finished at the university in five years! A great postscript to this moment was that five years later he visited us in Florida and then Cape Cod, and was as cheerful, warm and loving as we had remembered. An even later postscript had the then sixteen year old granddaughter, now twenty-two, visit us in Italy; she was shown around Rome on this young man's motorcycle and they both seemed to have a wonderful evening!

One morning our friends invited us to go to the harbor in Civitavecchia where they keep their boat. On the way we drove to Cervetri to view the fascinating Etruscan tombs. Unfortunately it was Monday, the day the site is closed, but we took a fairly long walk through the areas not enclosed. We were told many people took refuge in the tombs during World War II for safety from the bombings.

The harbor at Civitavecchia is huge, holding one thousand pleasure boats. Extremely tidy, organized and efficient, it is surrounded by laundromats, stores, and restaurants. After a great lunch while we overlooked the water, we were all set to go out on Fabio's boat. We had brought jackets and bathing suits, but while we were having food, our friend said he was sorry but he wasn't feeling well and we would have to go back to Rome; he'd take us out at another time.

We were concerned, but he went to see his doctor after taking us back to his house. A month before we arrived he had undergone eye surgery, and the affected eye had become very inflamed; naturally he was worried. Two hours later he returned with a huge smile. The ophthalmologist told him he had "pink eye" or conjunctivitis. He had medicine and had bought three pairs of dark glasses for various degrees of light. The doctor said it was almost epidemic in Rome at this time, and to be sure that no one near him was infected, no one should kiss him and we should all wash our hands as much as possible. Our friend was obviously so relieved it was not the surgery gone awry.

He stopped at his restaurant on the way back and brought steak filets and *vitello tonnato* to his house; his lovely wife made soup, a truly picturesque salad, a colorful fruit platter, a sumptuous cheese tray and we feasted well. Fabio usually drinks very little wine, but on this night he had several glasses, laughing and saying, "My doctor said to drink wine!" He felt so much better, and we did as well.

I mentioned earlier in this chapter that as I search through years and years of journals I have kept during Italian visits, I notice an interesting dearth of description of Roman monuments and tourists destinations, but a plethora of vivid and palate pleasing descriptions of meals consumed in this city, of evenings spent happily with friends, and of wanderings in and around this special city. Perhaps I have not felt the need to more than simply and briefly mention what is endlessly described in guide books, novels, and occasionally films.

I am not implying that visiting the Via Veneto, Piazza Di Spagna, the Church of Saint Peter in Chains with Michelangelo's statue of Moses, the Colosseum and Forum, and Ara Pacis are not important and worth visiting; they are. We have seen them all and have appreciated each. However, this has taken place over many years. I believe that visitors often get mental indigestion when all the sights they feel should be seen are visited in a short period of time. This is an impossible or at the very least, a troublesome situation, not only in Rome, but in London, Paris, New York or any other great city in the world.

We try to see at least two new sites on each visit as well as revisiting some of our old favorites. For example, in March of 2002 we went to the Galleria Nazionale d'Arte Modern or Delle Belle Arti to an extremely interesting exhibit of paintings from around 1880 to the 1930's. We especially liked the Italian impressionists and think they are excellent, but have never received the attention they deserved in the shadow of the French impressionist painters. At the end of the tour I bought a tee shirt in the bookstore with the lion logo of the museum which restores the memory of a most pleasant afternoon at this museum when I wear it.

Several days later we made a visit to the Palazzo delle Esposizioni to see the exhibition of "Roma—1948-1959—La Dolce Vita." Great photos were on display of Federico Fellini and his wife, Giuletta Massina; others of Gina Lollobrigida, Sophia Loren, Frank Sinatra, Tyrone Power and so many more celebrities of the period. Movies of that same time were shown on large overhead screens; also effectively presented were costumes, fashions, and perfectly restored period cars and Vespas. The entire showing was excellent and a wonderful trip down memory lane!

Etruscan artifacts are not of great interest to everyone, but if they are, a visit to Villa Giula is in order. Built in 1550, originally the summer residence of Pope Julius III, the building alone is magnificent, but additionally it now houses the largest Etruscan collection in Italy. I find these pre-Roman artifacts quite interesting and we have made visits to other museums in Tuscany with similar, but infinitely smaller collections. The history of the Villa is separate, but fascinating in itself. Apparently the Pope had an enormous collection of statues, which after his death, were transferred to the Vatican. Queen Christiana of Sweden, the principal subject of the previously mentioned lavish painting in the Museum of Rome, was housed in this building when she visited Rome in 1655. A trivia touch!

There was a great exhibit of paintings by Gaspare Vanvitelli during the winter of 2003 in the Chiostro (Cloister) del Bramante. Roger loved his style and the paintings of Rome in the late seventeenth and early eighteenth centuries. We bought a large poster of one of his works showing the Tiber by the Aventino part of the city; this painting depicts life of the common working people as a boat is being unloaded, others are continuing on the river, children play and a dog sniffs the ground. We found his work an interesting change from the grandeur of so much art depicting rulers or religious subjects. Once home, we framed it and hung in our bedroom, and thus, we are in some way, perhaps spiritually or psychologically, attached to Rome. The attraction is more potent than that of putting a coin in the Trevi, although we have done that often!

Rome is like no other place on this planet Earth; at once it is grand, exciting, beautiful, inspiring and breath-taking. As with any large city it can also be frustrating and annoying at times, but most often, it gives back a satisfaction as one is reminded of so much of the ancient world which has influenced and continues to influence our government, philosophy, entertainment, gastronomy, military, law, literature, architecture, economics, public services, and for many, religion. To visit Italy without seeing Rome is to miss the point; whether one loves it or leaves it forever alone, it must be experienced.

ROME—EVER ETERNAL

From the hotel roof top's bright breakfast room
I spy the sunlight splashed great granite Dome
Of Saint Peter's Basilica, and smile
With immense, and happy satisfaction
On my return to Rome, the Eternal.

Our first visit here, most memorable
Thirty-six years ago, instilled a love
Ever deepening for this city, this
Land, this country, its people, our true friends.

Spectacular ancient sites, Pantheon,
Colosseum, Forum, Tomb of Hadrian
We visit again and again. Then on
To Renaissance wonders—the Vatican,
Villa Borghese and Gardens, and more.

But it is not only the monuments
Or the art which entrance us, however
Magnificent they are! It's the rhythm
Of life being lived! Food, wine, all enjoyed
By not only us, but by its loyal
And patriotic Roman populace.

The Hotel Isa is our headquarters
And respite in Rome, when the structures, so
Dramatic, begin to overwhelm one.
Our host, Maurizio, together with
Family and staff, give us rest and peace.
We are at home in this tranquil haven.

No place on this Earth has experienced
More of the positives as well as the
Negatives of life than this entity,
Rome. Its legendary, spectacular
History, Law, Literature, Drama,
Architecture, sometimes punctuated
By anarchy, destruction, cruelty
And defeat. Beliefs of Paganism,
Catholicism, Fascism, Communism,
Socialism, have each defined a time
Political or pious, and troubled
Many people who have ventured through the
Abyss or success of the Roman life.
Continue on, my love, my Rome, my big
Happiness. I count minutes 'til return. Geralyn Peterkin

SOME ITALIAN PEOPLE

"We are such stuff
As dreams are made on."
Shakespeare

THE TEMPEST IV, i

"Thou Paradise of exiles, Italy!"

Percy Bysshe Shelley
Julian and Maddalo, line 57

Roger and I are "temporary voluntary exiles" in Italy almost every year. In one of the Dik Browne "Hagar" cartoons of which we are so fond, Hagar is asked where the stars go in the daytime. He replies, "Italy." His long-suffering and understanding wife Helga explains to the children that their father thinks that everyone would go to Italy if he could. Our sentiments entirely. Why is this so? Of course the scenery is spectacular, the cuisine divine and the wine pleasing to Bacchus himself, but one of the best reasons for being there is to interact with the people.

The National Police or *Carabinieri*

Like "innocents abroad" we were driving towards Sicily on our very first Italian excursion in 1971. The Autostrada of the South was partially opened but most of the services, such as gasoline, food and rest stops, were not yet in place. We had gotten a late start because we had stopped in Pompeii for longer than we had planned. It was essential that we reach our next stop, Cosenza, so that we could proceed on the next day in time to get the ferry across the Straits of Messina into Sicily. Reservations had been made for us, and with a limited time, there could be a dearth of lingering.

Dusk was approaching and Roger mentioned that our fuel was dangerously low. The road was essentially empty; no cars, trucks or people. We spied an exit and decided to drive down hoping that we might find a town and therefore a gas station. A long, winding exit led to nothing. Trees, some cultivation, but not a building or a human in sight. We went back on to the high autostrada and slowly proceeded. Several miles down the road, parked on the side of the road was a police car with two officers inside. We pulled up behind them and Roger got out and went to their car and tried to explain our predicament. The senior man got out of his vehicle, frowned, and asked if we were French. We shook our heads no. He frowned again and asked if we were German. We began to get his drift. Roger pulled out his American passport and it was magic! A big smile came across his face; "Americano!" He pointed to the gas cap on our car, and by hand signals, indicated that we should follow him. We did; he led us off the main highway, down an unfinished road to an incomplete and unopened gas station. There were working pumps in front, I suppose for the use of the police. They unlocked them and filled the tank of our tiny Fiat. Roger tried to pay. "No, No, No," the senior man kept saying, moving his hand gently in a left to right motion. I wanted to thank him properly, but at this point in my life knew about four words in Italian. I remembered that Italian people like children and respect family. I whipped out pictures of our four children, showed him, and said the only fairly appropriate word I could think of: "*Bambini*!" He looked at the pictures, smiled and there was a genuine responsiveness.

After many "*grazie*"—thank you's—on our part, and mutual handshakes, we parted. This was our third day in a country we had never been to before, and to be treated so well by the national, elite police force, the *carabinieri*, was an experience we shall never forget. And we haven't for thirty years.

A postman in Montevarchi and a museum guide

This kind of experience was not unique; kindness and generosity have been extended to us on so many occasions. Several years ago we drove to the small town of Montevarchi near Arezzo to go to the Museo Paleontologico. We had a difficult time finding it until we saw a postman and we asked for directions. He told us where to park our car in a nearby car park; he then walked up to where we were, and on foot, directed us to the museum. We have found time and time again that many people are so considerate. Because we had a delayed start, we arrived at the museum shortly before they closed for lunch and the afternoon. The young woman in charge enthusiastically allowed us to enter, but told us we could stay only about twenty minutes as she was required to lock the doors, making certain no one remained inside. Because the time of our visit was going to be necessarily brief, she wouldn't allow us to pay, and guided us around by herself after giving us brochures. It was a delightful, small tour. She pointed out the remains of mastodons, tigers, and deer, which she delightedly exclaimed were "Bambi!" When she showed us fossil remains of grape vines, Roger's comment, "*vino antico*" (antique wine), got a big laugh from her. Another pleasant experience.

A city traffic policeman

Returning from the deep South towards Rome about twenty-five years ago, we found ourselves in the midst of the worst of Naples traffic. There was one intersection which might have been designed by Dante as he outlined the sixth circle of Hell in the INFERNO; five streets converged into a labyrinth attempting to become a circle. In the center of this maze of countless and clamorous cars, trucks, buses, motorcycles, motor scooters and even brave souls on bicycles, stood a traffic policeman on an elevated stand so that he could be seen by all the operators of the various vehicles. With his immaculate uniform he wore a white cap similar to those I've seen on British policemen, and a pair of white gloves. He was the essence of calm as he directed this incredible throng around him. We had a problem; we were lost. Totally and completely. An almost perfect sense of direction has always been one of Roger's very useful talents, but on that day, it had disappeared. Finally, after going around and around this almost circle and not knowing which way to go on, he found a semi-legal place to briefly park. Dangerously making his way through the traffic to the center post where the policeman managed the mechanical menagerie with the style and grace of a conductor of a great symphony orchestra, Roger finally managed to inquire directions by shrugging his shoulders and saying, *"Dove Roma?"*

(Where is Rome?)

With great aplomb, this wizard of Neopolitan traffic organization held up his hands and stopped all traffic coming into the circle from all five streets. He motioned to Roger to return to his car, then, pointing at one of the roads, loudly said, "Roma!" Can you imagine having this happen in New York?

A gentleman selling *cappelli* (hats) in a posh establishment

Walking in Rome one morning in the mid 1980's we passed the Borsolino store. This very name conjured up romantic visions of elegance, and now, except in movies of the thirties and forties, men in hats of this ilk are seen less frequently every year. In my sometime overactive imagination I would conjure up visions of gentlemen removing these fabled fedoras as they entered Rolls Royces on their way to the Excelsior in Rome, the George V in Paris, or the Plaza in New York.

We entered the shop and I immediately spotted and fell in love with a wide-brimmed, brown felt hat—made for a woman! The material was doe-skin soft; one felt as if it could be drunk like cream. Normally I am not a hat person, but when I put this on my head, I created a new persona, at once genteel and mysterious. I felt like a movie queen from time past—perhaps Ingrid Bergman in CASABLANCA.

Strongly encouraged by Roger who thought it looked great on me, I decided to buy it. Just out for a morning stroll after cappuccino, neither of us had brought cash, credit cards or checks. I had left my purse in the hotel. I asked the gentleman who was waiting on me if he would be so kind as to put the hat aside for me and we would return after the siesta hour when the store would re-open, to buy the most glamourous, chic hat I'd ever seen and actually held in my hand.

He insisted that this would not be necessary. He said he was going home for the extended Roman lunch/siesta time and he would stop at our hotel. We could leave a check in American dollars with the concierge and he would pick it up.

We warmly thanked him for his thoughtfulness and turned to leave the shop. Immediately he called out, "*Signora,* you forgot your hat!" Incredulous, I reminded him that I hadn't paid for it. Patiently, as if he were explaining to a five year old, he told me he was going to pick up the check at my hotel. I couldn't imagine walking out of an elegant New York boutique with an expensive item neither having signed a credit card nor given a check or cash for the item. I'd never experienced that level of trust with complete strangers—let alone in a foreign country. I walked back to our hotel clutching my glamorous hat in a box with the wondrous Borselino name, full of admiration for the gesture of kindness exhibited by the gentleman of the Roman Borselino shop.

Safely stowing my hat in our room, I left the check with the hotel's concierge. After returning from lunch, we were told that he had indeed collected the check due him. No problem.

A vendor of leather goods

In a colonnaded area near the Uffizi Museum in Florence there used to be a number of stalls in which exquisite leather items, handbags, attache' cases, suitcases, wallets, belts and the like were sold. These leather items were often so beautifully wrought they seemed to sing out, "Buy me—take me home with you!"

We couldn't resist and in a burst of leather mania we chose two attache' cases as well as numerous small items for gifts. We were due to leave for Rome the following morning and then to New York two days after that. This had been a very brief trip, mostly relating to the travel business with which Roger was involved at that time. Getting low on *lire,* Italian money at that time, and having no more travelers checks, we decided to use our credit card for the purchases. It was Saturday afternoon and the banks were closed. We did have some regular checks from our bank in New York.

During an animated, friendly conversation with the proprietor, I remarked on his fluent, idiomatic English. Laughing, he told me he had lived in Brooklyn for fifteen years, but that life in New York was just too hectic. He missed Italy and returned here several years ago. At that time we too lived in New York, not the city, but in a small town on the Hudson River near West Point where the United States Military Academy is located. Nonetheless, we exchanged reminiscences of places we had commonly known. After a time, he let it be known that he would prefer cash to a credit card as it cost him a great deal in service fees, and he more than hinted that he had already given us such rock bottom bargain prices that his profit was slight. Gingerly, we offered him a personal check, guessing he would probably refuse. This would have been reasonable and would not have surprised us. We explained that we had *lire* enough only for tonight and barely through the next day, Sunday. Had we been staying until Monday when the banks would re-open, this would not have been a problem; but we weren't. We would be in Rome by then.

He not only said he would accept a personal check for the leather articles, but that he would be happy to cash a check for us so that we would have enough *lire* to feel comfortable for the next few days until we could get to a bank. I was astounded! "Do you trust us?" I asked.

"Why? Are you going to cheat me?" he replied, smiling. Effusively we assured him we were not. He began to laugh and said, "I know that. I can tell a phony or a cheat miles away. I have been fooled very few times in my life."

Happily we returned to our hotel laden with our beautiful leather items, plus enough Italian money to carry us to the end of our trip. No one had ever given us such a generous offer in our own country unless of course we were well known to them. Incidentally, that happened more than nineteen years ago and I am still using the handsome leather attache' case. It's in great shape!

Fabio of the great Roman restaurant and his wonderful family!

Many people do not care to drive in Rome. Roger loves it. Our very first trip developed and confirmed this. Exploring Rome in our tiny Fiat during that first jaunt, we came upon an area typically unknown to most tourists. The Parioli district is mainly comprised of many luxurious apartment buildings, embassies, and restaurants patronized almost exclusively by the people living in the area. We were driving through this attractive area about lunch time. Believing that not only armies march on their stomachs as Napoleon stated, Roger never misses a meal. He spotted a restaurant with an outdoor section covered with large canvas umbrellas and tables with spotless linens, and decided we would lunch there. We did and it was heavenly. That was in 1971.

Never would we go to Italy without having at least one, but as many meals as we could at this special place. Dining there one evening in 1975, we noticed a car with a ski rack on top which was parked in the driveway. We began a conversation with the young man who was obviously in charge and learned that it was his car, and that the owner of the restaurant was his father. He had been sent to Switzerland for training in the hotel and restaurant business, hence the ski rack, but his father decided that it was now time for him to relate to the family business.

Over the years we became more friendly. There was a six year period when we were unable to travel, but we never forgot this wonderful restaurant. When we once again began in earnest to be diligent travelers to Italy, this, our favorite dining spot in all the world, was a destination first on our agenda. The father of the younger man, Rino, was semi-retired we were told; his mother, delightful Giuseppina and he related to the restaurant usually only two days a week. Our relationship with Fabio, the son, grew; we met his attractive wife and young daughter. We began to exchange postcards and Christmas cards after we returned home. Eventually, our friendship became so sincere, that a most incredible event happened. He invited us to his own home for dinner on the night the restaurant was closed. Never had we had a meal in a private home in Italy, and, for this to happen with someone who had the finest restaurant in Rome, or probably in all of Italy in our opinion, was an honor that overwhelmed us. On top of that, this generous man drove to our hotel to pick us up and take us to his home.

After a warm, most delightful evening, our friendship grew closer. We invited them to visit us. A few years later this couple sent their then nineteen year old daughter, Valentina, to spend three weeks with us on Cape Cod. It was such a memorable visit that after ten days she telephoned her father and suggested that he visit too. He did and what a super time we had.

I was a bit paranoid at first that I might have to cook for this man whose restaurant is legendary. But I needed not worry. Before he arrived, his genial and lovely daughter told me I cooked like an Italian woman! He loved some of the local seafood we have on Cape Cod. We took him to our favorite summer restaurant there and he enjoyed Maine lobsters and especially, scallops, which he ordered on three occasions.

When we returned to Rome, nothing would do but that we stay with their family. For us, it was like being in the home of a favorite relative. The welcome was genuine, warm and beyond kind.

We have become close to Fabio's parents as well; they are more than generous, kind and gracious. The extended friendship shown to us has been a rare and delightful gift. We are always touched by their genuine warmth.

Fabio is a boat aficionado, having been raised in a village on the shores of Lake Como; now he keeps a large boat in the port of Civitavecchia. It was only natural therefore that he was interested in seeing places in New England where boating is important, so he and his daughter rented a car and explored Mystic, Connecticut, and Newport, Rhode Island. He seemed delighted with all he saw. When he was a young boy he had a small boat with a Johnson outboard motor. When we were at a restaurant one evening which was located on a boat filled harbor, he saw an identical boat and motor exactly like he had as a kid. Nothing would do but to get into it. Watching him sitting there and smiling so broadly and genuinely, we took his photograph. Six months later when we went to Rome, we presented that picture to him, enlarged and framed. It was his favorite thing!

Before he arrived we took his daughter who is an animal enthusiast to the aquarium in Boston, and to the Bronx Zoo in New York. We also made forays to Martha's Vineyard and to Woods Hole where the Marine Biological Laboratories are located as well as the Woods Hole Oceanographic Institute. A trip to New York was a must to visit our older daughter who is a high school teacher of Italian; we wanted the two to meet, and they did most successfully.

Trying to show her what is available in a small town, we attended a drama presented by a local theatre group, had lunch in area restaurants and visited art galleries. We explored the inlets surrounding our house in our small boat, and simply tried to give her the feeling of the local life in a small New England town. Having grown up and lived in the huge and well-named eternal city of Rome, it had to be a total change. Of course she was used to the small towns where her father grew up as well as the village in Switzerland where her mother's family lives, but this was Massachusetts in the United States, and although our town was small, it was a different world from the small towns of Europe.

Valentina happily discovered the world of the designer discount mall. She had a ball buying a backpack, a baseball cap, warm-up trousers and other trendy items a nineteen year old would buy, as well as gifts for her parents. The store where CD's were sold was a tremendous hit with her. She bought many as they are so much less expensive here than in Italy, which pleased her tremendously.

We had a standing joke. Whenever her father 'phoned us, he would invariably ask, "Is she helping you?" I would assure him that she was. In reality, Valentina was a more than an ideal guest. Not only did she help in the kitchen, she offered to do almost any other thing that needed doing—shopping, laundry, or whatever was required. We decided to make a photo record of her doing housework to show her dad. First, we took pictures of her washing windows—that for a joke; then cooking pasta; baby-sitting for one of our young grandsons; and so many other household chores so that we could spoof her parents. When both her mother and father finally saw them, they were very amused.

A happy post script; Valentina and a friend visited us in Florida during the winter a year following her summer visit. We went to museums, the "safari" park, and the beach; they played tennis and visited our younger daughter and her family who live there. A special outing to a restaurant was memorable for its name "Bellagio," as this is the name of the town next to the village where her grandparents have vacation houses on Lake Como.

I must mention that on the occasion of our first visit to our good friend Fabio's restaurant in Rome in 1971, when actually he was not yet working there, a most pleasant man was our waiter. His name was Giuseppe, and I am deeply pleased to say, that he is still very much involved with the restaurant, and that each time we return, he makes a great effort to greet us and if possible to wait on our table. We are all hugs and kisses, and this, in a rather formal restaurant in the classy Parioli. But, the other restaurant patrons, well-to-do Italian nationals, are indulgent of us and our behavior; they have heard that we are not only good friends with the proprietor and his family, we have firm bonds with Giuseppe, and furthermore, we are the laughing, friendly, if slightly *pazzi* (crazy) Americans who happily return here year after year. And each year we become close to the other men who serve this restaurant; each is a professional and the essence of kindness. Some have begun to tease me and correct my pronunciation; Carlo especially makes me repeat, "*zuppa di verdura*" (vegetable soup) until I improve. Italians pronounce every consonant distinctly whereas Americans tend to slide over many of them. When he tried to teach me to say "*aglio*" (garlic) we all giggled at my verbal efforts.

Fabio and his lovely wife Tiziana visited us in Tuscany. Most of their vacation days are spent on the boat, at the Lake Como house, or in Switzerland visiting her family. We had a marvelous day with them going to historic towns and a few tiny villages through the countryside. Roger and I have spent much time throughout this area, and since he knows his way around so well, it was no problem for him to drive like a native tour guide. And, he seems to enjoy it so much!One night in Rome, Fabio's home, Roger had to direct him to our hotel. After the tour in Tuscany and Roger's directions in his own city, Fabio bought a new car with a GPS, or ground positioning system; he calls it his "Roger!"

While our dear friends from Rome were with us, I took the liberty of reading parts of my journals from years past I thought might amuse them. Before we left Cape Cod I had xeroxed sections which pertained to their restaurant from 1971 through recent visits. My entries lack literary niceties, but I consistently record every dish from every meal we have ever eaten in Italy. When I read this aloud at home, this record of nostalgia is brain pleasing, emotionally fulfilling, and obviously, mouth-watering! Consequently Fabio and Tiziana heard about our favorite things on their menus of twenty years and more ago. The tastes of the public change with time, and therefore some of the things we had so loved from the 70's and early 80's were no longer trendy and so disappeared from the offered cuisine. My all time favorite was *cannelloni* (a small sheet of pasta rolled around a stuffing of meat and herbs, covered with a nutmeg-flavored creamy white sauce, a touch of Bolognese sauce and parmigiano reggiano cheese); I had never had it before I visited that restaurant and afterward ordered it each time we returned. I was devastated when it disappeared during the 80's. Roger's favorite was *pollo arosto*—roasted chicken, but different from any we have ever eaten on this side of the Atlantic. I loved it too.

The happy ending to this saga was that when we returned to Rome we again were invited to our friends' house for dinner. They surprised us with, you guessed it, *cannelloni* and *pollo arosto!* Of course, being super hosts, they presented many other courses and specialties, but to remember our favorites and to re-create them just for us was a treat we'll never forget.

This memorable meal took place the night before we had to return to the United States. When we arrived home we discovered that we left our camera. What was worse, it was one we had borrowed from our son. The good news was that we remembered exactly where we left it! At Fabio and Tiziana's home! We 'phoned them and indeed found out that it was there. They offered to send it to us, but we declined, saying that we would return as soon as possible and retrieve it ourselves. This reminded me of an incredibly good teacher I had at college many years ago. She taught psychology and I elected every course she offered. I remember during the time I was taking her class in adolescent psychology, I continually left one of my belongings in her classroom, and each class day I had to return to gather whatever it was I "forgot."

This continued on for some time until she laughingly remarked that when one leaves an item behind, it frequently suggests that the person wants to return to that place. She was right in my case. I disliked the class I had scheduled after hers. In the tale of the forgotten camera, I'm afraid that her theory is again, only too correct. We want to return! Please, dear friends, we said, Fabio,

Tiziana and Valentina, hold on to the camera; we will be there to get it, which we are using just as an excuse to see you all once again in your beautiful land!

Rosalba and her family in the Marche'

Many years ago as a post graduate student, I took many courses in the evening at the state university near to my home. Our children were grown and so Roger would go with me and while I was in class he would go to the library and catch up on the newspapers and magazines he couldn't thoroughly read during the week, being too involved with business. After class we would meet for dinner with several of the professors with whom we had become friendly. It would be almost redundant but accurate to state that they were from the Italian department! Both of our daughters had been involved in the summer program in Italy offered by this university, and one year, Roger and I had attended the six week summer program as well, so we were all well acquainted.

During one semester we became friendly with an exchange student from Urbania, Italy who often would join our dinner group. She was studying here after having gotten an undergraduate degree in Italy, in preparation for a PhD in economics. The following summer we met again at a reunion in Italy, and we kept in touch from time to time. A few years later we met once more, this time in her town, Urbania in the Marche', for dinner with her and her fiancé. Then came that time when we were not able to go to Italy for six years and we almost lost touch. We found that we were going to be in the area of the Marche' in 1996 and were most anxious to see her and renew our acquaintance. At that time, it was my sad chore to tell her of the death of the Italian professor who had introduced us. We met and talked for hours and promised that we would have a family visit the next time we were in the Urbino/Urbania area.

Our mutual friendship grew into something very special. We invited her and by now, her husband, to dinner the next time when we were in that beautiful part of Italy, but she declined; she said that we should meet her family and that her parents would love to have us come to their house for Sunday dinner. We accepted!

Her mother was not only a lovely woman, but an accomplished cook. We began this memorable meal with an excellent *brodo* (soup) and homemade *passetelli* (a small pasta). Then we had turkey, rabbit, and quail; the quail was roasted directly over the coals in the open fireplace. Along with the meats, spinach, carrots, potatoes and pickled eggplant were served. We finished with fresh fruit, a heavenly homemade cake and a platter of Italian pastries. After a while, *signora* roasted chestnuts over the fire which we had with *limoncello* (a drink made of lemons, sugar and vodka)! What a repast!

Even better than this incredible meal was the extreme pleasure of meeting Rosalba's family. Her father is a charming, handsome man; a retired carabinieri officer. At that time her sister Gloria was recently engaged and we were instantly comfortable with her and her fiancé, Gianluca. We became so friendly during the course of the day that Roger told them that if they invited him to their wedding, he would come. P.S. Three months later an invitation arrived at our home in Massachusetts, and on May 1st, there we were in the cathedral in Urbania, guests at their wedding! That day was one we shall never forget; spectacular from beginning to end in every way possible! Food, friendship, laughter and genuine good feelings throughout the day.

We also met several of Rosalba's brothers at this time, and all in all, it was not only another unforgettable Italian experience, it firmed our good and growing friendship with another congenial and kind family.

About six miles outside of the town, her father owns an old house and extensive acreage. It is where he grew up, and now that he is retired, he raises some sheep, goats, pigs, chickens and rabbits there. He goes there everyday to feed and care for them. The week before we got there, though it was only November, a surprise blizzard had covered the ground with more than two feet of snow; this caused him to walk the distance from his house and back to make sure the animals were fed and safe. We drove out there after the huge Sunday afternoon meal; the countryside was luminous with white hillsides and pure, clear air.

The house on this farm land has been abandoned for years. It has neither running water, plumbing, heat or electricity. Architecturally it is a gem and could be made into a delightful get-away. So many people in Italy left their farms after World War II for other jobs in the cities or abroad. Throughout Italy there are thousands of homes similar to this one that are no longer lived in. Many people though, are restoring homes that belonged to their parents or grandparents, some to live there or others for use as weekend or vacation retreats. Rosalba's father has plans to do this with his childhood home. The location is superb and it would be an oasis. Many old buildings have been bought by people from other countries and restored; this is especially evident in Umbria and Tuscany—parts of Tuscany are jokingly called "Chianti—shire" because of the many British who live there—but this trend is being slowly evidenced throughout all of Italy and not just in those provinces.

Our friend Rosalba's house is a restored sixteenth century convent with modern heat, electricity, kitchen and bathrooms. A professor at the local university, she manages her professional life with the life of a young mother of now four young, beautiful daughters, and of a wife, and all seems to be in balance. We have come to know and admire her husband; watching him with his children is to know a good person.

A grace note recently occurred. The couple whose wedding we attended visited us in Florida accompanied by their five year old daughter and two year old son. We were honored to be among the first to be told that by the next summer, baby number three would come to them! Rosalba and her family promise to visit us next summer on Cape Cod. We are blessed.

Cathy and Giorgio of Urbino

While we were at Gloria and Gianluca's wedding dinner we were seated across from a young couple who are friends of the family. Our friend Rosalba arranged that we meet them after the ceremony to insure that we would be comfortable. Both Giorgio and his wife Cathy are professors in the University at Urbino. Cathy is an American woman, originally from Wisconsin, and Giorgio, totally fluent in English, became our interpreters during the course of this incredible party. We needed some help in translating as relatives of the wedding party and some of their friends acted out skits reenacting the lives of the bride and groom; some friends gave speeches for the benefit of the entire assemblage, and much of this would have been lost on non-Italian speakers. By the end of the evening, we had become friends with both translators and their darling young daughter, and decided that we would have dinner together on the following Monday. When we telephoned to ascertain the time and place, they insisted that we come to their house rather than to a restaurant. It was the most delightful evening one could wish for. Cathy had made spaghetti *carbonara* among many other things, which is Roger's favorite pasta! This heavenly sauce is comprised of eggs, *pancetta*—a kind of bacon, and cheese. Since that time we have met each time we go back to Urbino.

Cathy invited me to Madison a few summers ago to attend a writers' conference at the university. She invited me to stay with her aunt and uncle as her parents were in the process of building a new house. Not only was the conference totally satisfying, but I had the pleasure of meeting her extended American family—great people! Another plus was that I was awarded with two honors for my writing!

Cathy's husband Giorgio recently attended a conference in the United States and he and another professor visited us on Cape Cod for several days. The good world becomes smaller through friendship!

The Wedding in Urbania

For those who have never been to a wedding in Italy, I feel compelled to share the things I found so interesting. Before the wedding itself, most of the guests gathered in front of the *duomo* or cathedral. The groom was making the rounds, greeting friends and smiling, although he seemed typically in the daze of a man just about to be married. Gloria, the bride, was escorted by her father from their home conveniently located across the street from the cathedral, to the church door, where Gianluca, the groom awaited her. They walked down the aisle together; there was no wedding procession such as we are used to in the United States. There were no bridesmaids or ushers. The ceremony was rather long, but easy to follow as everyone was given a complete program with the entire service written out and then printed, in the handwriting of both the bride and groom. There was no recessional at the end of the service; instead, most of the guests walked up toward the altar where the newly married couple remained for endless hugs and kisses and best wishes. Finally it was time, as if by some unseen but mutual agreement, that all should leave the church and proceed to the reception.

The hotel located just outside of Urbania is placed on a hill overlooking an incredibly breathtaking scene of greenery—trees, pastures, soft hills and the beauty of *primavera* or spring in the Marche'. (The Italian word for spring is so appropriate as it translates literally to "first green"!) Many kinds of *aperatif* (before dinner wines) and hors d'oeuvres were served on a patio above a swimming pool. The sun was glorious; the day perfection.

The matrimonial feast followed in the large dining room. Waiters served one *crostino* (a small slice of toasted bread),with tomato and mozzarella cheese to each person. After that, another came with chopped *funghi,* mushrooms, in a delicious sauce; next a *crostino* with pate'. On each table there were bottles of white wine, red wine, a sparkling white wine and mineral water.

The next four dishes—or *piatti,* were then served. The first, a local specialty, was made of two incredibly thin sheets of pasta enclosing a stuffing of herbs and cheese. Heavenly! Next there was a totally *bianco* or white lasagne with a cream sauce, peas and cheese. "To die for," as my children used to describe something they loved! Then a Milanese risotto (Arborio rice patiently cooked in broth) with perfectly prepared mushrooms, and lastly, miniature *gnocci (a special homemade pasta made with either potatoes or ricotta cheese)* served in a very light covering of tomato sauce.

Next we had a lemon sorbet, to clear the palate, I presume. This was followed by a most tender filet of beef with special mushrooms called *porcini;* then grilled lamb, pigeon and herb-stuffed rabbit. The vegetables accompanying the meats were spinach, salad, and fried potatoes.

But we weren't yet finished! Delectable local varieties of cheeses made up the next offering; this was followed by homemade *gelato,* or ice cream, in tiny, edible chocolate cups. The wedding cake was covered with fruit; the texture almost like that of cookies, and this dessert was served with champagne. Then coffee! What was truly amazing was that the timing of this huge meal was so ordered and leisurely, that we were happily ready and able to consume all.

Then came the show! Apparently it is customary for weddings in the provinces, or the "country" as our friends explained to us, to have skits performed. We were told that this would not be done in Rome or Milano as the city population considered themselves too sophisticated for this kind of happening. We watched the re-enactment of the births of both bride and groom, complete with doctors and nurses in gowns and masks; then, depicted as children, getting on the school bus; the bride's dancing lessons; as young adults, the couple dancing at the disco; the groom's job in China where he lived for several years, and on and on until the present. Each sketch was accompanied by appropriate music; the final one ended with the song from A CHORUS LINE, "She's the One."

At one point the bride's sister, our friend Rosalba, with several friends, all dressed in Spanish dancer costumes, went through the dining room selling aprons and baseball caps with the names of the bride and groom and the date of their wedding to the guests. Of course we bought both. And treasure them!

It was then about seven in the evening. The wedding ceremony had taken place at eleven in the morning and we had been dining since two in the afternoon. An announcement was made. Everyone should clear the dining room until half past eight so that the staff could clean up. Unbelievably, all guests were expected to return at that time.

We walked around the grounds of the hotel for awhile, wondering what could possibly follow? We didn't have a clue, but certainly we weren't going to miss anything! Our hotel in Urbino, about ten miles away from the reception, has its doors locked at ten in the evening. This is quite typical of small Italian hotels. When we left at ten that morning the proprietor asked us if we'd like a key in the event we would be late. Assuring him that no wedding could last that long, we declined. Now, at seven thirty, we realized that we would be past the lock-up "curfew". We had chatted with Erica, a woman from Verona whose daughter was dating Rosalba's brother. Although Italian, she had grown up in South Africa and had impeccable English. Our new pals from the long afternoon repast, Cathy and Giorgio, had taken their young daughter home to bed, and so we were in need of another interpreter! We asked Erica if she would telephone our hotel and ask someone to please wait for us. We wouldn't be later than eleven. She did and assured us that Gianfranco at the hotel was happy we were having so good a time and that he would wait for us. He must have realized that morning how late we might be; we had no idea.

At eight thirty the great majority of afternoon guests returned; many lived in the vicinity or were staying at this hotel and I noticed that a number of these guests had returned to their homes or hotel rooms and had changed into casual attire. It helps to know the routine!

Phase two, reception, began with music for dancing; another skit was presented, and then, unbelievably, what was termed a" light buffet" featuring cold meats, cheeses, breads, salads, many types of cakes and desserts, soda, juice, wine and beer were offered at full buffet tables. We finally gave up at ten after dancing, and only being able to nibble on the quantity of the delicious food offerings; we drove back to Urbino, complete with the experiences of an unusual and most satisfying day. Having arrived from Boston on the afternoon before, we were jet-lagged and it had been a very long day. We were expected at the home of the bride for brunch the following morning so we decided that some sleep time was very much in order; the party was not yet over! This wedding was an event we would not have missed for anything, and as the only American couple there, we felt indeed privileged to have been a part of it.

Gloria and Gianluca of Imola

We return each year to Urbino and every year for the past four we have given a dinner party at a local restaurant or agriturismo. Our friends there always invite us to dinner at their respective homes and since we usually stay in a hotel in that town, it is impossible to reciprocate from one's home, hence we invite all to a Sunday dinner at a special place. At the end of dinner, the couple whose wedding we attended asked us to visit them in their new home in the city of Imola. Their daughter was then two and Gloria was only a week or two away from delivering their son. We were hesitant about bothering them at a time when a new baby was imminently due, but they insisted and we were treated to a special few days.

Imola is an impressive city of 65,000 inhabitants; Roger and I walked through the old part of the city and when he returned from work, Gianluca gave us a tour in his car. The weekend following our visit, the Formula One race was to be held here and preparations were visible throughout the town. We saw the track, which was huge, and the vast stands for thousands of fans.

Their house was absolutely lovely; bedrooms, great kitchen, living room with fireplace, private garden and two huge garages; as if that weren't enough, Gloria is a fantastic cook!

We explored the area on our own the following day to give Gloria a bit of free time to rest. We tried to visit the local museums, but found they are open only on weekends in the off-season, so although the tourists are fewer, except for the major cities, the sites are often on a much reduced schedule during the rest of the year. When we returned to their house in late afternoon, Gloria had a fire going and we all had tea as we sat in front of its warmth. Repeatedly, we invited them to go out to dinner as our guests, but they would not budge, so that night, our hostess made great spaghetti carbonara after Gianluca gave us some crostini with smoked salmon and others with truffle paste! Fantastic! Full of wonderful food, pleased with the company of good people, we fell into bed about ten o'clock.

Maurizio, the owner of our favorite hotel in Rome

What would your reaction be, if upon checking into a hotel, the owner smiled as he enthusiastically greeted you and told you that you people were the oldest guests he had? That happened to us, but it was not as it first sounded! When we went to Rome in 1976 with a student group from the State University of New York, we all stayed at a modest hotel which catered mostly to student groups. In the years since that time we have stayed there many, many times. Each time, the services, the decor, in short absolutely everything in this hotel, has been upgraded to the point where it is now rather luxurious, but still intimate and friendly. Student groups, needless to say, no longer stay there, nor could they afford to. The rooms and baths are elegance itself; the location is ideal, and in addition to that, the staff is marvelous, but best of all, we have become very good friends with the owner, Maurizio, and recently also with his delightful wife, Raili. What this charming and cosmopolitan man was saying and we understood perfectly, was that we have been coming to his hotel continually more than any other guest he has. We chat with him on the telephone occasionally, and never, ever, would we stop in Rome without staying for at least a few nights in his wonderful establishment where we feel totally at home. We alternate taking each other to dinner; we have met his handsome son and lovely daughter, and most of all, we count him as another good Italian friend. We are blessed.

An unfortunate incident made less by a kind woman

Is Italy perfect? Hardly. Our car, which stupidly we left, fully packed with all our suitcases fully visible, was broken into and burgled as it was parked on a busy street in Florence. We knew better; we should have left it in a parking garage or in an attended lot.

Having had this exact episode happen to our cars in New York City on four different occasions, including one as far back as 1955 when we were returning from our honeymoon, once in Boston in the 1980's, and even once in the "*tres chic*" enclave of Palm Beach, Florida, directly in front of the gracious co-operative apartment building where Roger's distinguished aunt lived, we should have known better. At that time in Florida a mean Scrooge swiped all the Christmas toys we had purchased for our then four young children at the local F.A.O. Schwartz's. Sadly, the policeman who took the information said that some people especially came to this area before Christmas with the specific intention of doing just that.

When we lived in a small city on the Hudson River in New York State our house was ransacked twice before we installed an elaborate alarm system, and even then, it was tried, although the intruders were frightened off by the screeching alarm. A pickup truck used in my husband's business at that time had the window deliberately smashed and materials stolen; his car 'phone was stolen from his new car. Both of these incidents involving our vehicles occurred as the truck and car sat in our driveway and we were in the house. I mention these incidents only to show first, that crime, unfortunately, happens all over. Second, I am delighted to say that the Italian police recovered my suitcase, one piece of jewelry, and most of my clothing. Not one thing illegally taken from us in the United States in nine separate events was ever returned. Not flatware, nor electronic items, jewelry, nothing. Perhaps the Italian police are more efficient?

Not to continue needlessly in this vein, but I must tell of a woman who aided us immediately after the car burglary in Florence. Returning from a super lunch only to find the car empty was devastating. A woman who owned a shop featuring accessories such as scarves, gloves and handbags for sale, noticed our chagrin. She spoke English and offered to escort us to the police station where we could make a report. She locked up her shop and took almost an hour to go with us, translate, and generally help us. Among other things, Roger's passport, which was in his suitcase, was also missing. She helped the police with our information so they could fill out forms which enabled him to be "legal" until he got back to Rome and the American Embassy to replace his passport. Months later, after we were notified that the police had recovered some of our belongings, Roger was in Florence and picked them up. He then went to the shop to thank the woman who helped us so much. In appreciation, he bought two magnificent silk scarves for me, one in navy blue and the other a golden beige with a black design. I treasure them; they are timeless, and they will always remind me, not of loss, but of the kindness of one who unhesitatingly came to the aid of two confused temporary exiles. This is the Italy of people who have heart and feeling. The vast majority.

Elena, *simpatico* (pleasant), friendly, shop proprietor

We have come to know Elena quite well; she has a small ceramics shop in Castellina-in-Chianti. We first met six years ago and we never went to that delightful town without seeing her at the very least, once. That was in the beginning; now we visit often, share dinners and enjoy the company of her most congenial husband Giuseppe and their two children. We correspond and exchange Christmas greetings.

About seven years ago there was a tragic accident of truly horrifying proportion at her father's factory, and her brother lost his life. Naturally her parents were devastated at losing their only son in an indescribable manner. I am not certain whether by Divine Intervention, design, or accident, but in any event, the next year our friend Elena gave birth to a son. Certainly no one person can replace the loss of another, but this baby has done so much to ease the pain from a beloved sister, as well as from the parents of the lost son. Now they all have a beautiful little boy to love and care for, and he has a teen-aged sister, excellent parents and loving grandparents. I think he will be a *principe* (an Italianprince)!Thousands of miles away, I think of this family everyday as I look at some of the most unusual ceramic pieces happily hanging on my kitchen walls which were acquired from Elena's shop; a perfect string of garlic bulbs, an Italian artichoke, and an artistically arranged group of vegetables looking more real than real, and a magnificent centerpiece of lemons in a basket, and again I turn to Shakespeare:

> *How beauteous mankind is! O brave new world,*
> *That hath such people in't!* (THE TEMPEST V,1)
> and I am glad that I get to be an exile in this Paradise!

Several years ago this couple purchased a house in a wooded area several miles from the village. They restored it with perfect bathrooms and kitchens, and now, in an apartment separate from the family quarters but within the same building, we have rented from these kind and generous people. From the bedroom window as well as from outside, the towers of Siena are visible; the views outstanding. A delight for us to be here!

Sacha, artist and boutique proprietor

Adorable Sacha, the artist in Florence is a young friend who will continue to be a special person to us for many years. We now have five of her paintings on our walls in Cape Cod, as we seem to add another on each trip! One is a bowl of delicious looking cherries, another of ripe vegetables, one of a character from La Commedia dell'arte, and most recently, two of toys reminiscent of the 1940's Roger liked so very much as it reminded him of things he had as a young child. With luck we may have more in the future—keep painting, Sacha!

We have shared an evening with her parents and began to solidify another Italian friendship. A note from her arrived recently showing her in a wedding gown as she was married in Mexico. We'll have to catch up!

She now lives in The Netherlands and a few weeks ago we received news that she now has a baby boy!

Federico, energetic, young restauranteur and some of his relatives

Pestello-Antico Ristorante is our favorite restaurant in Chianti country. The food is superb and beautifully presented, the atmosphere perfect, the wine cellar abundant, but best of all, the young proprietor, Federico, is not only a marvelous host but has become a good friend. We discovered his restaurant in 1997 and have become regulars each time we've been in the region. Incidentally, it's one of the favorite places of my son-in-law Michael as well, who appreciates good food and wine with the Italian ambiance.

On one visit we took a group photo of Federico, some of his staff and us. At home we had it enlarged and framed and on our next Italian trip we took it to him. He deeply appreciated the gesture and today it hangs in his office. In the winter of 2000 the restaurant was closed for extensive alteration and now it is more perfect than ever. Of course we stopped by to chat with the host while it was undergoing restoration and promised him we would return as soon as possible. In the autumn we did, and it was not only beautifully designed and appointed, the cuisine was better than ever—it that was possible.

It has become our habit to bring small tokens of appreciation to some of the people in Italy who have been so kind to us. Usually these are souvenir items from either Cape Cod or from Florida where we spend some time each year—tee shirts, key rings, calendars, hats or canvas carry-bags. We brought a shirt to Federico and the most amazing reaction occurred. The genial estate owner from whom we were renting our Chianti cottage, 'phoned us and said there were flowers for me. A young man had delivered them to the manor house, he told us, but explained that they were for the Peterkins. We walked down to see what he was talking about, and there was a bouquet of yellow chrysanthemums and tiny orange pumpkins wrapped in a straw-like twine. Beautiful! Federico's work! But that was not the end. The next day pink tulips arrived together with another bouquet of large scarlet and white lilies.

The explanation for two together was that the restaurant was closed on the next day and he wanted us to have flowers for every day we were in the area. We went to the restaurant the following evening and there on the table lay perfect *girasole* or sunflowers wrapped with tiny yellow peppers. I thanked Federico profusely, but begged him to stop. The flowers were wonderful, but too much. Sternly, he told me to sit down and be quiet! A perfect rose surrounded by small flowers followed the next day and then ruby colored lilies; large pink daisies were next followed by delicate white flowers the following afternoon; then yellow iris with small lavender flowers, next an exquisite orchid, and finally, pink roses with purple chrysanthemums. Eleven flower arrangements, more than I ever have received in my life, one after another, day by day! It was a truly overwhelming experience!

Fedcrico introduced us to his mother and to his sister Maria Pia, both of whom are instrumental in the kitchen of the restaurant. One night Maria Pia's daughter, Asia, was there. A young girl at that time of about six, she was waiting for her father to pick her up when he finished work.

Almost without exception, Italian nationals have a favorite bar. These bars are entirely different from American bars; one goes there for morning coffee, for pastry, for ice cream, and occasionally for a beer or glass of wine. We have always had a favorite bar in Castellina, the Chianti Bar, where invariably we go about ten o'clock every morning for cappuccini and for Roger, a *mele pasta (apple pastry)*. The family owners, a man and woman and their two sons, are friendly and always welcome us enthusiastically, especially after an absence. We exchange Christmas cards and post cards with them as we now do with so many Italian friends. While waiting for our caffe' to brew, Roger noticed a child's drawing hanging on the wall. The name on the paper was "Asia." Suddenly we realized that Federico's niece was the grandchild of the senior couple of the Chianti Bar, and that their son Gino was Maria Pia's husband and the father of the little girl whose primary school drawing was pinned up for display!Happy discovery to find two of our favorite places in Chianti country related, as it were, to each other!

Since that time we have been guests at Maria Pia's and Gino's house for a dinner to remember forever; we have become friendly with a friend of Federico's, Serena, and happily, we have gotten to know Mamma Theresa, Federico and Maria Pia's warm, lovely mother and their charming father, Franco.

One evening in May 2004 while we were dining at this restaurant, Federico came over to our table and asked if we would come next door to the attached informal bar when we finished our meal as he wanted to tell us something. When we entered, he had a secret smile as he told us that he and Serena were engaged and would be married in January when the restaurant was closed. As we hugged him and offered our best wishes, he added that he would like us to attend! Thrilled by the invitation, we assured both him and Serena who had entered, that we would be there!

We booked our plane and house reservations the moment we returned home. The invitation arrived in November and two months later we were present at the beautiful ceremony and lavish reception which followed. This ceremony and subsequent celebration were slightly different from the one in the Marche' as each area has slightly different customs and traditions. However, the glorious menu, congenial guests and warm family combined to make this day so happy, so fulfilling, we shall never forget it.

Immediately after the ceremony the reception began at an incredibly gorgeous resort hotel. A large room was the setting for an array of hors d'oeuvres pleasing to the eye and enchanting to the stomach. Musicians entertained, wine flowed and all waited for the entrance of the bridal couple. Eventually, together with the bride and groom we all moved to a formal dining room. Each place was adorned with a printed menu and a gift from the couple.

We began with a polenta filled with mushrooms before moving on to a farro soup with different varieties of mushrooms. Then a lasagne arrived with a unusual ragu; following this, tortelli pasta with truffles. This must be what is served in heaven! But of course we were no where near finished!Faraona, a type of fowl was served next with various kinds of vegetables and then beef with potatoes and baked vegetables. The wine flowed and eventually, but not hurriedly, the lavish wedding cake appeared accompanied by coffee and a variety of after dinner libations.

The wedding ceremony had taken place at half past three; dinner was complete at midnight. But the party was not yet over! Many of the older people kissed the bride and groom and departed, but all the young and many others retreated to the room that had served earlier for the antipasto delicacies. The musicians returned, dancing began, more wine appeared and the party continued. We finally gave in to fatigue at three A.M. after many good-byes, kisses and hugs. We felt honored and privileged to be included in another wedding of people of whom we are so fond, and again, for the second time, we were the only Americans! A happy P.S. to this is that Serena and Federico are now the parents of two beautiful little ones—a girl and a boy!

A sympathetic gentleman hotel manager

I hate to generalize, but often do, and so if I had to choose two words which describe the Italian character more often than not, I would choose, generosity and amiability. During November of 2000 we found ourselves once again in Sicily for the second extensive visit in eight months.

We were driving from Siracusa to Palermo through Catania and decided to stop for our typical morning cappuccini break at a large hotel which caters mostly to business travelers. It is located at the entrance to the Catania-Palermo motorway. We had stopped there on a previous trip and found the surroundings and staff pleasant. When we walked to the lobby bar the barman apologetically stated that service was limited to hotel residents. There were four of us at the time and everyone except me began to leave. I spotted an official looking, handsomely suited man behind the main desk. Catching his eye, I pantomimed a tear from my eye and said, "No coffee?"

Immediately he came to the front and indicated that we should wait. I explained that we had been here in February. He smiled, spoke a few words to the barman and directed us back to the bar. The cappuccini were delicious! I thanked him for his kindness and understanding as we left; his warm smile and handshake acknowledged my appreciation. Generosity and amiability! Italy!

A special taxi man in Siracusa, Sicily

Anyone who travels or who lives or works in large cities is well-acquainted with taxis. Although we live in a small town and rarely use them on a regular basis, we are very familiar with this mode of transportation throughout the United States as well as in various European countries. We've experienced few problems excluding once being badly cheated in a late night cab from Heathrow to London, but that's another story from another country!

While in Siracusa we met two taxi drivers, Salvatore and Giuseppe who became our pals and guides. Roger and I have minimal Italian language, mostly we "speak" menu, and have no Sicilian dialect whatsoever, but we were in luck as these two men had a friend, Benny, who had moved to Rhode Island as a child and had recently retired and come back to Sicily. He became the translator for us as well as for Salvatore and Giuseppe. If Salvatore, who called himself our "*sera*" or afternoon driver took us to a restaurant for dinner, Giuseppe would estimate the time we would finish, and he would be waiting for us near the restaurant at the piazza where the taxis gathered. If he had another call, he always reminded us that we had his cell 'phone number and if we needed him he would respond promptly. He called himself our "*notte*" or night driver. One evening after dinner, having become more comfortable with us, he suggested that on our next visit we might consider staying in a different hotel, one less oriented to the commercial traveler. He drove us to a grand old 18th century villa converted to a luxurious hotel where we had a tour of the beautifully appointed public rooms. He was proud to announce that Winston Churchill had once been here and the smoking room was named for him!

On our last morning in this historical and enchanting city by the sea, we were having breakfast in the dining room when Giuseppe came in and presented me with a medal of the city of Siracusa. On the "head" side there was a profile of Athena with an inscription in Greek, and on the "tail" side, the words, "Azienda Provinciale Turismo Siracusa" in Italian. I was so delighted with this thoughtful and most unusual gift I ran up to our room to search for something I could put through the clasps and wear immediately. I found silver colored twine which had come on another gift and threaded it through the loop and ran down to show him. It has since become one of my favorite and very unusual pieces of jewelry, eliciting comments from strangers as well as from friends. Again, thank you Giuseppe!

On a follow up trip to Siracusa we met Giuseppe again and this kind man took us for coffee, gave us a shell with the symbol of Sicily, and as a parting gift on the day we were leaving, a bottle of limoncello. Before he drove away to take clients to the airport in Catania, he opened the trunk of his taxi and removed a small portfolio; he opened it and took out every letter, photo, and Christmas card we had sent to him during the past few years. And despite the fact that I am redundant in my praise, I must reiterate the fact that most Italian people are, generous and amiable, and to add to that I would say, kind and loving.

On our most recent Sicilian visit, we invited Giuseppe and his wife Rosa to dinner. We had never met her before. An attractive, charming woman, we now had the pleasure of knowing another warm, loving person as we dined and later walked through the narrow street of Siracusa to the Piazza Archimede. The evening was totally satisfying, yet again. Friendly, kind people! Plus, the following morning we met the friendly other taxi man, Salvatore, for a coffee and fine visit.

And despite the fact that I am redundant in my praise, I must reiterate the fact that most Italian people are, generous and amiable, and to add to that I would say, kind and loving.

Friends at the hotel we prefer in Urbino

No listing of congenial people from Italy would be complete without mentioning Gianfranco and his wife Iole of the hotel in Urbino. Together with Barbara, their right-hand woman, this triumvirate smoothly direct the operation of this charming hill-top hostelry. We celebrated our wedding anniversary while staying here and they, having discovered that, placed a beautiful bouquet of flowers in our room and a bottle of vin santo as well. This gesture is only one of so many kindnesses shown to us. A hotel should be a home away from home, and this is made so by the people who make their guests feel special, welcome and truly like a part of their family. That's what happens here! The hotel has recently been sold, but we continue to visit with Gianfranco as often as we can.

Gianni and Vincenzo of the Osteria

The Osteria di Fonterutoli, was a small restaurant located very close by the estate in Tuscany where we often stay. I say "was" because they have moved to much larger quarters, Il Mulino in Quercegrossa. Gianni and his brother Vincenzo are the efficient and most friendly operators. We had an unusual experience years ago at the small osteria. Not realizing that we should have made reservations, we arrived to find every table full. Gianni, ever accommodating, asked us to wait for a few minutes while he produced another table and covered it with linen, silverware and glasses and invited us to sit. We were considered "regulars" by this time and the welcome was sincere. Their former restaurant is associated with a winery, Mazzei, founded in 1435 and its excellent fruit of the vine demonstrates the good use of practicing for almost 600 years!

Gioia, young, bright, entrepreneur in Pesaro

Seated in a favorite and unusual restaurant in the Marche' one evening, an attractive young woman at a nearby table spoke to us. She heard our American English and began a conversation; we learned that she was a highly educated person and was in the process of opening an unusual galleria in the resort town of Pesaro. Since then we have visited her unusual shop filled with art, crystal, china and special items perfect for wedding or other gifts; in addition we have met for dinner with her and her fiancé and exchange letters and greeting at Christmas. We always look forward to seeing her again.

Mario and family and friends in Abruzzo

No listing of good friends in Italy would be complete without including Mario in Abruzzo as well as his wife Gabriella, his mother-in-law Olga, father-in-law Vincenzo, and his marvelously talented musician friends, Lucio and Carmine. But I speak of them effusively, in the Abruzzo chapter!

A restaurant manager and headwaiter in the Marche'

Can you imagine walking into a restaurant far out in the countryside to a tiny village called Castel Cavallino, and having been there only once which was a year before, hear the headwaiter exclaim, "Massachusetts!" when he recognized us? This brought not only gales of laughter from all of us, but happy memories of our first visit there as well. Recommended by our hotel owner, we followed his directions which were certainly off the proverbial "beaten path", through a November night permeated with fog so thick we were unable to see more than twenty feet ahead; high piles of snow on both sides of the road impeded our vision as well as we crept along in our tiny Fiat. Just as we were in the midst of what we thought must be the near end of the earth, suddenly, seemingly from no where, appeared a well-lit and appointed restaurant.

Seated, and sipping on wine, we heard music coming from one of the speakers in the outer room. Listening, we dissolved into spasms of hearty laughter, gaining the attention of a party of eight seated nearby. When they began looking at us rather quizzically, we explained that the recorded song was, "Oh, to be Home in Massachusetts" and that we live there, but never, ever expected it to be played here so very, very far from home in a tiny village in Italy! Incidentally, the food couldn't have been better; the staff were totally accommodating and as a result, we've returned there each time we are in the area, which is actually every time we go to Italy!

I realize that so many people with whom we have become acquainted, including more than a few we are very close to, have a common denominator, and that is food. But that is not unusual in this country I love; food is important. Italians feel that it must be grown or raised properly, prepared well, and presented with care and often with affection. Restaurant proprietors take great pains to insure that their patrons are pleased. This is sometimes difficult in large city restaurants which cater to tour groups as, unfortunately, many tourists are not used to a different cuisine or customs and complain vociferously if food is not presented precisely as they are used to in their hometowns. Traveling alone, we strongly feel, especially away from the well-trodden tourist destinations, is the only way to see the "real" country, whether that be Italy, France, England or wherever.

Eva and Alex, transplanted from Britain to Tuscany and now back to Britain

I hesitated about including our very dear friends, Eva and Alex, in this chapter, "Some Italian People" as they are not Italian nationals, but British, but my best friend in Rome dissuaded me from placing them otherwise by saying, "Gerry, they have lived in Italy for more than forty years, they speak Italian, they own seventy acres of Tuscany, they produce superb olive oil on their exquisite *podere* or farm, they never miss the opera performed in *Firenze* or Florence, Venice is where they celebrated their fiftieth wedding anniversary,—they're Italian!" So here they are.

Actually this extraordinary couple whose manners, refinement and cultural interests are of a calibre found most infrequently, could be citizens of the world, or at the least, of Europe. Speaking perfect English, German, Italian, and I believe French, they are "at home" in London, Rome, Paris or Vienna, as well as all places between those.

We became acquainted with Eva and Alex when our good friends in California, Susan and Terry, 'phoned a number of years ago and asked if we'd be interested in sharing a cottage with two bedrooms, two baths, living room and full kitchen, in Castellina-in-Chianti, Tuscany. This perfect cottage was a rental on Eva and Alex's estate. We've been pals with our California friends across the miles dating back to our junior high days, so we immediately agreed. People whom they knew had stayed here and highly recommended the accommodations, the area, and the hosts. They were correct and so began a most happy and satisfying relationship.

Eva is an artist, demure, petite and attractive; her paintings have been displayed in shows throughout Europe. When we first met she offered to give us a tour of her ample studio and

I fell in love with so much of her work. Her subjects vary but concentrate mainly on scenes of Tuscany, the various operations of the farm and its workers, and the lush flowers ubiquitous to her estate and the area. The prices of the large oils, especially of the sunflowers I adored and really coveted, were beyond my budget, but I purchased a great print and told her I was going to return home, don a ski mask, hold up the local bank, and return with the money for the painting. She was very amused and thus began a fast friendship. (By the way, I was joking in case there are covert operations on Cape Cod!)

We returned to this enchanting spot in Tuscany time and time again. Recently our friends sold their estate and moved to Florence, but our recollections of our many visits to this idyllic oasis will never be out of our memories.

Alex is an intelligent, handsome man whose twinkling eyes belie the seriousness of his visage. A thoughtful story-teller, a superb host, and for many years the efficient owner-manager of a gorgeous piece of real estate which my grandchildren would describe as, "awesome," are descriptions of him which immediately come to my mind. Formerly an interior designer, their luxurious but intensely comfortable and livable home showcases his talent for design, as well as being a perfect setting for much of Eva's work.

This farm produced, and we are told still does under the new owners, wonderful olive oil, but I like the story about how this came to pass. When this couple bought the estate it had lain abandoned for more than ten years; the olive trees were congested by wild shrubs and trees. The groves had stood deserted for more than fifty years and while a few had not survived, most needed tender loving care to become productive once more. Gradually, the surviving trees were coaxed, pruned, and encouraged back to productivity; new trees were planted, terraces perhaps centuries old were found and cleared, and ultimately, through painstaking care and much labor intensive effort, a yearly crop of olives is produced. This, of course, is the basis of their delicious, extra-virgin, first-pressing olive oil.

I can only imagine what the buildings on the estate must have looked like when this couple first purchased what is now an ideal haven. I've been told the dining room had a trough for animals, there was no running water or electricity, and a true horror, there were bullet scars around the doorway from the German occupation in World War II.

Eva and Alex created a paradise; we are so grateful to have known them, and from time to time, to have stayed here, gazing from the windows at the beauty of the silvery olive trees, the brook, the lake, the magnificent architecture, the flowers and to be greeted by their contented black dogs, Raffi and Mora.

A footnote explains why this congenial couple sold their wonderful Tuscan estate. They decided that they had heard of too many people who waited too long to make a change as they grew older, and whose effects after decades of effort ended negatively. They then became ensconced in a lovely home in Florence enhanced by an unsurpassed view of the city, and busily spend their time in cultural activities and travel.

Recently, they have acquired a second home in England near to their children and grandchildren where they plan to divide the year between Italy and England.

Daniela and Paolo, a very special couple

Two who have been so close to us and whom we met through the marvels of the crystal industry in Colle Val d'Elsa, are Daniela and Paolo and their beautiful daughter and handsome son. We have shared many dinners with them, have watched as they had a historic Tuscan house renovated and now anticipate returning so that we can truly appreciate seeing their completed new home and the family of four happily inhabited there. They are the epitome of hospitality and friendship which we treasure.

Enrico of Urbino

Several years ago a large package arrived from Italy containing an exquisite original painting of sunflowers in the Marche'. We were overwhelmed. The sender was a gentleman from the Urbino area we met only briefly. Two months previously, while seated in a pizza restaurant this young man, Enrico, and his girlfriend came over to our table and greeted us. They said they heard we were speaking English and guessed we were Americans; we chatted and exchanged addresses. After a meeting this brief, this gentleman sent us a painting we have had framed, hung and absolutely love. We thank him for his incredibly kind and overwhelmingly thoughtful act.

Others: Described in Various Chapters, or Held Warmly in our Hearts and Minds!

Fabio R. of our hotel in Rome and his wife Barbara, as well as Angelo, Sylvana, Linda, Willy, Alessandro P., Mimo and Pina; Franco and his mother Antonietta at Tre Rose in Nesso; Aurelio, his mother Margherita, and Sarah at Trattoria San Giacomo in Bellagio; Paola, Franco and Ilenia in Castellina; Pasquale and Valeria in Poggibonsi; Francesca and Giuseppe and baby Valerio of Rome and his parents in the country; a woman and her husband whom we met at a restaurant and who insisted on meeting us the following morning with their two young children in tow, to direct us to the Museo Villa Medicea in Cerreto Guidi, near Vinci; Luanne, a transplanted American; Alberto, the artist; Mirella, the cosmetician; Marco, the barman; David, Allessandro, and Antonello, university students; Alessandro's mother Franca, sister MariaGrazia, friend Nicoletta, and friend Pino; Gaetano, handsome hotel man; and the staff of Tinello's trattoria. The wonderful people of the Cardano Hotel, owner Patrizio, his wife Gabriella, his son Alessandro, and Bruno, Corrado, Anna, Luciano, Fortunato and many others. I could not omit Carlo and his pizzeria near the Cardano as well as the hotels in Piacenza, the Ovest and Nord, where we find Claudia, and Liza. Anna and Sergio in Florence, Marco and Donatella in Castello di Rivalta, the great staff at Riserva di Fizzano including Jho, Elena, Roberta and Ilaria; Anastazija with her ceramic creations; Fabio of the Trattoria Marione; Azzura, a young woman we met at Federico's wedding; Rachid in Siracusa; Alessia and Francesca in the tourist office in Castellina; Simonetta and Andrea whom we met at a Cinghiale Festival in Capalbio; Frank and Maureen of the gorgeous estate in Radda, Sergio, Gianni, Renato and the staff at La Bilancia and so many more. Chef Stefano in Castellina; Luigi, Roberto, Francesco, Angelo, Carlo, Gianni, Stefano and Giuseppe in Rome; chefs Caesare, Angelo, Giovanni, Adep and Ismael also in Rome and Rosaria at coat check. We exchange post cards, Christmas cards and often e-mails. You have enriched our lives; thank you. I apologize if I have omitted some.

Our Third Wedding in Italy!

Another adventure! I am a life long amateur actress. About six years ago I had a featured role in a play in the Woods Hole Theatre in Cape Cod. A young woman, Tara, was in the cast and after weeks of rehearsals, nine performances and a party for the cast at our house, we became very compatible despite the fact that there was a considerable difference in our ages. At the end of the play's run, she asked me for my telephone number and I hurriedly wrote it on a scrap of paper. I did not see or hear from her again for at least six years and heard that she had moved to California.

Two days before we left for a recent Italian trip my 'phone rang. It was Tara. She first asked if I remembered her. I assured her that I certainly did and still had the newspaper reviews and photos of our theatrical adventure. She told me that she still had my telephone number on the same piece of paper on which I had written it, and also that she remembered that we loved Italy. She excitedly stated that she now lived in Italy and would love to see us if we returned. I told her we were leaving in two days and that I would call her the moment we arrived at our hotel near Milan. She said she lived very near there and we would meet.

We made a date to meet for dinner when I 'phoned her. She explained that her boyfriend who is in the film industry had been so busy with a project that he might not be able to come, but that she would. That evening we waited for her in the hotel lobby and suddenly not only Tara, but her charming and most delightful companion, Laszlo, appeared. He told us that she was so excited to see us and that he didn't want to disappoint her even if he was letting some work lapse. We four had a fantastic and totally happy evening and great reunion with Tara. She told us that she was in language school everyday, learning to speak Italian.

We left the area the following day but stayed in touch by telephone and e-mail. We were not able to get together again but I assured her that we would get together soon, either at our home on Cape Cod or in Italy. She said she was very busy as they were moving to Rome.

A few months later we received a very happy and exciting e-mail from her. She announced that she and Laszlo were being married in September in the town of Capalbio near the sea in Tuscany and that she would love to have us come! Roger immediately made plane reservations, reserved a car and arranged hotel bookings in the town where the wedding would be held. This would be our third wedding in Italy and we anticipated the pleasure, happiness and joy we have come to expect with each. Thank you Tara for remembering us and our Italian connection!

September found us in Capalbio where we attended their wedding and glorious reception at the villa of the groom's relatives. The countryside of Tuscany is incredibly beautiful and the area around Capalbio was no exception. The main difference to us was that half of the large number of guests were of course Americans! We were not the unique ones at this event as many of Tara's family, relatives, friends, and some bridal attendants were from the U.S. as we would expect.

Italy is the beauty of its many waters, the mountains, the lush productive fields, vines, groves; its art, music, and monuments. It is all that, but more, much more; it is the land in which we feel friendships and kindness and where we return time after time. Italy is people we have come to know, to respect, and in many cases, to truly love. Without them, Italy would be scenery, a wondrous cuisine and works of art. Magnificent perhaps, but static. And that is never, never enough, for it is the people who make a country alive and who have made it for us the special place where we are so very contented to be exiles.

ABRUZZO—BEAUTIFUL AND RUGGED

"You may as well forbid the mountain pines
To wag their high tops, and to make no noise,
When they are fretten with the gusts of heaven."

THE MERCHANT OF
VENICE, IV, i, Shakespeare

When we announced Abruzzo as our next destination as we parted from the estate in Tuscany where we often have rented a small cottage, our hostess looked, if not horrified, then at the very least, askance. This very cultured British woman, artist and music scholar, stated that she had never known anyone who had gone there, and this delightful person had lived in Italy for almost forty years!

Next she advised me to buy heavy woolen sox, long underwear, and to make sure that I had very warm, preferably down-filled jackets packed in my luggage. The date was November first; Abruzzo is south of Tuscany and as we departed, the sun was strong and bright. We were coatless with only a sweater over our shirts and slacks. We hugged our good-byes and I promised to write. I began to wonder what we might expect.

Leaving Tuscany, we continued toward Rome on the autostrada. The terrain had changed from the area near Siena with its rich looking soil supporting grape vines, grains and olives, to the south of Tuscany in which the earth is grey-colored; some of the hills are virtually bare, known as La Crete. Through Umbria and then to Lazio the appearance of the landscape changed slightly again but became utterly dramatic when we entered Abruzzo. Huge, snow-capped mountains which reminded me of the Alps, thick forests, and large uninhabited areas interspersed with ancient hill towns surrounded with new construction outside the old city walls, were among the sites viewed from the autostrada. Dozens of bridges over severely deep crevasses and innumerable tunnels through the mountains—one more than two miles long—, were pervasive. There was very little traffic unlike the very busy Italian north and we guessed that this was because the first of November is All Saints Day, a national holiday.

We arrived at our destination, an *agriturismo* in Loreto Aprutino; it was an interesting and comforting place. We liked it so much we have returned ten times since our initial visit. These kinds of accommodations are regulated by the Italian government and vary widely from the ultra simple to the nearly luxurious. In the main they consist of rental apartments on a working farm. If meals are offered they must primarily consist of items grown or raised on the premises, or at the least, in the province in which the farm is located. We have appreciated the quality and freshness of this requirement every time we have had the opportunity to dine here. The estate where we frequently sojourn in Tuscany is what I would describe as a gentleman's farm. Quantities of olives are produced, elegant rental apartments as well as a cottage we have always preferred are available, but it is extremely genteel. There are no animals except two lovingly pampered dogs. Meals are not available; it is not an *agriturismo*. In Abruzzo this farm was more rustic, but totally comfortable and most hospitable. Just different.

Mario, the genial, bearded, grey-haired owner and manager, together with his attractive wife Gabriella, purchased this farm about twenty years ago, and began the *agriturismo* about fifteen years ago. We were told that it had been a convent, now abandoned, with two fairly large buildings on the property. Since then the restoration has been remarkable and never ending. From our first visit we found it totally comfortable, restful and enjoyable. Each time we have returned the estate looks ever better. The large communal living room was always filled with furniture, a television, books, games and best of all a huge fireplace which glowed each evening. Now this large space has been decorated with impressive modern metal sculptures, finer furniture, a VCR and DVD and hundreds of videos. Three new apartments have been built as well as a laundry, a structure for housing farm machinery, a large outdoor barbeque area with sink, grill, and pizza oven, and perhaps most impressive, a large swimming pool surrounded by gorgeous plantings. Mario has planted hundreds of new trees throughout his property enhancing the beauty as well as the environment.

As we approached this farm for the first time down a long dirt road, about eight hundred meters, and bordered by tall, slim cypress trees, I noticed an elaborate structure somewhat like a large grape arbor on one side of the road. I commented on this unusual structure and wondered what it was. As I looked closely I mentioned to Roger that something was growing on it which looked liked kiwi fruit. I immediately said to myself that this was ridiculous; we're in Abruzzo! As students are often told before multiple choice tests including the SAT, one's first choice is usually correct more often than not; Mario told us that kiwis they were! Several days later we watched a group of men and women pick and sort the fuzzy brown fruit. Huge open plastic containers held them until they were shipped to market.

This farm also produces award winning olive oil which is available for sale. Mario is agreeable about shipping it throughout the world for those of us who do not want to carry bottles on planes when we return home. Gabriella has been a prime mover in the women's oil association. She travels throughout Italy with other women as a judge of olive oil. While we were visiting she was sent to Spoleto to judge; when she returned I was curious to know how this was done. She explained that oils are evaluated by smell and taste; this is accomplished by putting the various oils from all over Italy into dark colored glasses as color has nothing to do with quality; she told us that it is a common misconception that green oil is superior, and that some producers have been known to add green dye to their oil to further the idea among consumers that green is better. She said that in this particular year the best oils were Sicilian, Sardinian and Tuscan. Her position as judge has naturally eliminated her from judging the oil from their farm. Mario went into his office and returned with a magazine, *GAMBERO ROSSO,* which seems to be like the American magazine GOURMET. There were five women on the cover and one was his wife. She hated the cover picture of herself, but on pages 50 to 53, there was another better picture of her with a bottle of their oil, and smaller photos of Mario, her mother Olga, and scenes of their farm, as well as including three pages of text with explanation of her role in the newly formed women's oil association.

In addition to the cultivation of kiwis and olives, chickens, ducks and turkeys meander behind a huge fenced in area, often appearing on the dining room table in a much altered and delicious state. Large parcels of ground are devoted to raising fruit and vegetables for the dining room as well. In the autumn strings of tomatoes and chili peppers are arranged in abundant cornucopias of reds and greens and hung from hooks underneath the roof of the protected area next to the dining room.

Olga, Mario's mother-in-law, known as the "iron woman" as she rarely stops working, is a cook beyond compare. Seated in the dining room, its stone arches supporting the attractively designed stone ceiling, one is given food lovingly prepared and delicious beyond belief. A typical meal we shared with other guests began with a glass of *prosecco,* a sparkling white wine, together with pieces of locally produced cheese. Then for *antipasto* a plate of cured meats, mozzarella and a green vegetable preserved in sweet vinegar. Next, two different pasta courses were offered; one a *gnocci* made with ricotta cheese and mixed with broccoli rabe, and the other a specialty which looked like lasagne, but was called *timballo.* This truly heavenly concoction was made with about twenty layers of paper thin crepes and not pasta. Between each layer there were ragu and cheese; it was incredibly light and totally delicious. That evening there were sixteen guests at the table and I wondered how long it would have taken to make enough crepes to feed us, as well as Olga, her husband Vincenzo, her two helpers, Mario and Gabriella, and the two musicians who were helping serve, but also sharing the table when they could. The dinner, or feast actually, continued with hundreds of tiny wooden sticks threaded with very small pieces of marinated and herb-scented lamb, cooked outside over a wood fire. Without exception, it was the best tasting lamb I have ever eaten. Wonderfully fresh salad greens accompanied the meat. Needless to say, excellent wines were poured without reservation.

We were then invited into an adjoining room; a large oval table was at the center and a piano at the side. The two musicians, Lucio and Carmine, were pianists, friends of the family and both conservatory trained; they began an entertainment which lasted well into the late evening. One man had played for years on American cruise ships and locally at weddings, and the other had played in many of the world's best known cities. Now, one was teaching music, and performing in the Abruzzo province; the other had a career as an accountant, but played for his pleasure. Each man performed alone, and then together, they created glorious duets. One of the guests that evening, an American attorney who had also been conservatory trained as a young man, joined them, and separately and often in tandem, the three played jazz, standards, classics, and upon request, some Neopolitan favorites. An added attraction was the wife of the American pianist; she had been a professional singer and she entertained all with a marvelous repertoire of song. Of course, not every night is filled with such spectacular entertainment as this special one, but even the quiet evenings with Olga's cuisine are nights to remember for a long time after. On this evening we devoured homemade apple torte accompanied by white wine, and then an amber colored dessert wine throughout the duration of this incredible concert. No one had to worry about over-indulging and driving as we all had apartments one flight up from the dining room.

There was a recent and most delightful postscript to one of these friendships. When we last visited Abruzzo and Mario's wonderful *agriturismo,* we of course had a reunion with Carmine and Lucio, and now Lucio's bride, beautiful Marielena! Carmine told us he had relatives on Cape Cod; he held some old family photographs in his hand and asked if we had time when we returned to the Cape if we could look him up and give him the photos. Of course we did; Carmine's cousin Gildo told us that his granddaughter was being married in a month and he would love to have Carmine attend. E-mails and telephone calls went back and forth and Carmine decided to visit.

We offered to pick him up at the airport and told his cousin Gildo that he could stay at our house until after the wedding as his house was busy with guests and family. Invitations began to arrive for us! We explained to Carmine's family that we did not have to be included; we did not know the bride or groom or in fact any of the family. Of course, that wouldn't do! We were told we would attend the rehearsal dinner, the wedding and reception as

well as the day after luncheon party for the bridal couple. This was
the way—the Italian way—of thanking us for bringing together
cousins who hadn't seen each other for thirty years. A marvelous
experience for us, not only for the *matrimonio,* but for the genuine
pleasure of seeing the reunion of loving family members! Truly a
small world—Abruzzo meets Cape Cod! A wonderful plus for us
was that Carmine played the piano in our house everyday, often
for hours. It was truly a joy to have him here!

When I dream and reflect on Mario's wondrous niche in
Abruzzo, "Le Magnolie," I am reminded of the Italian proverb
which came to me in translation. "Trifles make perfection, but
perfection is no trifle." This accurately describes the unceasing
efforts of Mario, his family and his helpers. They have created an
almost perfect retreat; a place of peace. Each apartment is well-
appointed with comfortable beds, well-equipped kitchens and
bathrooms, and telephone.

Inviting grounds extend for acres for wandering, exploring
or just plain viewing. One afternoon as we wandered we found
an open staircase on the grounds which led to a small reflecting
pool, a summer gazebo type structure and a grotto. We weren't
sure whether this was a part of the religious format of the previous
tenant or a pagan oriented shrine, as some of the faces carved
in stone were obviously not saintly. Later we asked Mario about
this and he said he intends to restore this area in the future. He
will undoubtedly do a thorough and accurate rebuilding after
researching its origins. Another reason, as if we needed one, to
return to view the finished product!

As we got more and more acquainted with Olga and she
realized I loved to cook, she would knock on our kitchen door
and present me with produce from her gardens and the farm.
Depending on the season I would receive lettuce, tomatoes, kiwis,

broccoli and the freshest eggs. The first time she brought me two huge eggs I had no idea what they were but soon discovered they were goose eggs!

At the end of March one year she asked if we would be staying for "Pasqua" or Easter. When I said we couldn't she was quite disappointed until I said we were meeting one of our daughters and her husband in Tuscany. I told her that this daughter was the Italian teacher and Olga looked so puzzled; she asked why she hadn't taught us the language. I tried to explain with my minuscule Italian vocabulary that the school where she teaches is an hour away from her house, she has three active sons and lives five hours away from us by car. I think she understood!

Abruzzo is a large province with spectacular scenery. Each area of Italy differs from others in so many ways, and of course, this is no exception. We enjoy exploring and so one morning of our first visit we set off to see the city of Sulmona. The end of World War I, Armistice Day, was being celebrated and we observed two uniformed soldiers at attention in front of the war memorial and many flags in the town center. A statue honoring the Latin poet Ovid who was born here stands in a small park. An outstanding feature of medieval architecture is the impressive aqueduct built in the 1200's which goes through the town center. There are several notable churches which have been built and re-built after suffering damages in earthquakes; a modest civic museum containing religious ornaments made by goldsmiths during the Renaissance is worth a visit. This small city changed rulers many, many times from ancient history through the *Risorgimento,* from the Italic tribes, the Romans, Frederick II, the Angevins, the Spanish, the Bourbons, to the Kingdom of Naples and more. I've probably omitted more than a half dozen. A visit to the local tourist office was a great help. Often in the more provincial towns there are few if any English speakers, but we were lucky. A young woman, extremely friendly, informed and most helpful, gave us brochures and a quick guide to the main points of interest. She also directed us to a restaurant where we enjoyed an excellent lunch. This is always important to Roger! Sulmona is probably best known today for the production of the sugar coated almonds known as *confetti,* an almost required addition to Italian weddings and christenings.

The city of L'Aquila is considered to be the grande dame of Abruzzo; it is a center of great culture, and according to the guide books, devoted to music. It is located at a high altitude; I tend to be frightened of mountain roads with sheer drop offs and as a result, my husband often calls me "Gasperina" as I tend to loudly inhale as we drive by seemingly bottomless cliffs, but my faithful, considerate driver and husband of many years as well, studied the map and found we could get there by motorway rather than by local roads. This route was a good choice, including a part through the longest tunnel we had ever been in up to this time, about seven miles. The road through the tunnel was well lighted and not at all frightening to me.

Perhaps it was the grey, fairly cold day in the mountains, or maybe we just missed what was important, but we were not overly thrilled with L'Aquila although we faithfully trudged around for three hours. We were most impressed with The Basilica of Santa Maria di Collemaggio; built of pink and white marble, and erected in a space with mountains in the background, this edifice evokes a dramatic and moving image. When we returned to Mario's, he laughingly asked if we had been cold in that city. It was a very knowing laugh!

The road from Loreto Aprutino to Chieti is surrounded on both sides with an abundance of attractive agriculture. The ever present construction industry is constantly observed as new apartment houses and large, luxurious private residences are being built or are newly built. We have seen fewer older houses being restored than is typical in Tuscany or Umbria. Chieti is a city both Roger and I liked very much; it's a provincial capital, an old city, whose glory is in its past. This part of the town, with its splendid monuments and architecture is surrounded by many, but not all non-distinctive building outside of the city walls. The views from the overlook, or *belvedere,* of the old town show the tremendous population growth of this entire area.

The archeological museum in Chieti houses the famous Capestrano Warrior statue; this work, a product of the Picene culture of the 6th century B.C.E. is often used as a symbol of Abruzzo. More than seven feet high, the Warrior, according to one story, was found by a farmer in 1935 as he plowed his field. Others claim it was found in a necropolis used by these people of Italic stock at least several hundred years before the Romans ruled here. I wanted a small copy of this statue as my tie with Abruzzo, and in the train station in Pescara I found a shop specializing in the products of the province which included copies of the tan-colored icon sternly upright in meticulous armor. His sword is clutched across his chest over a breastplate. I chuckled as I held this warrior in my hand, thinking that perhaps I'd be the only woman on Cape Cod with this statue. He now stands at attention on top of the glass-fronted china cabinet in my house. Bravo!

Although we have visited in this part of Italy in four different months, I began to understand why our friend in Tuscany had urged us to bring many warm clothes to Abruzzo. In October, early November, and several times in April we found it to be almost balmy during the day with one notable exception when a rainstorm accompanied by winds turned the local rain into sleet, and covered the distant mountains with snow. There is ample heat provided in the apartments but we often turned the radiators off during these months. The fireplace in the living room was always pleasant and we were never chilly. However, there are many ski resorts in the mountains and these are what many people think of when they speak of Abruzzo. Naturally warm clothing would be needed for winter sports just as they would in the Alps or the many mountain ski havens in the United States. Skiing and other recreational facilities are doing a big part in bringing the economy of the Abruzzo forward. The National Parks of Abruzzo, though often struggling under the auspices of different authorities, have made strides in protecting natural resources. Threatened animal species, including the elusive chamois, have been returned; constant disagreements with people still living in these areas have hampered full progress, but progress it is, however slow. This region of magnificent snow-capped mountains and immaculately tilled fields is still in many ways, a land unto itself.

Gran Sasso is the highest peak in the Apennines and Roger is anxious to make a pilgrimage there. I must admit that I am not yet sure whether or not I will go; as I have mentioned, high places are not my favorite, however, if I do not go, I know I shall be disappointed. It's a bit like flying; I do not care for it, but I care less for staying home and away from Italy, so I gasp and go.

In Italy there are twenty-seven cities known as "pottery towns" recognized by the National Pottery Council. In contrast to the thousands of factories which turn out ceramics labeled "Made in Italy" to the world, and which vary greatly in quality, the "pottery towns" represent the best in artistic craft. One of these special towns is Castelli. Since the time of the Renaissance the works of art from here have been displayed in many of the museums of the world. This noted center of majolica, located near the base of Gran Sasso, is firmly if seemingly precariously perched on the side of a steep precipice, with fantastic if breath taking views of the surrounding area. Dozens of shops offer all kinds of ceramic objects from the useful to the merely decorative. I wanted a tile for my collection and had a difficult time deciding just which shop I should enter. A sign caught my eye, "Mancini-Carbone" and that convinced me; I admit to a decision emotionally and sentimentally based. "Carbone" is the name of my older son's best friend from the time they were teenagers; I also remembered that his family has roots in Abruzzo. It was a fortuitous choice! I bought several beautiful tiles and had an extremely pleasant visit with the woman who owned the shop. I have a habit of taking informal photos of shopkeepers who are pleasant, of various friendly employees of restaurants and hotels, and after I return home, I have copies made and send them to those whom I photographed. It has always been a pleasant entree on our next visit. Sixteen months later we returned to the same shop in Castelli. This delightful lady immediately recognized us and greeted us with kisses. Ever since we had been here we had talked of something we wanted to buy. We did not know what it was called, but it was a beautifully decorated ceramic container which holds water, and is hung on radiators by a special hook to add humidity to the heated air of houses. We do not have radiators in our house, but figured we could hang it on the wall as a vase for fresh flowers. The designer and artist was the husband of the woman who also told us that their son was now at the university studying ceramic art. We chose a beautifully decorated piece which we continue to enjoy. Before we left, this congenial woman insisted on giving me a gift—a small ceramic lidded dish for jewelry. These kinds of gestures simply do not happen in the United States, but have occurred time after time in Italy. If an Italian likes you, he or she makes no bones about it; hugs, kisses, food, or gifts are forthcoming. We return to this delightful shop every time we go to Abruzzo and are never disappointed.

The first time we visited Castelli sixteen months earlier we arranged to meet with a young couple from Illinois; university

dance instructors and choreographers, they were spending four
months in Italy with their precocious four year old daughter as
the husband was on a Guggenheim fellowship and writing a
book. They were staying at Mario's but like us, they had heard
of Castelli and wanted to see the town in person. Other people
at the *agriturismo* had been there on the previous day buying an
array of beautiful ceramic items and had recommended a small
family restaurant as excellent. Actually, they said they walked away
pleasantly "stuffed." We met the dancers and their lively youngster
and proceeded to the restaurant. Lunch was a total joy from start
to finish; the friendliness of the entire staff was genuine. We all
decided to skip the antipasto as our acquaintances who had been
here yesterday counted fourteen different items presented to them
in this course. We immediately went directly to the pasta course;
three were brought to us! The first a *tagliatelle con pomidori,* a
flat noodle with tomato sauce, and then *chitarre ragu,* a pasta
resembling guitar strings with a meat sauce, and finally, ravioli.
All were wonderful! Next, four vegetables were presented followed
by salad, French fries, lamb chops, pork chops, and veal with a
cheese sauce. Only the slim dancer Cathy, managed dessert.

As we were leaving, we were asked into the kitchen for an after
meal drink, *limoncello,* and friendship. There were two women
who obviously were responsible for the cooking; one older woman
who seemed to have much authority, and a fairly young one who
waited on us. We were asked where we had shopped. When I
mentioned "Carbone" this brought enthusiastic approvals and
assurances that their quality was of the best. Later in the day we
stopped at a few other shops and the difference in quality, and
therefore price, was patently obvious.

Whenever we re-visit Castelli we naturally return to the small
family restaurant where we had previously dined. The cook, her
husband and her daughter rush out of the kitchen with big hugs,

kisses and a very warm welcome for us. The father, husband of the cook, whom we had met only briefly on the first visit, always cheers us with big smiles and greetings. They always thank us for sending them photos and postcards. We enjoy another fabulous lunch at each visit, and just as we had been told much before, we leave delightfully "stuffed."

Not far from Loreto Aprutino, on the Adriatic coast, there is the large city of Pescara. A resort area, it is also a growing, busy industrial center with an increasing population and expanding economy. I must admit that on our first visit there in 1997 we were not overly impressed. The streets seemed a bit unkempt, the buildings a bit of a hodge-podge and cars parked illegally. But times change!

Our recent calls on Pescara were so very different. The streets were immaculate, new buildings emerged everywhere, older buildings were freshly cleaned if stone, and painted if stucco, and cars parked illegally were being ticketed, or in some cases, towed away. We planned on visiting the *Museo delle Genti d'Abruzzo,* or the Museum of the People of Abruzzo, but the day was warm for March, the sun was brilliant and since I had packed a picnic we decided to lunch by the sea. We found the marina or yacht club, parked and enjoyed our repast while looking at the sea and a collection of attractive boats. The marina itself was super tidy; no litter, no graffiti, no disorder. We walked around admiring the view and enjoying the sunshine. Time passed and we were certain the museum would be closed, so we decided to return the next day.

On the way to Pescara the following morning we stopped in the bar in Montesilvano for a coffee or cappuccino as we always do when we are in the vicinity. This particular bar is also a pasticceria; one side is devoted to glass cases with the best looking cakes, pies, desserts and ice cream one could wish for. At Easter time we discovered they also make chocolate eggs in sizes and ornamentation we had never seen before. There were hundreds of them and we were amazed at the variety and luscious appearance! Many were well over three feet high and any of them could be, and many were, personally dedicated to a child, a family, or a special love. The barman Marco, a delightful young fellow, was amazed that the shops in the United States were not also filled with three and four feet high chocolate eggs when we expressed amazement at the ones in the pastry section. There were also smaller ones as well and we ordered one for Mario's family for a special night.

We found what we thought was the museum, entered and paid, and immediately realized it was the wrong museum. This rather small but what turned out to be a most interesting place was an art collection of six artists, painters, sculptors and ceramicists of the same family, called the *Museo Civico 'B. Cascella'*. Only one of the six is still alive we were told by an engaging staff, but I wouldn't swear to this as their command of English was about the same as mine of Italian, not impressive. The museum contains only the works of these six men, representing three generations of the same family. Many of these compositions were most striking and at the end of the tour I purchased more than a dozen post cards with reproductions of many of the paintings. By the reaction of the staff, I got the feeling that this was probably more than they had sold in months. They asked if we were British; we said no that we were Americans. They were so very pleased. I don't believe they have many visitors from the United States. We spent a delightful morning there and only by accident, but that is part of the excitement of discovery in an unfamiliar place.

The following morning we were determined to go to the museum we had set out to see on the two previous days. Stopping first for coffee and a chat with Marco at the Easter egg bar we encountered a smiling, friendly older man—about our age—who was enjoying a coffee. Marco told him a bit about us, where we were from, and how we return to Italy and now to Abruzzo year after year. We began a halting conversation with this man, or as much as our language gaps would permit. He left early as Marco explained to us he had an appointment. When Roger began to pay for our coffee and pastry, we were told that the kindly gentleman with the warm smile had already paid for us.

Driving to Pescara and trying faithfully to follow signs for the museum, we were rewarded for our patience and finally located the building. It was located on a very narrow, "walking only" street which I might describe as "arty." There were antique stores with exquisite furniture, art shops, restaurants and a rather elegant pub advertising itself as "jazz club." The museum was excellent; there were no explanations in English, but for about fifty cents we bought a guide in English which was detailed and explained the various exhibits clearly and succinctly. This institution described through superb displays the history of the people of Abruzzo from the first humans to appear here about 700,000 years ago, to the cultural development of the twentieth century.

I was most fascinated with the history of sheep raising in Abruzzo. This was the main activity of the rural population for three thousand years. During the bronze and iron ages new populations entered the area and interrupted much of the agricultural activity. These new people were sheep-rearing and this activity continued as economic activity almost until the end of World War II. Cheese and wool provided the livelihood for more than half of the population of Abruzzo until agriculture and industrialization became a force in the beginning of the nineteenth century. A tradition or method of driving the flocks from winter pastures to summer pastures and returning again is known as "transhumance." In the summers the sheep were grazed in the high mountainous areas and then in the winter to the lower grazing fields. This migration was vast and went from northern Abruzzo to what is now Apulia. The routes, known as "tratturi" and often more than three hundred feet wide, were fixed and firmly established by Roman law and were continued and strengthened by the Aragon rulers. Benedictine Cistercians built monasteries along some of these paths and were instrumental in making this area the number one producer of wool in Europe. The high pastures were much too cold and often laden with snow in the winter, but abundant with grass in the summer. Conversely the southern pastures became dry and desert like in summer, but were grass covered during the winter. Driving the flocks covered almost one hundred and fifty miles and were fraught with hardships for the shepherds and the flocks. Dogs were used to manage and guide the sheep and to guard against wolves; an anti-wolf collar worn by the dogs is shown in one of the displays in this well-organized museum. Currently there are still enormous numbers of sheep in Abruzzo, however, as one man explained to me, if it is necessary to move the flocks from one area to another, it is now done by truck.

The building housing this museum used to be a prison during the period when this Italian province were trying to unshackle itself from the Bourbon monarchy and achieve Unification; one hundred men were jailed here for revolutionary activity. The urban parts of Abruzzo were rife with secret societies and liberal thinking as the movement grew to become independent, while the more rural societies did not want to overthrow the governing body.

It took several tries before we found this museum, but it was worth the time and effort. We were so pleased that we returned there several days later and chatted with a young man who is employed there part time while he finishes his university degree in

English Literature! I bought a beautifully made tile of a sunburst and a tee shirt for one of our grandchildren.

I like to record the day's activities, meals, the people we talk with, actually almost everything that happens as we travel. Often afterward, on quiet evenings at home, especially in the winter by the fire, I read them aloud to Roger and then we look at photographs of the same time period. One afternoon I decided to leave our small apartment at the agriturismo and go downstairs to the large rooms where dinner is served, entertainment is sometimes offered, and guests often congregate. The table height for writing was more comfortable for my height—or lack of it—and I knew no one was around so I wouldn't be bothering anyone. Soon however, Mario appeared and played a compact disc of good listening music. Roger came down a bit later to see how I was doing with the writing. A bit later Mario reappeared with a platter of cake and cookies and a bottle of Sardinian wine for the three of us. It was a dessert wine, smooth and excellent with cake and cookies! We had only a small taste as Olga began cooking in the kitchen next to us and we were dining here this evening. I would never want to spoil my appetite when that gifted woman offers dinner.

Mario is generous in sharing the use of his computer. Roger went to check on our e-mail and brought me a note from one of our grandsons who was reading ROMEO AND JULIET in his freshman English class at school. He said he had to correct the instructor as she was mispronouncing the name of the character, Tybalt as "Tie-balt." He was well aware of the correct way to say the names as we have the grandchildren visit us in the summer and after five days of practice, they perform an abbreviated Shakespearean play. He happened to play the character of Mercutio in that play a few years ago and knew the play well. He was also the one who, upon receiving a worksheet in that class with the unidentified quote at the top: "On your imaginary forces work" raised his hand and told the teacher that it was from the Prologue of HENRY V. The unfortunate teacher never knew that he had played the character of Henry V during the previous summer. "Nanny, she almost had a heart attack," was his comment.

We both heard hard rain during one night which precipitated a drastic change in the spring weather. We had been in Abruzzo at this point for eight days; the days were mild and sunny and we referred to it as "golf shirt" weather. When we began driving toward the town of Citta San Angelo we noticed a change in the mountains and realized that while it had rained where we were, snow in quantity had fallen on the high elevation. The sights were dramatic as the peaks were whiter and the lower mountain slopes, previously bare, were now snow covered. That evening a snow shower fell on the farm though we were fairly near the sea.

The small town of Citta San Angelo was one we had viewed high in the hills from where we often drove below. One morning it became our destination as we were curious about it perched high above the main road. As we walked around this tidy area and tried not to shiver too much, we noticed many attractive restaurants and pricey stores. Flowers were planted and bloomed in the park and along the side of many streets. We walked through a municipal building which used to be the Convent of San Francesco. Totally and beautifully restored, it now houses a library, offices and a courtyard garden with a graceful fountain. From an overlook in front of a hotel there was a smashing view of the Adriatic Sea; the sun was now shining but we noticed very heavy surf on the water which was the result of the storm the night before. We intend to return here but hope the day is a bit warmer.

The town of Loreto Aprutino, a few miles from our *agriturismo*, is in the center of many olive producing farms. Known throughout

Abruzzo as the place where each year an ox kneels in front of the relics of Saint Zopito, this small center with medieval origins is quiet and unassuming. Walking through the narrow streets, some of which could not be used by anything other than people walking or by bicycles, though the steepness of some would preclude even bikes, a well-dressed, smiling middle-aged woman approached me, spoke in Italian and handed me a spray of lovely yellow flowers. The gesture was so immediate and gracious, I was deeply touched and murmured a succession of *"grazie."* Later I discovered that the flowers were called mimosa; they were not the same variety found in the USA, but a specie abundant in Italy from February to April depending on location. That particular week in March was devoted to honoring women throughout Italy and those flowers signified that.

One morning we went into Loreto Aprutino for our morning coffee at our favorite bar and found a street market in full operation. These markets continue to exist in many towns, especially the smaller ones, throughout Italy and are great fun and most interesting. We always try to visit them wherever we are and buy something whether vegetables or a pair of sox. On this particular morning there was music and singing coming from an amplifier in the market piazza which intrigued Roger; he traced the sound to a truck selling CD's and tapes, and after a quick search, the proprietor found the same tape which we had heard and liked, and which Rog then quickly bought. Each time since when we play it and listen to the sound of the singer and the music, we recall the day, the market, Loreto Aprutino, Abruzzo, and all the enjoyment we have found there.

As I have often noted, Italians tend to have a favorite bar; they go for a mid-morning coffee, a soft drink, or frequently an ice cream. Pastries are often sold and on Sundays people buy all kinds of cakes and cookies for dessert, and especially if they dine at a home other than their own, they bring a *dolce,* a sweet. It's a pleasant and happy tradition. We try to follow this practice when we stay in a town, and of course then return to that town for a visit year after year; we usually go to the same bar for our after breakfast coffee. Most bars are closed one day per week and this enables one to see another, but we tend to be loyal visitors to the same bar day after day. In Loreto Aprutino, although we had not been to "our" bar for sixteen months, as we walked in the proprietor behind the counter broadly smiled and cheerfully spoke the name of the *agriturismo* where we stay. The recognition is comforting and delightful.

Late one afternoon Olga tapped on our door. By a few words and hand motions she indicated that we should come down to the dining room. A local priest who had dined here with a group of men the night before had brought two paintings, beautifully wrought copies, and he wanted Mario's family to see them. One was Fra Angelico's "Annunciation" which I instantly remembered from art history classes; the priest corrected my "Fra" with "Beato." Perhaps this artist is on the road to saintliness? The other work I immediately recognized as it was reproduced in my high school Latin text and depicted a noble Roman woman. We were pleased that Olga wanted to share the viewing experience with us.

Eating well in Italy is not difficult, which is perhaps the understatement of the century. When we do not dine at the farm as Olga does not cook every night during the "off" season, which is when we prefer to visit Italy, we have a favorite restaurant in the area, La Bilancia. The entire staff, owner, head waiter, waiters, cooks, barman, in short, all the employees now know us and greet us like family. On our last visit just after we were seated, Renato, a waiter indicated that we should follow him to the bar. When we got there he showed us that a photograph of the two of us was displayed on the wall. I always send photos of the wait staff, but on this visit I asked Gianni, the head waiter if I might be able to photograph the entire staff including all who worked in the kitchen. We made lunch reservations for the following day and arranged to come early before the dining room was officially open. Gianni had everyone line up in front of the open fire where much of the meat is grilled and we happily snapped away.

On the evening five years ago when we entered a local restaurant and were seated, a cheerful young man greeted us in perfect, unaccented English. He explained when we looked startled that his family had left Abruzzo when he was two years old; they had moved to Canada for work, but now that his father was retired, the entire family had moved back to Italy the year before. Statistics estimate that after the Second World War when Italy was suffering the devastating effects of the German occupation and Allied rebuttals, almost eight million people emigrated. This movement was quite different from that of the late nineteenth and early twentieth centuries when most emigration was to North or South America. Unlike this particular family, the latter emigration tended to other more prosperous European countries. More than half of those who departed since the late 1940's have returned to their homeland, Italy. His family was unusual for this time as they emigrated to Canada for more than twenty years, but typical, as they returned.

During the two weeks we were in Abruzzo on our last visit, we often dined at this restaurant which incidentally is also a small hotel and has banquet facilities for weddings, anniversaries or other parties. After our fourth dinner Roger went to the cashier's desk, which tonight was staffed by the owner, Sergio, to pay for our meal. Roger was told, "No charge." Incredulously, he said, "Thank you, but this is business." The owner replied, "But this is Italian business!"

After weeks of glorious meals, we felt we were getting a trifle thick around the middle and decided to cut back on the number of courses we would order no matter how enticing and delicious. This didn't work at this excellent facility! The next evening we told Antonio our waiter that we did not want an antipasto; the next thing we knew bruscetta with grilled peppers arrived at our table followed by mozzarella cheese arranged in a spiral with ham and arugula between. Gianni came by and told us not to worry that it wasn't on the bill. We tried to explain that this was not the problem, but he wasn't listening. The waiter put bread on our table in the usual fashion, and Gianni came by and whisked it off. A few minutes later he returned with other bread and whispered that this was better. We then ordered a small pasta to share. No way! First came spaghetti with ceci beans and broth, then a tagliatelle with asparagus and cheese in a rich white sauce and then parpardelle lepre (a wide pasta with hare sauce) for me, and because they knew Roger loves gnocci, a platter of that delicacy with tomato sauce was set before him. We were groaning with pleasure as well as overly filled stomachs when Gianni appeared with a salad of crisp, ultra fresh greens, carrots, fennel, and tomatoes dressed perfectly with excellent olive oil and Balsamic vinegar. It would have been enough for a family of six. We managed to finish it and I suppose at that point our dear headwaiter finally realized that if he brought a meat entree we might expire. We rested for a bit and ordered espresso. Renato walked by and didn't give us so much as glance; after passing our table he abruptly turned around, plumped two pieces of cake on our table and seemed to run off before we could recover. And so it went. The meals were fabulous, the staff as kind and friendly as one could ever want, and if those are not reasons to return, I couldn't imagine what would be. Many hugs, kisses and *arrivederci* as we said our good-byes.

Our last night at Mario's was one to remember. Earlier in the week I had asked Olga if she were cooking that night. She said she was and I told her it was Roger's birthday and that I would order a cake for all at the bar in Montesilvano. There would be six at the table that evening. We began with eight different dishes of various antipasti including cured meats, frittata, bruschetta, olive balls and pickled beets. Next we were served some of the lightest, most delicate ravioli I have ever had in a sauce which must have been made by pasta angels directed by Olga! This was followed by a green salad and roasted chicken. We had birthday cake for dessert, sang the typical happy birthday and finished with dessert wine from Sicily. I asked Olga, and Gabriella who had helped her mother with dinner, to please come out, join us and have some cake and wine. They did, and it was another memorable Italian evening.

Many people visiting Italy for the first time never see Abruzzo; understandingly the tours are arranged so that the world famous sights of Rome, Florence and Venice can be seen. I would encourage those who wish to return, especially third or more time tourists, to forget the organized tours, rent a car, make reservations at more obscure and less famous places, especially at *agriturismos,* and become acquainted with local restaurants and their operators. There is so much more to Italy than the Rialto, "David," or Saint Peter's, as wonderful as they are. We are anxious to return to Abruzzo as there is so much we have not yet experienced, and all which we want to enjoy again. In this rugged, beautiful, as well as seaside province, if the mountain pines bend with the wind, it really might be from a heavenly gust.

ABRUZZO HOLIDAY

An *agriturismo* in Abruzzo
With Mario and Gabriella is
An enchanting respite from all tourist
Obligations, destinations, and the
Typical programs required by tour guides.

A gastronomic fantasy appears
From the kitchen, directed by Olga's
Culinary genius. On great, special
Evenings we are treated to a concert
Of piano music emanating
From the nimble fingers of two men, both
Talented musicians and friends of the
Proprietors; Carmine and Lucio.

This farm is devoted to olive oil.
The trees, which produce precious fruit, are viewed
As covered with gray-tinged, green leaves, spring pruned,
And lovingly cared for until autumn
When the ripe olives are picked, carefully
Pressed, expressing the extra virgin oil.

This fantastic process, ultimately
Delighting our taste buds enhances, enchants
Soup, salad, vegetables, pasta and more!

During the day one is free to wander,
Explore the orchards, admire kiwi vines,
Toss bread to the flock of chickens and ducks,
Admire and talk to the four large, gentle
Dogs, or watch the cats snoozing, when not on
The hunt for a perpetual handout
From friendly guests, or a lethargic mouse.

Day trips from Mario's are possible
To many parts of Abruzzo. Some are
Sulmona, Pescara, Chieti, Penne,
L'Aquila, Castelli, Ortona, plus,
Castles, churches and museums. Rugged
Mountains, massive, and often snow-covered
Even in warm weather, always amaze.
Often covered with evergreen trees, yet
Seemingly growing from earth-free granite.
The sea, Adriatic, colored turquoise
Tinged with heavenly blue—a great vision.

Cordiality, friendliness, kindness,
And generosity characterize
The Abruzzi people, their food, their land.
A journey here is an education,
An experience, different from Rome,
Florence or Venice, but well-worth taking! Geralyn Peterkin

IF NOT UGLY, THEN AT LEAST UNATTRACTIVE

"This was the most unkindest cut of all."

JULIUS CAESAR III, ii, Shakespeare

"To suckle fools and chronicle small beer."

OTHELLO II, i, Shakespeare

Some people should never leave home, or at least, their homeland. They would be much more content visiting Disneyland, Las Vegas or any American seashore. Abroad, they find fault with almost everything and are a continual embarrassment to others. I might add that this behavior is not limited to a very few Americans, but has been observed in many nationalities; perhaps those whose senses of humor were either surgically removed or absent from birth.

Every country has its own culture, customs, dress, way of behaving in various situations, food styles and other habits which go toward making national characteristics. Otherwise why would anyone want to visit another country if that place were exactly and precisely like the one left behind? Some misguided travelers however seem to want everything to be an exact match for the place they came from; it's difficult to comprehend why would they then travel far, when staying home or at least near to home would be so much more pleasant for them? A mystery! I have observed this unsettling phenomenon, fortunately not often, but nevertheless disturbing and frequently embarrassing when it does occur.

Examples:

1. While touring Pompeii, after the guide described and explained some of the Roman paintings and referenced Michelangelo in his friendly lecture, a tourist asked if that artist were still working. When he was told how long ago that man had died, he became extremely annoyed as if it had been the guide's fault.

2. In an extraordinarily fine restaurant in Tuscany, a meal of many courses was served to a small tour group of perhaps ten people. It had been prearranged and was served family style. When platters of the various meat courses arrived, one woman asked what one particular dish contained. She was told it was "*coniglio*" or rabbit; she literally screamed loudly, "BUNNY!" and pretended to vomit.

3. In an informal, but good restaurant near Milan, a patron ordered a pizza with sausage. When it arrived he proceeded to remove all of the sausage and told the waiter to have the chef cook it more thoroughly. The waiter tried to explain that it was already well-cooked and that the texture was different from American sausage. Nothing would do. The waiter removed it and the chef cooked it more. When it was returned to the table, again this man refused it, telling all it wasn't done enough. The chef came from the kitchen and he tried to explain, but, it was like talking to the proverbial wall. This fellow should stay home and order the pie he was used to from his local pizzeria chain.

4. Seated in an art filled gourmet restaurant near Siena, a woman
    who looked like a "Vogue" model wannabe caught my eye
    from her table and began complaining:

    A. The menus in Italy are all alike.
    B. I hate it when the stores are closed in the afternoon.
       Why do they do that? They don't do that at home.
    C. It's so cold here. I thought it was sunny Italy, etc. (It
       was mid-November.)

5. In a small hotel in Lucca, a Protestant minister who had
    never learned charity, became irate, unkind and unpleasant
    to the young boy who served him morning coffee. The
    youngster, who could not have been more than fourteen,
    did not understand English and couldn't fathom that the
    man wanted a large cup of American type coffee and not
    a small espresso cup typical in Italy. This rude man felt if
    he just kept raising the pitch and volume of his words they
    would be understood. I couldn't stand his treatment of this
    boy and I finally interrupted to explain the situation, but he
    didn't want to hear anything but what he said. No wonder
    he seemed to be traveling alone!

6. Having lunch outside by the Piazza del Campo on an
    unbelievably warm, sunny day in Siena during March,
    most of the diners were being greatly amused by a street
    entertainer. He had a small bottle of water and he would
    gently squirt random pedestrians on their heads; when they
    turned to look as they felt their hair, he would point at the
    numerous pigeons flying in the area. He would also find a
    couple and when they weren't paying attention, he would
    hold the hand of the man who of course would think it was
    his female companion. When the situation became apparent
    and the hand was abruptly dropped, the crowd roared with
    laughter. After this type of amusement continued for about

a half hour, the entertainer walked among the diners for tips. At every table but one, he received a small but happily given reward for his efforts. The occupants of this odd table sternly looked at him and shook their heads in a universally understood, NO. A few minutes later the man returned and left a one thousand lire note (then about sixty cents) on *their* table.

7.   Many restaurants in Italy require reservations simply because they are totally filled at the evening meal and there are no available tables. Diners are free to linger and many do for an unusually long time after they finish the meal; this is part of the culture. In the USA it is usually necessary to turn the tables over many times in an evening to cover the costs of running a restaurant. People are rarely encouraged to remain after the meal is completed. The waiters in our country usually hint by placing the bill for the meal on the table after the last swallow or so.

We had reservations at our favorite restaurant in Rome one evening when a group of six arrived at the door just behind us. Literally, there wasn't a space left that was not reserved. This group became annoyed and disparaging. They pointed out that there were two empty tables in the dining room. The owner tried to explain that they were reserved for nine o'clock, and that it was eight thirty and the people who had reserved were not yet there. The bad manners of this group continued and eventually they left. Again, I was embarrassed at the arrogance and rudeness of some of my countrymen. Doesn't anyone remember, "When in Rome, . . . ?"

8.   I observed a scene which could have been made into a comic part in a movie. This occurred in a very busy and excellent trattoria in Florence. Seated at the next table were three people from a large country in Europe known for its snobbishness. A woman in the party took her linen dinner napkin and proceeded to polish each glass, each piece of

flatware and each dish before water, wine or food touched them. Needless to say, each was perfectly immaculate before she began. We have patronized this establishment for eight years and know its standards to be tops. After that group left, I went to the owner and told him of my embarrassment at the woman's behavior. He smiled, shrugged his shoulders, and said, that it was just part of the business.

9. Their cruise ship stopped in Venice, and a couple from New Jersey interrupted their exploration of this fabled city for lunch. We had been there for about fifteen minutes when they entered this small, upscale and perfectly designed and decorated restaurant. The gentleman, who wasn't, verbally accosted the maitre d'hotel because he couldn't find "chicken parm" on the menu. This strangely named dish which in American restaurants is usually covered with melted mozzarella cheese and not parmigiano-reggiano, or parmesan as it is commonly known in the United States, is simply not found in the north of Italy. It may exist in the south, but certainly not by that name, and actually, I have never seen or heard of it there. Loudly, this obnoxious man tried to tell the headwaiter what is was and when the restauranteur gently shook his head in disbelief and dismay, the angry customer forcefully announced that if all the Italian restaurants he knew in New Jersey made this, why didn't the ones in Venice? Didn't they know how to cook Italian food?

    We cringed in embarrassment and hoped that Venice was their last port of call before returning to Newark, Bloomfield or Secaucus.

10. A very successful business woman from New York was visiting Italy for the first time. At dinner she angrily demanded butter and proceeded to berate the waiter for not having provided it in the first place. He brought her butter but tried to explain that he didn't have it on the table as butter was typically not used at the evening meal. The poor fellow then had to endure another tirade.

A small charge is automatic at all restaurants; it is called "*coperto*" and is used to cover the costs of the linen and bread. Some Americans do not understand this concept and become abusive when they see this small charge on their dinner checks. Again I cringe with embarrassment when I hear a countryman do this. How much more pleasant life would be if these people had just taken the time to find out a few of the customs in a country they are visiting. Their ignorance is replaced with arrogance and creates a situation remembered with repugnance.

Such people should stay home; they are not interested in a different culture and lifestyle. Can you imagine their reactions if one from Lucca became abusive in a hotel in Cleveland because his morning coffee was large, weak and unfamiliar? Or if one from Bari asked if George Washington were still working and became extremely annoyed when told he had passed away two hundred years ago? Or if one from Florence was enraged because there was no authentic prosciutto on the menu or in the restaurant?

What did the man say? (Or should have) Get a life!

TUSCANY

"Age cannot wither her, nor custom stale
Her infinite variety."

ANTONY AND CLEOPATRA II, ii
Shakespeare

Tuscany has been the subject of so much lyrical and colorful writing in recent years, I was hesitant to include anything about this wondrous land. However, the more I thought about it, I decided that to write about Italy and exclude Tuscany would be like serving dry rice or pasta. Truly, her "infinite variety" and matchless beauty can stir the heart and thrill the senses, and in a very personal sense, we have been so very happily ensconced in this province so many times, to have omitted it would be tantamount to the refusal to recognize a close friend or relative.

When I think of Tuscany I think first of the landscape; the scenery is intensely and indelibly pictured in my mind. I see perfectly plowed hills and fields looking as if manicured; tall, straight, serious cypress trees with their no nonsense demeanor; the orderly vines supported on erect fences; shimmering silver-green olive trees; garden patches, or *orti,* as finely designed as knitted afghans; and in the autumn of the year, the agriculturally fascinating and immaculately groomed horticultural areas looking like gigantic quilts in earth tones, sewn by a giant seamstress. Even in the rain, the countryside is nothing short of exquisite, punctuated by Tuscan farmhouses, panoramic views and flowers.

In sunshine, the splendor of the green as it's seen in vines, mountains, trees, almost everywhere, is bathed in the play of variegated light.

To look over the magnificently cultivated land in Tuscany is to think of the perfectly fixed geometric lines of longitude and latitude as pictured on a map, and put there by a specially designed software program. But a second glance will evoke, not the absolute perfection of imaginary lines running over the earth or programmed ones from computers run by whiz kids, but artistically placed stripes painted by Leonardo or Raphael. These bands follow the contours of the rolling hills in so subtle a pattern it evokes a feeling of being touched by the supernatural. Farmers could not do this, I reason. These masterly lanes must have been placed by Renaissance artists or by angels with special agrarian assignments.

If that were not enough, the colors challenge the eyes making them try to absorb more shades than Nature intended eyes to see. And, then suddenly, a pang of anguished hurt is felt, thinking of the inhuman acts and resulting bloodshed this land has felt. The terrifying struggles to rule this terrain by peoples from afar, and as well by those within this large region as near as Florence, Siena, or Pisa, and the cruelties felt by the innocent victims, are almost lost as a vague, nebulous memory under the influence and cover of Nature's lavish artistry.

The first peoples in recorded history to inhabit Tuscany were the mysterious Etruscans whose tombs are found throughout the area. These early settlers, characterized by a mysterious language and Greek-influenced pottery, together with their cities and civilization, were annihilated by the Romans who re-named the area, Tuscia; centuries later it was conquered by Charlemagne after the Ostrogoths and Lombards had each had a turn in dominating the land. The last ruler in the feudal era was a powerful woman, Countess Matilda, who died in 1115; without direct heirs, or any who seemed to be peaceful inheritors, she willed her mighty lands to the Papacy. A discrepancy occurred after her death as her husband claimed she had changed her will and left her lands to him and not to the Pope; he then claimed them which, unfortunately, began centuries of struggle between the popes and lay rulers, mainly the German house, Hohenstaufen. A direct result was that the principal cities became independent and financially successful. Florence headed a league to resist the Germans and became an ally of the papacy. This political movement was known as the Guelf party. Supporters of the Emperor and against the papacy were known as the Ghibellines.

An interesting point about this schism occurred in the late 1200's. The Guelf party had divided into two factions, the black and the white. The great poet, Dante Aligheri, was allied with the "whites." When the "blacks" became predominant, Dante was exiled in 1302. He eventually settled in Ravenna and died there and a tomb was erected. For centuries the Florentines have tried to have his remains returned to his city in Tuscany, but the people of Ravenna have consistently refused. Apparently their feeling is that he was exiled from Florence when he was alive, so why should they have him returned now.

During the 1300's many powerful guilds of merchants and craftsmen emerged in Florence. Banking was paramount, but the woolen industry was extremely strong and influential as well. The wool guild alone employed almost thirty thousand workers during this period. Tuscany was finally united by Cosimo Medici in the 1430's; he was a merchant banker who allied himself with the non-wealthy classes against the wealthy aristocrats. Known as Cosimo the Elder, he upheld republican ideas and was strongly supported by the populace. Unfortunately, this trait was not true of all his successors. Cosimo was an able financier who was a strong patron of the arts, supporting, protecting, and subsidizing many great artists of the time including Ghiberti, Brunelleschi, Donatello and Luca Della Robbia.

Between this era and the vote by plebiscite more than four hundred years later to join the Kingdom of Italy in March of 1860, there were many stressful and agonizing periods under the Spanish, the French, Napoleon, and Austria. The present day tranquillity of the countryside does not reveal the anguish and suffering wrought against the inhabitants for millennia, but the silent land endures and survives.

Tuscany can be compared to the priceless crown of a ruler; Florence is the invaluable, predominant and rare jewel in the center which outshines the others; the smaller jewels, the lesser cities, town and villages, these supporting gems, precious in their own right, may not be as rich, important or famous, but are most valuable as part of the richly encrusted halo of Tuscany. As a result, at no time has this land been subjected to more invasion than has recently been observed. Fortunately, this invasion is peaceful; the popularity of this region among tourists has reached unprecedented heights, and the land seemingly more coveted at any time since the rule of the Medici family.

To think of Florence is to simultaneously think of the art treasures contained in its museums, churches and public buildings. A noted professor from Modena who had spent years studying in this city told us he had not seen it all, and he had worked at trying to do this for a very long time. The Uffizi Gallery is perhaps the most famous, not only in Florence, but in all of Italy as well as in the rest of the world. The collections are matchless and contain priceless works of art by Florentines, other Italians and Europeans. One drawback is that because it is so famous it often requires a lengthy wait in line to enter, and then having entered, a struggle to experience, let alone enjoy the masterpieces among the throngs of others trying to do the same. We have observed this from April until mid-November. In one of my journals I wrote that in September there were one million people on line to enter the Uffizi; of course I wildly exaggerated, but the line was extremely long. A pleasant distraction while waiting is that there are frequently several clever mimes as street entertainers one can watch and also cause one to wonder just how they can maintain one unmoving position for so long.

In the colder months when most of the tourist groups evaporate along with the entry lines, and the only museum goers seem to be in pairs as we are, it is pure pleasure to wander, not only in the Uffizi, but in the other galleries and churches of Florence as well. Several years ago at the end of November we enjoyed the relative solitude at the Uffizi as we roamed among the fabled works of art. We decided to interrupt our tour and enjoyed tea for two and a shared decadent chocolate dessert in their recently added tea room.

The down side of winter touring is that often one must be prepared for cold weather. On the other hand we have eaten lunch at the outdoor rooftop coffee shop in the Uffizi in mid-January while the sun was fully shining, and observed that good friends living in Castellina-in-Chianti set a table for lunch outside on their spacious patio in February. However, there are some winter days when the temperature dropped enough to freeze the puddles in the dirt road which led to our rented house and again, other days when we have been outdoors with only a blazer for additional covering. Living in the northeast United States winter is winter, and rarely if ever do we experience a break warm enough to picnic on a patio We have spent part of the winter in Sicily and even there winter is not swimming weather; coats are frequently needed. Many Americans think of Italy as somewhat tropical and that is completely incorrect. I have had people say to me that I was going to "sunny Italy" and would be warm all winter. Not quite.

One morning in Castellina during November I awoke to see snow covering the ground; everyone we knew told us that it was a most unusual event that early in the season, but it can happen. Planning ahead is essential; if it's winter, a heavy coat, gloves, scarf and an extra sweater is all that it takes to continue to enjoy Tuscany, indoors or out; the plus side is the absolute dearth of tourists.

I am especially fond of the Pitti Palace, or as Cole Porter wrote of it in the musical KISS ME KATE, "The pretty Pitti Palace." The incredible size is attributed to the fact that one Luca Pitti, antagonistic to the Medici family, wanted a residence which would dwarf theirs and so he built this magnificent structure on the left bank of the Arno River in Florence. The most important reason for people to visit this wondrous edifice now, other than to gape at its size and structure, is that it houses the Palatine Gallery as well as two other galleries where innumerable paintings and other objects d'art fill the opulent rooms. Two of my favorite Raphael works are here: "Madonna of the Chair" and "Madonna of the Grand Duke" as well as hundreds of other masterpieces.

An interesting note is that the original structure of the Pitti family was not as large as the palace is today. Historians note that due to the expenses involved in creating this residence as well as other economic disasters, the heirs to this palace became bankrupt and were forced to sell it to the Medici family, an ironic situation considering that Luca Pitti's original idea was to outshine the Medici with his brilliant dwelling. The Medici greatly expanded this palace during the latter 1500's, which continued with each ruler/occupant; after unification in 1860, the Italian royal family, the House of Savoy, moved paintings and furnishings here from the palace in Parma.

Behind this palace lie the Boboli Gardens; having been in Florence so many, many times we had never gone there until the winter of 2000. This is a great walk in the fresh air gazing at the fascinating sculptures, including some which are rather bizarre; the grottos, pools, the amphitheater and horticulture displays continually invite the visitor to explore the area. Two years after our initial visit, we were able to enjoy and experience a unique visit to these special gardens.

A friend, exceptional artist, historian, intellectual, teacher and super cook, Alberto, promised to give us a personal tour of the Boboli. We met him one morning and our private, personal excursion began with this man who knows every detail as well as every date of the objects in the garden; he is versed in details of the palace's construction, the architects, its former inhabitants, their rivalries, marriages, love affairs and, their obvious explained as well as a few unexplained deaths. We walked for several hours, looking at the flora and statuary and listening to this learned man expatiate about everything we could view.

He was very annoyed at what he considered to be a laxness and careless disregard for the garden's upkeep. Statues were re-arranged, some paths lacked gravel which caused messes of mud and erosion when it rained, the grotto had been opened only once in many years as far as he could remember, and he emphasized that he has lived in Florence since he was an infant. He has pleasant memories as a young child of coming here each Sunday with his father. Suddenly, he stopped and pointed to a statue which lay on its side in a parking area; hoping that it was a copy and not an original work of art, nevertheless he was visibly disturbed by what he considered to be the laxity of the management supervising the garden's upkeep. He went on to strongly state that he wished that Americans would purchase some of the statues as he knew they would be treasured and meticulously displayed in some of the famous museums in the States. I was rather amazed at this statement which is unusual for an Italian, and especially one so proud of the works of art wrought by his country's artists.

Interestingly, much later in the day after we lunched with Alberto, we were walking back to our car when we stopped in to say a hello to our young artist friend Sacha. She had a shop on the opposite side of the street which faces the Pitti Palace. Without prompting, she began to echo some of the same complaints we had earlier heard from our noted garden guide.

She was particularly annoyed about the vast paved area in front of the Palace; she strongly condemned those in charge for not having even one flower or plant or tree in the front area. The vast masonry could be enhanced, she reasoned, but now it's dark and dismal.

At dinner that evening as we related our day's adventure to a British gentleman who has lived in Tuscany for forty years, and repeated the complaints of the two young Italians we had been with that day, he heartily agreed. His many Florentine friends feel that this beautiful city is neglected by city services due to poor management. I don't pretend to know enough about the city or its political machinations to comment, but I have observed that compared to other cities, not only in Tuscany, but throughout Italy, the streets in Florence are less tidy, the dumpsters often overflowing, the re-cycle bins scattered and the dogs rarely curbed. It was interesting to us however, that the art historian, the artist/ shop keeper, and the landowner devoted to raising olives and attending the opera, were totally in agreement in their sincere words that there is a definite problem with city housekeeping. Despite this, Florence is a city not to be missed; it is unique, special, not only filled with art, but as another friend attested, it is virtually impossible to get a bad meal here!

Can anyone not think about Michelangelo's "David" when Florence is mentioned? I seriously doubt it. There is a large copy of this famous work in the Piazza della Signoria, and another of bronze on the high Piazzale Michelangelo which affords an incomparable sight of the city below. The "real" sculpture is housed in the Accademia, or gallery of the Academy. Last winter, having returned from visiting "David" once again, I mentioned to our British friend Alex that we checked on "him" and that we were happy to report that he was still there, ensconced in his glorious marble body. Dryly he replied in his crisp accent that he was glad to hear no one had carted him off!

A few years ago a Giotto exhibit attracted more people than the museum directors had imagined; we could not get tickets until the show was extended. This artist, one of the founders of early Renaissance painting, has always been fascinating to me, not only since art history classes, but especially since a visit to the Arena Chapel in Padua many years ago where his works fill the small place of worship. I was happily surprised when I was looking at one painting which had come from the Isabella Stewart Gardner Museum in Boston, not terribly far from our home on Cape Cod. I overheard an Italian woman say this in Italian, and surprised that I actually understood her words, I blurted out to her that I was from the Boston area. She smiled broadly and said that she had visited Boston and had been to the Gardner Museum and was so proud that the building itself was filled with Italian art. Moments like that make touring even more special than it normally is.

The Bargello, or National Museum, Roger's favorite, should not be overlooked, if for nothing else than for Donatello's two "Davids." The first, in marble, is very classical; the second, sculpted more than twenty years later, and in bronze, was the first nude statue since antiquity and constructed more than fifty years before Michelangelo's. From postcards I have made myself a framed "David" collection with the three mentioned above as well as Verocchio's and Bernini's. It cheerily hangs in my bedroom. David times five!

Well worth seeing in this museum is the Majolica Room with pieces from artists and artisans in the Urbino—Urbania, Faenza, Pesaro and other noted ceramic areas of this country. Perhaps because I have spent so much time in the Urbino area and am so fond of it, I tend to pay more attention to the works from here than from other places, but, in retrospect, I have become enamored of the ceramic work from Castelli in Abruzzo, Caltagirone in Sicily and Montelupo Fiorentino in Florence.

I have always been inordinately fond of the Della Robbia family works and this museum has an entire room devoted to these fabulous ceramics. For many years I would attempt to recreate the wreaths made famous by these artists by using many pieces of artificial fruit on an evergreen circle, which then would be the welcome sign on the front door.

There are times when even an inveterate art enthusiast is overcome with the surfeit of art, especially for a first time visitor. Trying to take in too much at once is like eating too many oysters; twelve might be fabulous whereas a gross is a disaster. If time permits, it is always better to re-visit museums in small doses, or better yet, off-season, to truly enjoy, digest and appreciate. Visits to "unpopular" museums can prove most interesting and often quite educational. Highly recommended and rarely inundated with visitors is the Science Museum. Beautifully arranged, uncrowded, and featuring Galileo's inventions for telescopes, barometers, as well as for other machines beyond my technological ken, it is more than well-worth a few hours. On another day we quite unexpectedly walked by, turned around, and then realized we were next to the National Museum of Anthropology and Ethnology and decided to enter. Although we hadn't planned on going to this particular museum, we spent a fascinating two hours within it. Except for the employees, we were the only visitors in the entire museum. There were extremely interesting collections from all over the globe brought back to Italy by explorers and we thoroughly enjoyed the clear displays and interesting subjects. The stop here was more than worth while.

I am definitely not a "shopaholic" but for those people who are, Florence can be heaven on earth. On the famous bridge, the Ponte Vecchio, which was the only bridge in Florence spared by the Germans in World War II, there are more jewelry stores filled with treasures in one fairly small place than one can imagine. Other shops in this "walking" city feature the best array and quality of leather goods found anywhere, and still others feature linens, ceramics, paintings, and quite naturally, the fabled clothing and accessories of silk or leather by those fabled Italian designers so easily identified by their famous names.

Almost every picture of Florence whether on postcard, book cover, watercolor, print or tourist guide shows the famous dome of the Duomo, or Cathedral, Santa Maria del Fiore. This incredible structure, in white, green and red-orange marble, was built under the direction of three architects and completed in 1369. The dome, or cupola however, was unfinished and uncovered for fifty years. A contest for its completion was won by Brunelleschi; the marvel of his ingeniously designed and dramatic engineering feat stands today as tribute to his vision and talent. The dome was the largest built since the Roman Pantheon and the highest to that date.

Two buildings related to the Duomo are the Baptistery and the Campanile, or bell tower. The Baptistery has remained one of the most admired and observed structures in Florence because of the magnificent bronze doors. The young artist Lorenzo Ghiberti won the competition for their design and labored on two sets of doors for almost thirty years. At the completion of the north door, Michelangelo is credited with announcing that they were fit to be "the door of Paradise." The Campanile, designed by Giotto, is more than five hundred years old and is considered to be one of the most spectacular structures in Italy.

So much of the Florentine Renaissance, an explosion of artistic talent in a relatively short period of time, transpired during the 1400's, mostly under the patronage of Lorenzo d'Medici, the grandson of Cosimo. This city, which is unlike any other, can be visited again and again. The Gothic and Renaissance buildings, palaces and churches never fail to awe one. Naming the painters, sculptors and other artists who worked in different media during this period would be to compile the best and the brightest of nearly all art history. It overwhelms. When I get to that point I like to think about the tombs of Michelangelo the sculptor, Rossini the composer, and Machiavelli the political philosopher, in the Church of San Lorenzo, and I imagine that the sculptor is creating still yet another masterpiece, the musician another opera, and the "ends justify the means" guy, is the agent who is finagling huge advances for the artists and large commissions for himself. And so, I relax.

Many visitors who come to Italy for stays of a month and more get what I call, "city fatigue" and as a result, desire to spend time in the fresh air and among the soothing scenes of the Tuscan countryside. Great numbers of cottages, houses and apartments which can accommodate between two and sixteen or more people are catering to this need, and have proliferated in the past decade as experienced travelers eschew the frantic tour pace. Although these residences have become popular throughout all of Italy, perhaps no where is this easier or more pleasant to do than in the small towns and villages of Tuscany.

Our favorite small town is Castellina-in-Chianti, another emotional choice I admit; we've acquired friends, several favorite restaurants, a great bar, wonderful ceramic shop, excellent barber and hairdresser, and feel totally comfortable in the grocery stores, wine shops, tiny supermarket and pharmacy. Best of all are the accommodations where we feel totally "at home" and actually are; the wife of our landlord told us we are so different from many visitors as we truly make the small house "ours" by cooking, entertaining guests, and buying flowers for the table, as opposed to those who just live out of a suitcase.

The town itself is small but delightful; anything one might need is available with the possible exception of a grand piano although I am certain this could quickly be procured and delivered from Florence within a few days if needed! Part of the main street is for pedestrians only which is perfect for strolling, window shopping, stopping for coffee, or merely enjoying the ambiance of the Tuscan day. The town's location is close to perfect we feel, with Siena twenty-five minutes away by car, and Florence less than one hour.

From this town forays can be made daily to almost all of Tuscany, although this is the largest province in Italy. Of necessity some require an early start, and I must confess that often we are not too good at that, especially when our bedroom windows are covered with shutters which efficiently hold out the morning light and indulgently allow us to sleep late. But, sooner or later we manage to visit the many small towns and cities we desire to see. If we don't accomplish all we plan on, then certainly we will on the next visit. Looking forward to future visits is always a pleasure.

Montepulciano, a high hilltop town known throughout the world for its special wine, *vino nobile,* is a jewel of a destination. Driving there towards the southern part of Tuscany, one is struck by the difference in color and texture in the surrounding countryside. The soil, seen in late October seems gray and at first glance looks barren, although it is not. The fields are freshly plowed.

The town is filled with palazzos; a long street, or *corso,* winds up to the top ending in a large square. I always think of the unusual and attractive metal sculpture on top of a large building by the square which is of a man with a large hammer which he bangs against the bell to note the hour. Many wine shops are located along this street, and some encourage tastings. On our first trip there we did not partake of this; it was pouring rain and getting dark and we were concerned about our drive back to Castellina. On later trips we explored this town in a more leisurely fashion and found the Church of San Biagio just outside of the city walls. An impressive and beautiful edifice, built by the architect Sangallo, and reputed to be built on the model of the never completed San Lorenze facade, it is well worth a visit.

Montepulciano was the home of the Renaissance poet Ambrogini, who was so proud of being its citizen, he changed his name to Poliziano, which is a nickname for the inhabitants of this town.

A modern reminder to visitors and townspeople are the memorials on the town walls to those local partisans who lost their lives fighting the Nazi party during World War II. One plaque names each person individually who gave his life.

Another truly beautiful medieval hill town is Montalcino; its reputation for the past two hundred years or so has comfortably rested on its wonderful wine, Brunello. This fortified municipality which lies south and west of Siena, is understandably proud of its wine which is aged in casks for years before being bottled, and is often kept for some time after that before it reaches the market. We first discovered this delightful place by accident in 1975; we had left Siena and taken a wrong turn, and by then it was lunch time and Roger decided that this would be the place. He was right! It was an oasis! And we have continued to enjoy the experience on many subsequent visits.

As a young child hearing the magical story of King Arthur and his removal of the sword embedded in the stone, then as a high school student reading Tennyson's IDYLLS OF THE KING, afterward seeing CAMELOT as an adult, and eventually sharing Disney's THE SWORD IN THE STONE with youngsters, I was stunned when I first heard the reverse of that myth in Italy. During the twelfth century, Galgano, a young man of noble heritage who became a knight, was saddened by what he considered to be his useless life spent either in warfare or in frivolous, unhealthy, non-spiritual activities. He renounced the life of this world and broke his sword against a stone, in which it became embedded. He became a hermit and devoted his life to prayer. After his death he was named a saint, and the land around his lonely hermitage became a monastery. Sacked by the Englishman, John Hawkwood, the abbey was destroyed in the fourteenth century. A chapel had been built above the abbey on the site of Galgano's hermitage and inside, there is a large stone with a sword planted in it. This story was the opposite of King Arthur's and I had to see it.

We drove to the site southwest of Siena and walked through the roofless abbey which the brochure informed us is being restored for an order of nuns, although the work did not appear to be quickly progressing. Then we went up to the chapel to see the famous sword in the stone. When we got there the chapel was locked and a young Italian couple who were also tourists said that the caretaker would open it in a few minutes. After forty minutes a window opened at her living quarters next to the chapel and she spoke in a loud voice. Not understanding the language, I had no idea what she was braying about, nevertheless we completely understood her cranky attitude. The young Italian tourists explained that the woman was annoyed because we were waiting and she was having her lunch! In a few minutes she did open the chapel doors and we finally entered and yes, saw the sword in the stone. I was entranced by these stories, similar, yet different with a reason. Arthur pulled his sword out to fight and Galgano pushed his sword in to seek peace.

After we had our fill of the sword and its surroundings, we next went into the small souvenir shop next to the chapel as I felt I had to buy a few things to assuage the signora's choleric disposition. I did and she softened, calmed down and became quite civil. Perhaps there was something more serious than an interrupted lunch which had upset her.

Our older daughter Leslie who is now an Italian language teacher in a New York State high school and the mother of three sons, spent a marvelous college semester—just ask her—in Siena as part of a group from the State University of New York. This interest began earlier when at seventeen, she spent the summer after high school graduation in Urbino, Italy and fell in love with the country. As a college sophomore she telephoned us and with great excitement announced that she wanted to spend the following semester in Siena. Puzzled, I asked her why she would want to go from Binghamton, New York where she was in school to Albany, New York the site of Siena College? It wasn't exactly an exotic location; I could have understood if she wanted to spend a semester in San Francisco, Chapel Hill, Boston or any place different from another upper New York State location. She giggled first and then said, "No, Mom! Not Siena in New York—Siena in Italy!"

She had gotten permission to attend this program sponsored by the SUNY system from the Chairperson of the Italian Department at her school as she had decided that Italian was to be her major, and now all she needed was the green light from her parents. Needless to say, this was speedily granted.

Each student was required to live with an Italian family and no two students could live together. This promoted learning the Italian language through constant practicing. Naturally, when American students live in dormitories together, it is only natural that they speak English to each other. This was not possible in a family with few English skills, and as a result she became actively verbal rather than only book literate. In addition, university classes were taken daily in the language, literature, art, history and culture of Italy.

A most pleasant footnote to this memory is that twenty years later, Leslie and her college roommate Pam, now an orthopedic surgeon and mother of four, who also went to Siena with our daughter during the same semester, had a joyous reunion together with their husbands in Italy. Much time was spent recalling their adventures at age nineteen through this land!

Siena's height as a major city occurred between 1260 and 1348; devastated by the plague in the following years, and then defeated by the long Florentine siege in the 1500's caused it to be the best preserved medieval city in Italy. After their victory, Florence refused to allow Siena to embark on new building projects, and the result, happily for us, is that this city became as a fly in amber; we can experience it almost as it was in the medieval period. Situated only a short drive from our rental in Castellina, it is a frequent attraction and we often go there for lunch, for the many historic and artistic treasures, or just to enjoy what we consider to be one of the most unique and dramatic piazzas, the Piazza del Campo, in Italy.

This piazza is the site of the famous horse race or *Palio,* held twice each summer. Siena is divided into seventeen districts, or *contrade,* and each submits a jockey and horse for the race which takes place around the precipitously slanted edge of the Campo. I have always been amazed that each horse is actually taken into the church of the district to be blessed before each race. This event elicits great competition among the inhabitants of each *contrade* and results in many wagers drawn among them. We have never attended this famous race as the descriptions defy comprehension; the city is filled with throngs of local Sienese, tourists and impassioned spectators. Often there are disastrous spills, and although the color and spectacle of the banners and medieval costumes and armor are splendid, we will continue to miss this event. The posters and post cards are sufficient!

Simply walking through the narrow streets and across the broad Campo can create a pleasant and enjoyable visit to Siena, but seeing only a few of its monuments and art can add another dimension to one's perspective on this fabled city. The black and white striped Duomo is a gem; gazing at the intricate floor patterns alone is worth the visit, as well as staring at the panels carved by Pisano on the eight sided pulpit showing scenes from the life of Christ. During one visit we felt almost invited to climb the tower next to this famous church. The totally clear day was filled with sunshine after a week of much fog and rain and we couldn't resist the promise of a spectacular view. We trudged mightily up the many harrowing flights of stairs, culminating in a circular tower climb. The exercise was more than worth it! Three hundred and sixty degrees of Siena! Absolutely spectacular!

The sunshine was appreciated by many beside us. The Campo that day was covered with people, mainly students we decided by their age and demeanor, sitting and absorbing the light and warmth. I thought of paleolithic people worshiping the return of the sun god after a prolonged absence. These young Tuscan people seemed to be in the same mode thanking Old Sol for returning to the land in an burst of warming, generous charity.

One of the most interesting stops in Siena is Santa Maria Della Scala, a hospital in the original meaning of the word; it was a place of "hospitality" to pilgrims along the Via Francigena which connected Siena with Rome and northern Europe. Begun in 1090, this notable institution cared for the poor, victims of famine or plague, and children orphaned or deserted. Now this famous structure houses a museum with an important art collection of the city and the very important and unusual history of this huge building. From its very beginning, the hospital was filled with notable works of art, many of which depicted the lives of the children housed here. The frescoes show wet nurses with babies, and continue through all activities caring for children up until the time in which they married, or entered the religious life. A famous chapel within the walls contains artistic masterpieces by notable artists of Siena; this entire building, Santa Maria Della Scala is considered to be the third most important building in Siena after the Duomo and the Palazzo Pubblico; its restoration has enhanced its physical structure as well as the frescoes and paintings, and is a most delightful place to spend a few hours.

The Palazzo Pubblico reigns over the Piazza del Campo; its brick facade and tower are so much a part and symbol of Siena it would be impossible to think of this city without both. Simone Martini and Ambrogio Lorenzetti are two of the most important painters whose works are found here. Especially notable as they are secular rather than religious paintings, are the Allegory of Good Government and of Bad Government by Lorenzetti.

Each Wednesday there is a huge street market by the Fortezza in Siena. Even if one doesn't shop, it is great fun to look at the various offerings whether food, household articles, flowers and plants or clothing. I also like to look at the patrons and the shop keepers as well. Being among the local people, and shopping as they shop, makes me feel even more at home than I usually am. We have bought many items at street markets; tablecloths, vegetables, flowers, long underwear one winter when it was colder than we had expected, extra kitchen items, sox, CD's, chestnut cookers, fireplace grills and probably many, many more I have forgotten.

In the larger cities in Italy there are bookstores with numerous books in English. I missed my Shakespeare books and in one store in Siena I found the complete works in one paperback edition. Granted the print is small, but for quick reference it's perfect. I had been reading Twain's A CONNECTICUT YANKEE IN KING ARTHUR'S COURT, and there was a line I was positive had been lifted, perhaps unconsciously, from MACBETH. Checking, I found it and e-mailed the information to one of my grandsons who was reading both works. I left the Shakespeare with the growing number of things we store in Italy for use on our next trip!

The small Tuscan town of Colle di Val d'Elsa is divided into two parts; the upper medieval and Renaissance section, and the newer, lower town. The high, older part is reached by the

Campana Bridge, named for the Campana Castello at the top, and is the entrance into the Via del Castello and its treasures of buildings hundreds of years old. This street enters into the Piazza del Duomo, again surrounded by interesting structures. One of these was our destination during our first visit here in 1998. The Palazzo del Podesta`, built in the 1400's and recently restored, became the Archeological Museum. We spent several hours here looking at many Etruscan tomb items, coins, pottery and shards of the past. Almost more interesting was the fact that formerly this building had been used as a prison; we could enter the cells and could only imagine the discomfort felt as they were incredibly small. Preserved behind clear plastic panels, are the writings of inmates who wrote Communist slogans on the walls during the 1920's.

This town has been the center of the Italian crystal industry for hundreds of years. Documents register that this was a taxed industry in 1406. Just off the Piazza Arnolfo, built in the middle of the 1800's and therefore located in the "new" town, a crystal museum was opened here in 2001 and it is a gem. The displays are well-lighted, there is a taped documentary shown on a televison about the development and growth of this activity, and booklets in many languages including English, which explain the displays. This museum is housed in a building appropriately built mostly of glass!

We visited this museum on a glorious, warm and sunny day; it was May 1st, which is Italian Labor Day, now celebrated mainly by workers and unionists. Many small commercial stores are open as customers are out in the street with balloons, pamphlets, etc. Interestingly, though, all of the groceries seem to be closed.

The very attractive, bright young woman in charge on the day of our visit was friendly and informative. After we concluded our museum tour we chatted and before leaving took a photo of her and her young daughter who was visiting as school was closed that day for the holiday. Happily, it was not farewell.

After we went home I sent her the photograph with a note. She responded immediately and we began a correspondence.

At Christmas she sent us a calendar seen throughout Italy celebrating the famous carabinieri. When we returned shortly after Christmas in early January I immediately got in touch with her and she offered to take us on a private tour of several of the crystal factories so that we could observe the process of making a molten material into beautiful and useful objects.

We met in the morning and the first stop took us to the only factory still operating here in which all crystal items are totally made by hand, and consequently are quite expensive. We watched a master craftsman from Venice fashion a sailboat from molten glass; this process mesmerized us with its skill and perfection. We were told that the hand made wine glasses are sold in the most elegant retail stores in London and New York for one hundred dollars each.

We continued on to the other factory and Daniela told us that her husband would meet us there and after the tour we would go to their favorite country restaurant for a good lunch. At the second crystal manufacturing facility we observed the process in which most of the labor is accomplished by hand with some machinery assistance. In the display room, Roger found a wine glass in a pattern he decided he couldn't, or actually didn't want to live without, so we are now the proud owners of crystal glasses from Colle di Val d'Elsa. Each night when we enjoy our dinner wine in the beautiful crystal glasses, we are so happily reminded of the day spent with our friends. These are the thoughts, the hard copies if you will, which revive and keep alive our happy Italian memories. Since then we have had a big Sunday dinner at their house, we have met some of their family and friends, and we hope that this charming couple and their adorable children will someday visit us on Cape Cod.

The day of our crystal factory observations was sunny, but a bit colder than usual; the thermometer hovered in the low forties F. However, we called our son on Cape Cod after we returned from lunch and he said it was two degrees below zero F. there! It didn't seem quite so cold in Tuscany after that report!

In 2003 we arrived in Italy at Malpensa airport and after several days began our drive toward Tuscany. We stopped for a few days in the beautiful town of Lucca. Driving toward this town from Piacenza we came over dramatic snow-covered mountains. The trees were white as were the fields and stones. Then, suddenly as we descended, the snow totally disappeared. The trees were bare and some looked as if it were November with brown leaves clinging to the branches.

Lucca, known to many as a music city as it was home to many famous musicians since the medieval period, but is mainly known now as the birthplace of Giacomo Puccini. A very attractive and upscale town, we immediately noticed that Lucca has many handsome clothing shops, as well as very good looking bars, fruit stores and butcher shops. The impressive walls surrounding the city were primarily built during the medieval period when it was rich from the silk industry and banking; this was the time of the development of buildings of stone and brick, many of which are still found, though somewhat in an altered form.

The Piazza del Mercato is of a most interesting shape, built over what was once a Roman amphitheatre, which historians state could hold up to ten thousand spectators. After the fall of Rome, the marble from the original structure was used for other buildings.

One morning as we left our hotel for the usual morning cappuccino at a bar we liked, we had to cross a large attractive square, Piazza Napoleone. On that morning several police persons were on duty on the piazza forbidding anyone to walk across; they signaled that one should walk around the perimeter and not cross on the hypotenuse. We couldn't imagine what the problem was, but obeyed the directive. Later we discovered the reason when we asked the barman; there had been a cold rain the night before and a large area of the center piazza was frozen. The police were assigned there to keep pedestrians off so they would not fall on the dangerous ice.

At the tourist office in Lucca there are Internet stations for the use of locals as well as tourists. Roger wanted to check on e-mail and we walked there. An Italian man spoke to us and mentioned that he worked at the "Bibliotecha Stadale," an important library in the town. After chatting for ten minutes he invited us there for a private tour. We accepted his kind offer, walked over to the library and were treated to a most special experience. Within the building there were archives with thousands and thousands of extremely old books. The entire building and contents had been restored in 1991 and was extremely impressive. The kind gentleman, Piero, thoughtfully took us around where few people, only certified scholars are allowed for research. Another wonderful, special Italian experience arranged by a thoughtful person for us.

The perhaps overused expression, "Small World," occasionally is very true. Roger took a nap one afternoon and I went to the small lobby of the hotel to write in my journal. Giorgio, the hotel employee at the desk, and I chatted and he told me his wife was from Hungary where they have a vacation house. His son and daughter were eleven and eight years old respectively. I always carry photos of our children and grandchildren and I showed him one of the family on our deck in Cape Cod. When I mentioned the name of our town he immediately said he knew a local man who spent much of the year in the same Cape town. Later Roger joined us and told Giorgio that he had met such a man a few years ago who was working part time in a drug store we patronize on the Cape. Giorgio mentioned his name and immediately Roger said, "Yes! I know him!" The world often seems smaller on such fortuitous occasions.

Two small Tuscan towns worth more than a mention are Pienza and Bonconvento. The Piccolomini Pope, Pius II, tried to establish the Papacy in his home town of Pienza and make it a model of a Renaissance city, but it never progressed beyond three beautiful buildings he commissioned, as he died shortly after their constructions. The lovely and grand piazza, the Duomo and the Palazzo Piccolomini are perfect destinations for a quiet touring day.

Perhaps more important now, the town is known for its wonderful Pecorino cheese. Throughout the town local stores sell many versions of this delectable food.

The first time we stopped in Bonconvento it was unplanned; simply, we were hungry, fairly typical for us and especially when Roger decides once again that it's time for a meal! After a hearty and delicious lunch at a small restaurant on the main street, we walked around this tiny, non-touristy town. Stopping in at the Church of Saints Peter and Paul, we were delightfully stunned to see the stained glass behind the altar. There, together with many known saints surrounding Jesus, were images in the richly colored glass of John Fitzgerald Kennedy, Martin Luther King,

Jr. and Mahatma Ghandi. We've returned on several visits to see this unusual sight. Very close by Bonconvento is Monte Oliveto Maggiore; this abbey from the thirteenth century seemed to beckon and we proceeded towards it. Situated on a mountain, the views driving up and back are unforgettable. We were first there in May and all shades of green in various plays of sunlight made this a most memorable visit, with the best sunshine appearing about one o'clock.

On a subsequent visit to this nifty town, Bonconvento, in January, we stopped by the side of the road and bought a crate of Sicilian oranges from a man who was selling them from his truck. They were superb! We shared some with the congenial couple who were renting our cottage to us.

We had a guest one year and wanted to show her the stained glass with the atypical faces, but on the way the police stopped us, along with many other motorists, as there was a bicycle race. The cyclists were escorted by many police vehicles and official sponsor cars who preceded the racers. We were there more than a half hour before the bicycles appeared, but finally they came; it was an intensely interesting sight. More than one hundred and fifty racers on bikes, more bikes on top of cars, and almost one hundred police. We finally did go to the church to show her the stained glass.

Who said you can't go home again? Our first trip to Italy more than thirty years ago began in Rome and continued for one night in the seaside town of Porto Ercole before we moved on. We were there in summer and considered it a romantic adventure; now, thirty years later in February, this seaside town was rather empty of people; we observed dramatic changes, but the original aura lingered. New villas, apartment houses and a plethora of boats anchored in the marina indicated the upward pattern of economic conditions in Italy. The winter day was sunny and warm enough for some restaurants and bars to serve outside, and for us, a happy reunion. We lunched at a restaurant overlooking the harbor and pleased with ourselves, returned to Castellina.

The street market in Castellina, small but comfortable and friendly, is held on Saturday. One morning I decided to buy a small, seasoned, rotisseried chicken for dinner that evening. Walking on among the stalls I came upon the flower and plant sellers and thought I would purchase a small flowering plant called "primula." I had seen them at several friends' houses, and although it was typical to buy four or six as they were small, I picked only one as we would be moving soon from one rental to another in a nearby town and we had so many things to transport. I chose a pretty, yellow flowered one and when Roger went to pay for it, the older gentleman whose booth it was, said, "No. This is an Italian gift."

I had never seen him before and I might never again; not that the plant was expensive, it wasn't, but the gesture was so kind, so thoughtful, I became teary. This man was not prosperous looking; his clothing was a bit frayed and he was badly in need of dental care, but his heart and soul were in perfect shape. Bless him!Examples like these are not atypical; we have experienced so many, and often. I am certain that one of the reasons, perhaps the main one, that we love Italy, is that we love the Italian people.

Driving toward Siena on the superstrada or highway which connects Florence and Siena, a massive fortress, Monterrigione abruptly and dramatically appears above the road. This huge fortification built in the early 1200's is mentioned by Dante in the INFERNO section of THE DIVINE COMEDY in Canto 31 as the poet compares this structure with the Giants inside the pit who guard the final deep circle of Hell.

"For just as at Montereggione the great towers
crown the encircling wall; so the grim giants
whom Jove still threatens when the thunder roars

raised from the rim of stone about that well
the upper halves of their bodies, which loomed up
like turrets through the murky air of Hell.

(Translation by John Ciardi, 1954)

Monterrigioni is fascinating, even for a brief stop. Recently this location has become more tourist friendly with parking areas and English language explanations on each building explaining the origin and use of each one. The circumference of Monterrigioni is about one half of a kilometer; the towers rather impressive though shorter now than originally built, the craft shops pleasant, and an interesting example of the lengths Siena took to keep Florence at bay.

Sitting majestically on the top of an impressive hill, the Certosa Monastery was home for centuries to Carthusian monks, but is now staffed and operated by the Cistercians. We had passed this imposing and huge edifice more than one hundred times as we passed from rural Tuscany into Florence on successive trips, but had never stopped. Finally, we made it the destination of the day.

Founded in 1342 by Niccolo' Acciaioli, Grand Senescal of the King of Naples and Viceroy of Apulia as a school for the purpose of teaching boys the liberal arts, it was eventually given over to the Carthusians. We arrived at the Monastery at ten thirty, and were told that the next tour would be held at eleven fifteen, so we spent some time in the amply sized bookshop. When it became time for the next group to be taken, we were the only ones, and so enjoyed a private tour. Our guide was a reserved, but pleasant man; we were not sure whether he was a monk, a resident priest, or a lay brother. He wore the simple habit of a brown robe as he took us through gorgeous courtyards, chapels, pointed out and explained the wondrous frescoes, and perhaps most interesting of all, he explained the life of the monks who, in previous time, lived in almost total isolation. Small cubicles within the walls were their homes; they were not allowed to speak or to see each other for six days of the week. On Sunday they were permitted to eat together with the other monks while listening to Scriptures being read. Food was prepared by lay brothers and delivered furtively and silently through an opening in the cubicle. To be surrounded with art treasures in the main rooms, as well as the incomparable views of the Tuscan countryside from its height on the mountain, and have these sights forbidden, seemed to me a punishment I could never hope to understand. I was gratified these practices had ended.

There are many perfectly maintained American military cemeteries in Europe as well as in other parts of the world, but the one in Impruneta, near Florence, is an impressive and moving site. The order of the entire area is stunningly beautiful; the care and upkeep faultless. There is a well-appointed visitors lounge which is helpful after a long walk through the area.

Covering seventy meticulous acres, the burial area is laid out in curved rows where more than four thousand military dead are laid to rest. An impressive memorial is located at the top of the hill; within this building, maps of campaigns made of marble and mosaic are found on the walls as well as inscriptions of prayers. A Tablet of the Missing names the 1409 service people who have never been found or were lost at sea.

We went into the office at the entrance to this site and began chatting with an Italian man who had lived in the United States for many years; his English was idiomatic and non-accented. We discovered that he had lived in a small town in the Hudson Valley of New York about fifteen miles from where we had lived for most of our lives. At age sixteen he had also visited Cape Cod and had great memories of the visit. He was a perfect employee for this position at the cemetery as most of the visitors were American and he could converse easily with all. A very well-informed gentleman, he discussed battles, generals, campaigns, and American political policies. We also asked him about life in Italy after growing up for many years in the United States. His memories of the American experiences were positive; now, married with children, living in Italy was great, he enthused, except for what he considered was the high cost of living and too much bureaucracy.

A few years later we re-visited the cemetery at Impruneta and found the order as stunningly beautiful and perfect as it had been on our last visit. Again we walked to the top of the Memorial; it is a touching moment to see the hundreds of names of the Missing or Unknown. The gentleman with whom we had spoken several years before wasn't at work that day, so we returned on the following morning to greet him, and enjoyed a half hour visit.

When our daughter attended a summer program in Urbino after high school in 1975, we visited her for a few days, and while there we met many of the teachers involved with the program and had an extended conversation with one young Italian woman who was teaching a course. She asked if we had ever been to the town of San Gimignano and when we said we had not, she enthusiastically suggested that we do.

Of course we did exactly that in a few days and found it to be an interesting, different and historic town. Known as the "City of Towers", San Gimignano originally boasted seventy-four towers, fourteen of which survive today. These towers were both fortresses and symbols of the wealth of their owners. There is a center square, Piazza della Cisterna, named for the well in the center. In 1975 we drove up to it, parked, and checked into a hotel for several days as we enjoyed the local museums, church art works and the surrounding country views.

Prosperity through tourism has changed this town; we re-visited San Gimingnano twenty-five years after our first visit and it is different in many ways, busier, more people, many more upscale shops, souvenir markets, stores selling local mushrooms, smoked meats and other local specialties, and restaurants, but it remains a great place to visit. We discovered first of all that no one can drive a car anywhere near the walled town. Parking areas are provided and one is required to walk in to it, which is not far.

A new museum had been added sometime in the years we had not been here, *Museo della tortura,* The Museum of Torture. Well done, if painfully grisly, showing the worst of man's inhumanity to man, these savage devices were sadly used in the inhuman, deviant, and heretical acts of the Inquisition. I thought of Mark Twain's remark that, "Man is the only animal that blushes—or needs to." The explanations in four languages further demonstrate the horror done by the machines designed to torment and slowly kill.

Later that year good friends of ours from Rome came to visit us in Tuscany. The wife said that her husband had promised for ten years to bring her here, but always something else got in the way. We had a wonderful visit and once again Roger was the tour guide; one of the places we visited with them was San Gimignano, and it was fun to be the foreigner showing the Italians around their own country!

I'm very fond of Volterra; known for its locally mined alabaster, which is carved into statues, lamp bases, jewelry and hundreds of other beautifully wrought objects. Many stores are filled with these wonderful items, and often one can watch the artists as they work and produce these creations. The city itself is Etruscan in origin and has an excellent museum filled with objects from this civilization. Monsignor Mario Guarnacci, (1701-85), a wealthy prelate who was interested in archeological research, and especially in items recovered from the Etruscan period, left a generous sum of money to Volterra to underwrite a museum devoted to the collection of items from this era. As a result the museum in Volterra houses the largest collection of Etruscan funerary urns and is considered the best museum of these rare items in Italy. One of the best known statues is the very slender, tall and naked figure known as the *Ombra della Sera,* Shadow of the Evening. Archeologists have tentatively dated it as the third century B.C.E., but that is uncertain. It was found by a farmer in the late nineteenth century and used as a fireplace poker for many years before it was identified as Etruscan. I found a copy in a richly filled gift store, bought it, brought it back to the Cape and named him, "Tarquinius."

On a subsequent trip to Volterra I found a small bronze *cinghiale,* or wild boar, whom I named "Bernini" to distinguish him from the larger boar I found in Florence sculpted in clay by Addriano; I gave that one the name "Botticelli." The year after that at the gift area of the Eurochianti Bar in Castellina, I saw a brown fur covered medium sized *cinghiale* that I just had to have, naming him "Boccaccio". Roger teased me when I seriously announced that I was probably the only woman on the Cape who owned three *cinghiale,* a Capostrano Warrior, a copy of an Etruscan statue, busts of "David" and Dante, and probably hundreds of other happy mementoes of our Italian visits.

The Pinacoteca, or art gallery, is filled with religious paintings from the twelfth to the sixteenth century. The rooms are not marked as well as those in the Etruscan museum, but perhaps this museum didn't enjoy a gift as generous as the Monsignor's.

We had observed an archeological dig on our first trip here in the early 1980's; now a Roman Theatre has been uncovered with its Corinthian columns in excellent condition considering that they are almost two thousand years old.

We drove to Volterra on a cold November morning; the scenery never ceases to deeply move me. Some fields are plowed with thick clods of earth; others are past this stage and are being tilled with sharp round wheels which cut up the large clumps. Others are being seeded and still others show a faint green on top of the soil as something is beginning to grow. What? This is November! I don't have any idea. Agriculture is a mystery and a continual struggle for those who deal with it daily. The seasons in Italy seem mysterious and the time for planting and harvesting are not in sync with what I have observed in the northeast United States. One more enigma, however pleasant.

Cleopatra, Shakespeare describes, and gives to the speech of Enobarbus, Antony's friend, as having "infinite variety;" I have no doubt of the wisdom of that statement, but I truly believe that if the varieties, the fascinations, the seductions, the beauties, the enigmas, the pleasures and all the extraordinary qualities of Tuscany were counted against those of the dramatist's rare Egyptian queen, the province of *Toscana* would be the winner. In addition to all the above delights of this province, one might also add, "Yes, the Tower in Pisa really does lean," despite the photo we took of it, and had enlarged and framed. Arranged crookedly, the tower became steadfastly straight; Pinocchio really "lives" in the town of Collodi—he has a park filled with sculptures of the characters in the children's classic tale; Vinci is the home to a museum devoted to reproductions of Leonardo's art, inventions, discoveries and some copies of his pictures by other artists such as one by Marcel du Champ of Mona Lisa with a mustache; Greve's piazza sports a sculpture that would make the religious fundamentalists gasp;Sansepolcro boasts of the work, "The Resurrection" by native son Piero della Francesco; Arezzo's Church of San Francesco is famed by the great fresco cycle, "Legend of the True Cross" also by Piero della Francesco; and on, and on, and on to yet more cities, towns, villages, waterfronts, parks and magnificent scenes of Tuscany. "Infinite variety?" Could there be a doubt?

PIGEONS FROM THE WINDOW IN FLORENCE

Through the kitchen windows the pigeons watch
As I slice cantaloupe—or *melone*
Called so by the Italians who live here.

Across the courtyard, towels, sheets and sox
Drip from the precariously hung lines,
But the pigeons pointedly ignore them.

The women who attach the still wet clothes
Bend dangerously out over the sills.
I shrink from watching them, afraid they'll fall.

Two floors beneath I spy a box filled with
Red, ripe, perfect tomatoes just waiting
To be transformed into ragu or salad.

Magically, their numbers diminish daily;
Deliciously enjoyed, no doubt, by those
Living and eating in that apartment.
As I slice plums for "*torte*" and more fruit
For "*macedonia*", I peek slyly
To see if the pigeons watch. Bored, they stare.

On Saturday I wake to see light rain
And rush to check those ubiquitous birds.
Not one in sight. They've split for the weekend.

VISIT IN CASTELLINA-IN-CHIANTI

In Chianti country, a small village
Of incredible loveliness is placed
Among medieval stone buildings; privileged,
We are visitors here and are yet graced
By its beauty, its warmth, and kind people.
Olive trees, young and old, thrive on the land
Surrounded by fields of grape vines which yield
The noted, famous wines, all which command
Well-deserved attention. *Bravo* the *vino*!
The scenery is totally awesome
And constantly delights one—eye to toe!
We stop at a villa, greeted by some
Friends who welcome us and bid we stay more,
Warmly smiling, they want to "bar the door"!

SIENA, THE WONDROUS

Distant glowing lights gleam from Siena;
I envision the *Campo*, the great square
Incredible, even in Italy,
Home to so many extraordinary
Constructions. The medieval heritage
So preserved, enchants our mind but prompts
The memories of the conflicts, battles,
Political machinations, hatreds
And the heinous black death, causing this place
To remain, much as a fly in amber,
As it was in majesty long ago.

Decades of competition, descending
Into siege; then ending with the huge force
Of Florence, victor, triumphant.

The titles, known names of its history,
The rulers, the religious, the artists
From the far distant past continue on
Consigned to narrative memory and
As background to the life the Sienese
Population, together with tourists,
Share, enjoy, work, play, and love in the now.

Home to the world famous race *Palio*,
This breath-taking horse and rider event
On lightly covered sloping cobblestones
Is dangerous, if exciting, and most
Important to the citizens of this
City. Ten *contrade* are picked to race

And the horses, along with their jockeys
Are taken into the church to be blessed.
The winning jockey, as well as the horse,
Are honored by dining at the head of
The banquet table. A celebration!

Our heritage is to perceive this place
In most of its original beauty.
This is a city of art; The Duomo,
Its zebra-striped marble sides memorable
In this country, a land with majestic,
Notable wonders. Stately *Palazzo*
Pubblico is symbol of Siena;
Restored, filled with fresco, oil, sculpture, is
Santa Maria Della Scala, once
The birthplace of blessed Saint Catherine,
And haven of true hospitality
To pilgrims, to orphans, the poor, victims
Of plague, famine, war and gross disaster-
All incorporated within these walls.

This magical Siena, the wondrous
Fascinating entity, capital
Of the blessed province of Tuscany,
A combination of elegance, grace,
And splendor remembered, defines this seat;
A genuine, true, Tuscan oasis.

DAVID—TIMES FIVE

I look up from the keyboard and I see
Arranged in a frame on the wall, "Davids."

First stands the pure, marble Donatello,
One of the earliest, and draped humbly,
Though his expression, tinged with vanity,
Seems to show boredom at those staring.

Another Donatello, this bronze nude
Created as a naked male statue
And the first since the ancient works, unclothed;
Beautiful boy, hand on hip, sword in hand.

The Verrocchio, bronze, similar to
The undressed Donatello as he holds
A sword and keeps the other hand to his side,
But modestly covered with brief costume.

Florence's pride, Michelangelo's work
More famous than any other David,
Stands calmly in the *Accademia*
While his proudly nude copy stops outside.
Bernini's David is active, forceful
As he uses the sling; his expression
And muscles clearly show his great power
And determination to be victor.

I look at these "Davids" and am happy
With memories of seeing each in Italy.

(Approximate dates of original sculptures)

Marble Donatello—1408;Bronze Donatello—1430's
Verrochio—1470; Michelangelo—1501-1504;
Bernini—1623

THE VENETO—VENICE AND THE VENETIAN ARC

"Venice is like eating an entire box of chocolate liqueurs in one go."

Truman Capote

"I stood in Venice on the Bridge of Sighs,
A palace and a prison on each hand."

George Gordon, Lord Byron,
"Childe Harold's Pilgrimage,"
Canto III, st. 45

I have never been a good street crosser. Often I wait for no traffic to appear until I cross, while at other times I know I can scoot quickly to the other side, just narrowly averting disaster. In London, it's worse; I always look the other way, uncomprehending of the "wrong" side of the street traffic. I always think of John Frederick Nims' "Love Poem" who describes a woman many of my friends think was someone just like me.; ". . . the taxi drivers' terror," . . . "A wrench in clocks and the solar system," . . . "And never on time." This behavior I must add is balanced by what the poet describes as, . . . "Only with words and people and love you move at ease." Well, with that in mind, of course I love Venice! If, for no other reason there are no streets, well, no streets with cars, trucks or busses. As Robert Benchley famously wired to his editor, "Streets flooded. Please advise."

About five years ago I read an article in a magazine lauding the small town of Asolo in the Veneto. Small and architecturally interesting, it was known also for several English writers who had spent time here, as well as a citadel over Roman foundations known as La Rocca. Extraordinary views were possible seen from this fortification. We booked a room in a hotel located on a street actually called, "R. Browning;" the hotel itself was named for the famous dancer, Eleanora Duse. Known as the "Town of a Hundred Horizons," Asolo is a delightful place from which to explore many places in the Veneto. Our hotel room was on the corner of the building and was a wonderful spot to look out to the piazza and do people watching.

We discovered several extraordinary restaurants here. Our favorite one was owned and run by a young, attractive woman who really knew her way around food. The cuisine was elegant, unusual and delicious. Again, an incredible gastronomic adventure. But, that of course, is Italy!

One vivid memory of Asolo is the sound of pigeons, especially in the morning as they nested? rested? slept? gossiped? along the gutters of the hotel. The sounds of their moans were reminiscent of someone with either a stomach disorder or of a sexual encounter, though pleasant, but not as yet having reached an ecstatic state.

The day after we arrived we made the acquaintance of a young woman from Toronto, Canada; our breakfast tables were inches apart and we began chatting and so the following day we three set out for the city of Treviso about twenty miles north of Venice. Though heavily bombed during World War II, this was a charming town with arcaded streets which seemed to be designed in erratic patterns, remnants of old city walls, lots of greenery and aged, but well-preserved buildings. The best part was discovering the many canals through the city which seemed to be filled with very clean water and many good-sized fish.

After a quick *panini* or sandwich lunch we drove to Castelfranco, a lovely find. This small town is surrounded by enormous walls, towers and ramparts; many upscale cafés and an extremely wide street most likely used as the weekly marketplace; we walked around looking in shop windows whose merchandise indicated much local prosperity. After stopping for ice cream and an espresso, we returned for a rest before the evening's activities.

Parking in Asolo can be a bit tricky. A parking area, Piazza Brugnoli, with meters which need to be fed on a fairly regular basis, was located on a hill above our hotel. After our return from Castelfranco and a rest and shower, I ran up the hill to feed money into the seemingly ravenous meter. I was delighted that I was successful as making machines work is not my strong suit with the exception of my food processor, mixer and a few others connected with food preparation. I was even more pleased with myself when I helped an Italian woman who was having trouble with the meter near her car!After I returned to the hotel I found out that parking was free from Saturday afternoon until Monday morning at eight A.M. Today was Saturday. My heroic feeling melted.

Our first trip to Venice took place in 1975, followed up by another in 1976, but we had not returned in more than twenty years. The early trips were filled with new and enjoyable experiences and still please the memory so very much—just as Truman Capote said! I understand what he meant. Sitting in the Piazza San Marco with an espresso, a splurge on an hour in a gondola (despite Byron's describing it "like a coffin clapt in a canoe"), vaporetto rides, the Lido, watching a ballet performance in the piazza while we sipped an after dinner brandy, buying a set of dessert dishes of Murano glass, hearing happy sounds from the streets until late at night from noisy vacationers and local young people, constant church bells, the Rialto, the ubiquitous pigeons, the beauty of the mosaics in the church of San Marco, the Ducal

Palace, and so many other places and experiences are memories securely and permanently embedded in my brain. I believe I felt like Byron's Childe Harold at times.

Now, years later, on a beautiful warm, Sunday in October, we drove, quite by accident, to a spot from which boats were available to transport passengers to Venice. The town was Mestre; we parked the car, got in the boat and off we were. Venice was packed with people; many were Italian day-trippers, plus tourists from all over Europe and North America. Every table in every outdoor café' was filled. We walked and walked all over, enjoying the sights and memories of past visits. We found a restaurant and had a great lunch and then discovered that we would literally have to run to catch the four o'clock boat, which we had been warned was the last one that day that would return to the place where we had left our car. We made it, just in time. As we were rushing to the embarkation point, Roger spotted it coming in to dock. He had generously tipped the driver in the morning, so he had confidence that if he saw us, he would wait. We waved; he saw us and we had a great and cooling ride back to Asolo for another night.

We decided that as much as we liked Venice, we would never go there on a one day basis, and furthermore, we would try to go in the unfashionable season when the crowds would be less so that we could re-visit all the historic and artistic places in relative peace. It is too much of an effort, we concluded, to spend only a partial day there. In addition to the enormous groups of tourists we did not see twenty years ago, we also did not see the number of sidewalk peddlers trying to market knock-off Fendi, Gucci and Prada articles. One stood right in front of the shop in which the real items were sold. Talk about nerve! These men were ever alert for the police who regularly rounded them up and scared them off, if only briefly, for they seemed to reappear with great frequency.

For us now, it was good-bye to Venice, but with a promise to return to this special place. In addition to its incredible architecture, art and ambiance, a city with no cars has an undeniable attraction for one with my affliction.

A delightful footnote to this adventure was that Lisa, our Canadian friend visited us at Cape Cod the following year. She is a travel writer and photographer and as a gift she brought us some amazing pictures of scenes we shared and enjoyed together in the Veneto. They hang in our house reminding us always of a very special few days.

A second delightful footnote to a Venetian adventure, though not ours, was the honor of our daughter Leslie receiving a Fulbright scholarship and studying for the summer in Venice. We were correctly proud of her and her achievements!

Who has not heard of Verona? Any high school student who has read Shakespeare's ROMEO AND JULIET with the constant warfare between the Capulets and Montagues counterpointed with the passionate love of the two young people, has a vague image of this city in his brain. The tourist bureau will give precise directions to the balcony where Juliet supposedly said all those wonderful things about Romeo, not knowing that he was listening in the garden. Post cards happily depict the scene, however vague or fictionalized.

Verona is so much more than this romantic fantasy; monuments and architecturally beautiful buildings and churches fill this delightful and recently ever more up-scale city. One of my best memories is of a night visit to the well-preserved Roman amphitheater; the opera MADAME BUTTERFLY was being performed in this huge and acoustically excellent facility. Entering, each person was given a small candle and at intermission, as the daylight dwindled, the candles were all lighted creating the most unusual and moving sight. Later as the opera progressed, a small pussycat, obviously lost, slowly wandered across the back of the stage. No one, not the singers nor the audience, seemed to mind. This was nature married to culture in typical, delightful Italian style.

Padua is the setting for THE TAMING OF THE SHREW; the main character Petruchio of Verona states: "I've come to wive it wealthily in Padua; / If wealthily, then happily in Padua." The other male lead Lucentio of Pisa, comes to Padua as well, but his reason, at least at first, is to attend the university, ". . . the great desire I had/ To see fair Padua, nursery of arts." Although Padua is now located in the Veneto, Shakespeare places Padua geographically in Lombardy as the republic of Venice then ruled over not only the Adriatic, but huge tracts of land including parts of Lombardy.

We first came to Padua with an Italian professor who wanted us to experience the magnificence of Giotto's famous frescoes on the walls of the Scrovegni chapel. The patriarch of this wealthy family had built a small chapel on the ruins of a Roman arena to atone for the corruption of his money lending father. Giotto's paintings were a fresh, bright interpretation of the Life of Christ and of his mother, the Virgin Mary. The poets and historians of the time were effusive in their praise of this master artist. Unlike the art works up to this period in which human figures were portrayed in the style of the Byzantine or Greek figures, stylized, flat and artificial, Giotto's figures were representative of real human forms, with darkness banished, vivid blue backgrounds and clear evidence of a story unfolding in each scene. Art historians give this artist credit for revolutionizing the entire art development of not only Italy, but of western Europe. He removed the medieval from art.

Every secondary school student in Italy has had to study the tome, I PROMESSI SPOSI (THE BETROTHED) by Manzoni.

Most young people I have spoken to admit that it was a bit tough going at times. Paramount in this novel is the theme of average people suffering physically, mentally and emotionally under the yoke of cruel rulers—aristocrats and titled despots. Italy wasn't free of so much of this injustice until after the Risorgimento which wasn't totally complete until the annexation of Venice in 1870.

I am not an opera buff, having attended only several in my life, and in all honesty, because they were performed in extraordinary outdoor arenas as in Verona or Rome. However, as I repeatedly clicked the TV control past channel after channel recently, I stopped at a public television station which was honoring the great composer Verdi; I became fascinated by the story of this dynamic person and his famous opera, RIGOLETTO. This filmed opera had been performed in England, but what grabbed my immediate attention was the presence of several experts whose erudition in explaining not only the story but the motivation of the composer caused me to remain stationary through the entire performance, and in addition, an English translation in sub-titles at the screen bottom greatly helped me understand the plot. RIGOLETTO was premiered at the *La Fenice* opera house in Venice; this work by the strongly nationalistic Verdi, forcefully demonstrated the horrors bestowed on the populace by certain elements of the ruling class.

We plan to re—visit Verona within the year, and perhaps Venice during the following year. The comparisons will be interesting, the differences noted, and I fully expect the experiences to be as fruitful, entertaining and educational as all Italian odysseys have been.

FAMILY

"The family [is] the first essential cell of human society."

Pope John XXIII, PACEM IN TERRIS, 10 April, 1963

"You don't choose your family. They are God's gift to you, as you are to them."

Desmond Tutu, Address at enthronement as Anglican Archbishop of Cape Town, 7 September, 1986

"The sons of Abraham have become quarrelsome, but remain family nonetheless."

Shimon Peres, Prime Minister of Israel, Address to The General Assembly, United Nations, 21 October, 1985

The novel BREAD AND WINE by Ignazio Silone depicts the Italy of the Mussolini era. Except for the major cities, the country was a country of poor people, eking out a living, especially in the chronically depressed South. The economy was mostly agrarian; the quality of life lacked much that was positive. At the end of World War II, having been trampled on by the Germans in the north, invaded by the Allies in the south, been bombed, beaten and with so much of their country either damaged or destroyed, the real fact that presently it is a major world economic power, above that of Great Britain according to some accounts, is a situation which can be described only in superlatives.

More than any other place I know, the presiding principle of cohesion which has kept a people together regardless of the perils, intrusions and horrors inflicted on them for thousands of years, is family. No where has this been so important or so apparent. From the time of the Etruscans, ". . . whom the Romans, in their usual neighborly fashion, wiped out entirely to make room for Rome . . ." according to D. H. Lawrence, to the twentieth century, this peninsula has been almost constantly subjected to invasion and upheaval.

Where rulers and therefore political systems have changed as often as seasons, and invasion and oppression are givens, and one doesn't know whom to trust, let alone depend upon, the only constants are oneself and one's family. For several thousand years allegiance to family has been the mainstay and principle of Italian life. Family, first, last and always. Survival depended on this code; existence required it. No matter how horrendous life was, safety, comfort and trust were found in family alone, and this often was evidenced at table. Sharing a meal, however meager or austere, cemented and enhanced this enduring relationship.

The economic change, or almost miracle which has occurred in Italy in just over fifty years has caused some changes in the Italian way of life which had not been noticeably altered in hundreds of years. The countryside was agrarian, and life, though often harsh, was fairly simple; most dwellings in the rural areas were without electricity, central heating or indoor plumbing. Cars were rare. This was not the situation in cities, but even there, conveniences were minimal. Now, life is different. Many people left the countryside for city jobs in the 1950's and have remained. The retirement age has been established and a pension legislated, so that much of the austere and often cruel burdens of life have been eased.

Young adults with families, many educated and professional, often now have a ready, able and willing source for child care while they are employed. It is usual to see grandmothers pushing strollers or grandfathers accompanying young children to the playgrounds. At school dismissal time, it is often the grandparents lined up to take the children home as the parents are working. Two income families are ever more typical as the standard of living continues to rise. During the seventies, cars were only beginning to be a normal part of family life outside of the major cities; it is now typical for families to have two cars, one for each spouse, and occasionally, one for the university student in the family as well.

Other changes are happening as well. For generations, it was almost unheard of for Italians to marry non-Italians. With more mobility, university education and travel abroad, there are more international unions being established. At one gathering we met an Italian man married to a German woman, an Italian woman married to a Canadian man, and an Italian man married to an American woman. A very close friend whose Roman restaurant is our favorite is married to a Swiss woman, and our favorite hotel is owned by an Italian man married to a woman from Finland. In a small town in Tuscany we met a couple neither of whom were Italian but who were thoroughly ensconced in the Italian life; she was originally from Austria and he from Iran. They met when both were studying art at a university in Florence and have remained in Italy for twenty-five years. They are both artists and have an art gallery in a small, but prosperous village and they have restored and live in a wonderful country house. Such marriages as these result in Italian children! Tim Parks maintains in his book, ITALIAN EDUCATION, that the real nationality of a child is determined by the place and environment in which he lives, plays, and goes to school. Thus, their children as well as those from other mixed nationalities growing up in Italy, are Italian.

Essentially, most Italians are bi-lingual; At home a child's first language is the local dialect; in school, and later, in dealing with others at university, business, and government, they speak "Italian." Most history buffs know that Italy was united as a country in the latter half of the nineteenth century; before, divided into many sections, city-states, protectorates and occupied lands, each area had its own dialect. I recently read that there are approximately one hundred different dialects in that country, but my older daughter, the Italian teacher, contradicted me by saying that her university language teachers said more accurately there were almost three hundred.

The Tuscan dialect, known as the literary language as it was the dialect in which Dante Aligheri wrote THE DIVINE COMEDY, became the "official" language of the country after Unification. Many provinces wanted their own dialects to receive this distinction, but the only one all could agree upon was the one Dante used. The government realized that it was necessary to have a single national language. Many older people who grew up between the two world wars were too poor to spend many years in school as they were needed on the farms or had to work to help keep the family together. The result was that many were unable to speak anything but their own local dialects. When television became popular in the 1950's and 1960's, the government decided that absolutely correct and perfectly enunciated Italian language would be spoken in broadcasting news and in many other forums as well. Broadcasters and announcers frequently were chosen by their ability to speak as correctly and clearly as possible, thereby becoming another medium in addition to the schools in which to teach children as well as the many adults who had not had the opportunity to learn the national language.

Perhaps because of this Italians are more than tolerant of others attempting to speak, or even attempting to say words in their language. We try to ask for things, or to order meals, or inquire about directions or ask questions in the little Italian we have. Most people are pleased by the effort. We have not found this to be true in a few other European countries. Only once I found it very funny when I asked for *macedonia,* and the waiter replied, "One fruit salad!" He was proud of the fact that he was learning English; I was glad I knew what fruit salad was in Italian! More and more, especially in the larger cities and tourist holiday areas, we have observed the tremendous increase in English speakers. The Italian schools seem to be doing a great job of teaching this to the young. A reason must be that today English is an international language necessary for commerce and government; Italians, although they love their language, *la bella musica,* the sounds of beautiful music, see the need as well as the advantage of speaking and understanding English in our ever more international world.

As well as being close to family, historically Italians are close to their home cities, towns or villages. This is an obvious holdover from the time when one's citizenship was determined by one's city or province. I remember asking acquaintances where they were from and being told proudly, "Modena is my city;" "Pisa is my city;" "Parma is my city," and so forth. There is a pride of belonging. Often a resident will gladly escort you to any historical or scenic parts of his town to show you the superiority of his part of the world and to share it with you, so that you too, will feel the pleasure and pride he has in his special place.

Most Americans, when abroad, whose ancestral backgrounds are more diversified, will answer, "The United States" when asked where they are from. Secondly, they might reply with their state, and only when pinned down, will mention the small city or town where they live. Naturally there are some exceptions; the answer New York, Boston, Chicago or San Francisco, for instance, will be first forthcoming as those places are universally recognized in Italy as in most of the world.

Christmas, or *Natale,* as well as other major holidays are spent with family. Italians who came to the United States continued this tradition for many years. Sunday especially, was the day for family to come together and share a meal which often lasted for hours. If children were grown and married with families of their own, they nonetheless were expected to attend these gatherings with their entire family. If both husband and wife were second generation Italian, it was expected that they would alternate Sundays from one family to the other. Since the end of the Second World War, much of this has deteriorated because of distance, and more recently, the same breakdown of this custom has occurred in Italy. Young people have found jobs in distant cities which has precluded the traditional gathering for Sunday dinner. These educated Italian professionals have found employment opportunities which have required mobility virtually unheard of in previous eras with the exception of the mass migrations in the face of devastating poverty. Most older people accept this, with a bit of, if not sadness, then at least nostalgia; at the same time they are proud that their children are making their successful way through the business or professional ranks and realize that this is simply the way it is in the world of today.

The circumstances surrounding and impacting on the family are different than they were a hundred or ever fifty years ago, but the strong bonds of family still exist as tightly as before. The telephone, and especially the ubiquitous cell phone, as well as e-mail are keeping these links firmly in place. Family is still paramount; if not face to face as in the past, then by electronics and emotions, heart to heart.

GRANDFATHER PIETRO

My paternal grandparents emigrated
Separately from Sicily to the
US about one hundred years ago.
Specifically I know very little
About why, but from studying, reading
And learning history, I can surmise
Obvious reason. Opportunity
Existed here, and many people came.

Married to Carolina in 08;
Then, a son, my father, born in New York
In 1909; his mother, six years
Later, died. The boy was small and suffered
From this loss. On my wall, her photo hangs;
I wish I had known her as I knew Grandpa.

Grandpa was a professional barber
As well as a fabulous cook and player
Of pinochle. As a child I often
Spent Sundays at his house for gourmet meals.
Italian dinners replete with soup, bread,
Lasagne, roasted meat and herbed chicken,
Oven cooked garlic potatoes, salad,
Always fruit and then cake. We kids
Were allowed unlimited amounts of
Soda pop, off limits at our own house—
Just on Sundays at Grandpa's happy house.
Adults refreshed their palates with red wine;
Usually homemade; sometimes store bought.
After dinner, Grandpa, the musician,
Brought out his magical guitar and made
Music we loved to hear and songs began.

Time passed; Grandpa was asked to babysit
My sister and me when our parents left
For a month in Florida. What great fun!
My boyfriend and Grandfather hit it off
Right away! He taught this guy Rog to play
Pinochle and made wonderful pasta
For him as often as he could dine here.
If studies or parental rule forbade
A meal at our house, Grandpa felt so sad
And asked, when would "Roja" come here again?

Pietro, my grandfather, known to most
In America as "Pete," was born on
January second in the year of
1882. We never knew the
Exact date because every year he gave
Himself a big birthday party on the
First day of the new year. Happy New Year
And Happy Birthday to Grandpa, well loved!

In 1957, at the age
Of seventy-five, dear Pietro passed
This life. Over the space of thirty years
We have made five fine Sicilian journeys
As we experience the island and
Always remember Pietro, Grandpa.

THAT'S AMORE'! OR
OTHER FAVORITES!

"Frame your mind to mirth and merriment, which bars a thousand harms and lengthens life."

THE TAMING OF THE SHREW, (Induction),
William Shakespeare

*"Italia! O Italia! Thou who hast
The fatal gift of beauty."*

George Gordon, Lord Byron from "Childe
Harold's Pilgrimage," Canto IV, st. 42
(Based on Vincenzo Da Filicaja's sonnet,
"Italia, Italia! O tu cui feo la sorte.")

Returning toward the north from one trip to Sicily, we decided for a change we would take the overnight boat from Palermo to Naples rather than drive up along the coast. The rooms for two people were all booked so we reserved one for four people for ourselves; it was perfectly adequate, but I think it would have been a problem for four adults to try to turn around or even move without bumping into each other. The boat was tidy, large as it carried many cars and trucks below decks, and efficient with bars and a very pleasant dining room.

That night the ship did some rolling, gently, which at first was unnerving, but eventually we both settled into a restful sleep. So restful in fact, that we awakened at seven to remember that it was required that we leave the boat by eight. We rushed to dress and swallow some coffee and went down to the area where our car was held. What a surprise! When we embarked last evening the holding area was totally filled with cars, a few tour buses and many large trucks, but when we arrived in that area to disembark our little red car was the only vehicle left on the boat! I had incorrectly guessed that no one would be in a rush to leave. I was totally wrong. We made the eight o'clock exit with two minutes to spare.

Amalfi was our next destination and we began climbing the Lattari Mountains on a curvy two lane road, not the kind of which I am inordinately fond. But finally we arrived at the apartment/hotel we had reserved and it was even better than the description from the catalogue. The view of the Tyrrhenian Sea stretched out in front of our rented apartment; we had a huge terrace, complete with tables and comfortable chairs; a party for twenty people could have been comfortably accommodated on this deck. The panorama of the unbelievably azure sea seemed endless. I was enchanted.

Although it was mid-November, the weather was mild, sunny and perfect for sitting on the wonderfully open terrace and enjoying the vista and ambiance, which we did for an hour before we went into town to explore. Amalfi was filled with tourists, ceramic shops, local ladies buying provisions for dinner, and children just released from school for lunch. The town was immaculate and quietly cheerful and we immediately felt at home.

Strolling on the main street through the town, we found a most delightful restaurant, small, and after lunching there, we decided, excellent.; liking the food and the staff so much, we returned five times during the week. There were never more than twelve patrons, often only six or eight, especially at the lunch hour. On our last night in Amalfi we decided to dine there with a cheerful young couple from Australia who were renting the apartment next to ours. We agreed to have a farewell dinner together before we parted. When we arrived at the restaurant for the sixth time we were amazed to see a large group seated in the dining room; a major local business was holding a dinner party and every table was filled. The four of us began to leave but the owner strongly indicated that we should not; quickly and efficiently he whisked every dish off the antipasto table and immediately set it for the four of us. This is so pleasantly typical in Italy of the gratitude and understanding shown to a faithful customer by the owner of a small establishment.

Watching the owner of this restaurant work and serve was somewhat akin to watching the conductor of a huge orchestra; his smooth moves were compelling and seemingly effortless. The result was a symphony of exceptional cuisine as well as something fascinating to behold. Verdi would have approved! Usually the boss had only a young busboy to help, but on that night he had called in another man to assist him serve. This person had no uniform, but obviously knew exactly what and how to do his job. We were quite certain that there was one lone chef, a woman in white we had glimpsed through the kitchen opening and who must have been a paragon of versatility, patience, efficiency and talent. The large group of thirty were ordering individually and receiving various antipastos, pastas, fish, meat, vegetables and salads. No one working in the restaurant seemed to get flustered, yet everything was prepared to order. We had observed this same kind of smooth proceeding in other restaurants throughout this country, and it has never ceased to impress us.

When it was our turn to choose, the first courses were just as diverse among the four of us, ranging from spaghetti carbonara and pizza Margarita, to seafood salad made with tiny clams, mussels, shrimp, sardines and calamari, all of which were still slightly warm so we knew they had just been cooked. Our second courses ranged from veal with lemon, to a filet steak and grilled vegetables. Peace reigned throughout. We enjoyed every bite.

Amalfi is reported to have been the first place in Italy to emerge from the Dark Ages; it was the first sea republic. Although only a small resort today, in the Middle Ages it rivaled Pisa and Genoa for control of the Mediterranean. Wars with its rivals as well as drastic tidal waves in the mid 1300's as well as one even before those, ended its supremacy. Because of its location, very high on the hills above the shore, the cathedral was saved; it is notable even in a country filled with notable cathedrals. Named for Saint Andrew, or as he is known here, Saint Andrea, his remains reside in a crypt under the basilica. Local lore maintains that his head was returned here from Constantinople in the thirteenth century.

Walking through town one morning we happened upon the Civic Museum. Officially it was closed as there was a conference being held, but the gentleman in charge insisted that we go in anyway. A very large room was filled with tables and chairs at the far end; men were seen discussing something with great seriousness, but we sat still at the other end of this huge room and looked at the paintings. No one attending the meeting seemed to notice us. Although we were given a pamphlet in English which explained the objects in the room, we couldn't look closely as many were in the section where the forum was being held. This brochure included an explanation about why a certain important manuscript of what I believe was the first constitution of Amalfi was not among the museum's artifacts. The papers were removed by the Pisans during the sacking of this town in 1135; somehow they were later removed to Florence; presumably they are still there. As a guide once explained to us when he talked of the beautiful bronze statues of the horses in the Piazza San Marco in Venice, "Spoils of war." Those horses were brought from Constantinople by Venetian soldiers in 1207 to celebrate their victory.

We drove to the picture postcard town of Positano, my heart in the proverbial throat. Horrendous would be my description of the road, but no one else seemed to mind; buses and cars tear along as if they were on the New York State Thruway. The spectacular scenery is like none other, and I am constantly annoyed with my paranoia about the sheer drop offs, as this detracts from totally enjoying the panorama of the sea, the thousands of lemon trees, and the houses placed at angles which defy, or seem to defy gravity.

This little town is filled with what seemed to me to be a thousand women's clothing shops; the dresses, lacy, dark and extremely beautiful. I immediately thought, "mother of the bride." We much preferred Amalfi, but perhaps did not give Positano enough time; I kept thinking of the return drive when we would be on the drop-off side of the road and this probably colored my feelings. Our older daughter had been here in the summer and loved the town and had recommended three restaurants; two were closed for the season as this area is primarily a warm weather resort, but we enjoyed a great meal at the third.

I always knew I could never pilot a plane as my sense of direction is practically non-existent. Nevertheless, I do know that the sun comes up in the east. After a few days of watching, I began to become really worried about my mental state. The sun, as I looked at it, rose as if it were coming up on the west coast. Fortunately, after I mentioned it, Roger who had a map, showed me why this was so; Amalfi faces southeast, or at least our apartment does. The town is located on a type of horseshoe bend; this explained it. I felt better knowing the sun was rising in its usual position and that dementia had not taken over my brain.

Paper making was an important craft in Amalfi for many centuries. At one time there were thirteen factories here; now, only one remains. A museum devoted to showing the history of this enterprise is located in a former factory which began in the fourteenth century and permanently closed in 1949. We wanted to see this and the guide was enthused with our interest and showed us the "new" machine brought from Holland in the eighteenth century. Later that day I bought a package of hand made Amalfi paper with the watermark one can see when held up to the light. I use it for handwritten notes for very special occasions.

After several days of rain the sea was rough and the waves were crashing high on the rocks of the shore. We had seen photos of this phenomenon in several restaurants and tourist shops and to say the least, it is very dramatic. Thoughts of tidal waves crossed my mind but were quickly replaced with wonderful thoughts of what I would have for dinner. Calamari? Veal marsala? Tortelloni stuffed with prosciutto and ricotta? Pasta with eggplant?

Flavio Gioia is an honored son of this city who is said to have invented the compass. A large bronze statue of him stands in Amalfi; he is holding a compass and an almost religious type hood surrounds his head. Controversy has surrounded the legends about this man; some scholars even insist there was no such person, but that his name was a confused amalgam of those of many other men. The actual origins of this invention, the compass, which changed the world, seem to be in China, but according to research, its improvements are largely thought to have occurred in the Mediterranean region. The great maritime centers such as Venice, Pisa, Genoa and certainly Amalfi, could not have happened without this important device. A fascinating book about this, THE RIDDLE OF THE COMPASS by Amir D. Aczel is a delightful read as the Professor examines the possibilities of the name as well as the incredible changes in trade, exploration and the rise and fall of so many historical centers which would not have happened without this device.

One of the symbols of Amalfi is naturally the compass, but now, if ever replaced, I feel it would be the lemon! Groves of these trees are found everywhere on the perfectly groomed terraces. At this time of the year, November, they are shrouded in black nets to protect them from sleet or freezing rain which sometimes happens, even here, in the winter. At least half of the stores in the area sell limoncello, the after dinner liqueur made of lemon juice, sugar and vodka. We found a small factory at the top of the town where some of this was made. Peeking in, we watched several women sitting and peeling lemons by hand. The ceramic shops sell hundreds of pieces of pottery decorated with lemons, from a very inexpensive but attractive tile, to huge vases costing hundreds of dollars. I bought a large platter beautifully decorated with the prescribed lemons; each time I use it, pleasant memories of Amalfi return. Lemons now rule here!

We had enjoyed a great visit to this old maritime center, but our week here was over and it was time to move on. We saluted the statue of Flavio Gioia, and drove away.

Many dogs seem to occupy a place of honor in Italy. Several instances showing this stand out in my mind. Walking along the Via Veneto in Rome on the way to an office where we had to check on airline tickets we were changing, we noticed a very well-dressed woman sitting at a table at a sidewalk café. It was chilly that morning in autumn, but not overly cold, at least not

by the standards which are more New England than Rome. This
woman was cradling something in her arms which I assumed was
an infant. A closer look revealed two small dogs securely wrapped
in plaid woolen pram robes, lovingly held in her arms.

Our friends in Tuscany were off to the opera one evening and
asked us if we would feed their dogs and put them in their pen
for the night. The food was left in an open, but at that time an
unoccupied apartment; all we had to do was to add water to the
dry food and mix, and leave them bowls of fresh water. Roger
didn't want to go back and forth to the apartment, so we brought
two large empty wine bottles from our cottage which we had filled
with water. After fixing the food and leaving ample quantities of
water in their bowls, I looked around the fenced pen area, not
having noticed it before. It was at least one quarter acre in size
complete with trees, bushes and grass. Within this area there
was a small "house" or shed actually, with a straw covered floor.
Within that small building there was a smaller dog house shelter to
protect them if it became very cold. This canine condo, complete
with the expanse of Tuscan greenery was lovingly arranged for the
dogs. I wondered if anyone saw us pour the water from the wine
jugs into the dog food and thought it was wine. Roger shrugged
when I mentioned this possibility and said, "Why not? They're
Italian dogs."

I left a note on their masters' door after we fed and put them in
their quarters. I said that we had given them supper and afterward
had tucked them into bed and that I had read two chapters of
LASSIE COME HOME, and a brief version of A HUNDRED
AND ONE DALMATIANS until they drifted off to sleep. The
next day they told us how much they enjoyed the note!

These lovely creatures were quite worldly; their sophisticated
owners told us these pampered but loving animals understood

three languages—Italian, English and German! Tri-lingual pups! Most impressive! We became very fond of them after visiting this estate for seven years; they became our pals. Each evening about five they would trek up the big hill to our cottage and patiently sit on the patio until they were noticed. Our dear landlord of whom we were very fond, had been very specific in the beginning about not allowing the dogs into the rental units or cottage, and forbidding anyone to feed them. We never did this in the earlier stays, but as the years went on and we began to stay for months at a time in the off-season when no one else was there, we began to cheat a bit about the snacks. Because I always made stocks, broth and minestrone, I usually would end up with cooked meat and heavy soup bones. These beautiful creatures shared the spoils! After a quick, small treat, they would scamper off down the hill to be put to "bed" in their comfortable quarters.

One evening I looked out from the kitchen window and saw the larger of the two dogs holding his head almost straight up and howling. I was alarmed that something was wrong with him and I telephoned his master. He chuckled and suggested I go outside and listen to something else besides the howls. I did, and from the small town a few miles away I could hear church bells. I had been told that he always accompanied the distant bells with a wailing solo. Italian opera dog? The Caruso canine of Chianti?

We have never forgotten going to a restaurant in Naples on our first Italian trip. It was a hot July night and all patrons were eating on tables set up outside in front of this trattoria. A couple next to us ordered in rapid Italian and in a short while the waiter came from the kitchen with three bowls of pasta on his tray; he placed two of them topped with delicious looking tomato sauce on the table for them. The third he put on the sidewalk beneath the table; we hadn't noticed before, but then we saw that they had a small terrier on a leash. The other pasta was his!

A young Italian friend drove up to our rented cottage one time and I noticed his dog in the back of his car. It was a Dalmatian; I asked for the name of the pup and was told, "Pongo." Just like ONE HUNDRED AND ONE DALMATIANS, he told me.

Although the situation is improving, I must admit there is a down side to this canine situation. Curbing one's dog has not caught on with every dog owner which makes some city walking a bit tricky at times. This varies widely we have noticed from place to place; some cities and particularly small towns are making big progress.

The city of Piacenza is not particularly noted as a tourist stop; we stopped here for the first time almost by accident, in 1996, found a comfortable, friendly hotel and discovered a busy center of business, industry and agriculture. Since then we have often made it a one or two day stop. The brochure of the city proclaims: PIACENZA "CITY OF ART": OVER TWO THOUSAND YEARS OF HISTORY.

Much of the old city of Piacenza is surrounded by still standing city walls. Some parts of these were in need of repair, but we have noticed on many subsequent visits they are actively being restored.

This city is noted for being the first Italian city in 1848 to vote for annexation with Piedmont in signing on for the Italian Union. "*Primogenita*" or first born, is the word often used to describe Piacenza for this reason. The long history of Piacenza is similar to many of the other cities in this region. From the time of the Romans, and even before, it was beset with political wars and struggles for rule, and culminating perhaps in the distaste for absolute monarchy, when in 1545, Pope Paul III, a Farnese, gave Piacenza to his ne'er—do—well son Pier Luigi. His exploits, corruptions and depravities were so offensive to the local nobility they showed their contempt by murdering him and throwing his body from a palace window.

A newer problem, not political dissent, has become a problem in this area in recent years—flooding. So many of the fields next to the waterways have been cultivated, so that the fall rains which swell the rivers, dangerously rip into residential and industrial areas. A study of the problem strongly condemns the excuses of the authorities and blames the destruction on the intentional and deliberate compression of the rivers and streams, to make room for the factories and housing requirements for an ever growing population at the expense of eliminating the necessary flood plains. Disasters in 1994 and 2000 were especially harmful; the last one killed more than twenty-five people and uprooted, either permanently or temporarily, many thousands.

We visited *La Galleria d'Arte Moderna Ricci Oddi*, and enjoyed the Italian impressionism so much we've returned on subsequent visits. We bought post cards and several books, but unfortunately for us, there were no English translations. So far, Piacenza has not been into the English-speaking tourist business, but as more people from the UK and the USA discover this interesting city, these translations will appear. Another engaging museum, this one of local history, is the *Civic Museo di Palazzo Farnese;* especially striking was the large exhibit of carriages and coaches drawn by horse, pony, or dog! A major section of this museum is the Museum of the Risorgimento, but it was closing time and we did not get to see it. Of course we shall return!

I tend to remember Piacenza as a bicycle town; the young, the old, men, women, it seems everyone in this city gets around on a bike. I always get a kick from watching women, many long past youth, well-dressed and frequently in high heeled shoes and some without backs to the shoes, competently and confidently pedal through the streets along with the motorized traffic.

Piazza Cavalli, or Horses Square, an attractive piazza with a "Gothic palace on one side and a seventeenth century building on the other," is dominated by two bronze equestrian statues. We enjoyed the morning as we walked around the square and then had coffee at the most elegant bar, which hearkens back to a by-gone era. The room had coffered ceilings interspersed with paintings. This sophisticated and beautiful setting set the pace for the beginning as well as the remainder of the day. The coffee was excellent and immediately afterward we decided to drive to find the Castle Rivalta.

This castle is located in the midst of a tiny picturesque settlement. We were too early in the year to visit it as it is open only from April to November, but we walked around the minute village and a very friendly woman standing in front of a restaurant began chatting with us. She began in French, but we told her we were Americans and she immediately switched to English. Because she saw us alight from our car with French license plates, which shows how tiny this settlement is, she naturally thought that was where we were from; we have successfully leased cars from a French rental company for many years which has caused many people to make the same mistake about our nationalities. That is, until they speak French to us and we answer unintelligibly.

Deciding to have lunch here, we entered the restaurant and found that the sociable woman we had spoken with earlier was the wife of the proprietor and chef. The month was January and the Christmas decorations were beautifully in place. I admired the wreaths which decorated the several large rooms in the restaurant. Donatella, by this time we were on a first name basis, told me they were made of braided bread, and each one, and there had to be more than twenty, were decorated differently and uniquely. She had made them all and I had never seen anything so unusual and beautifully adorned.

Lunch was one of the best! We ordered wine, but as it was mid-day, we did not finish it. When time came to pay the bill, Marco, the owner, said it was a "present" to us. We had never met him or his wife before this day, but we took photos of him and his wife, sent them and we will definitely return. The food, the people and the decor were superb, and, we would like to tour the castle.

One morning after our usual coffee stop at the unique bar we noticed there was an art exhibit next door. The sign advertised: "1948-1986 Paintings by Ludovico Moscani from those years." Of course we bought tickets and went to see the exhibition as soon as our coffee was finished! We viewed a most well arranged and interesting array, even if the artist's particular modern style is not our favorite. However, the building in which it was shown, the *Palazzo Gotico* was worth the price of the exhibit. Hundreds of years ago the walls were decorated as were each of the high ceiling beams and these interesting embellishments still existed. I wanted to know more of this edifice, but stumbled over the language barrier with the kindly and pleasant guides.

The art treasures and buildings of this ancient city are not all its attractions. I have pamphlets of the local dramatic and musical offerings and they are indeed impressive. Tennessee Williams', SUDDENLY LAST SUMMER, was featured at one theatre and at another there were many shows scheduled from October through April including KING LEAR, AMADEUS, WAITING FOR GODOT, and CYRANO DE BERGERAC.

Cremona, the famous violin town, is near Piacenza and we drove there for a look. On the way we crossed the Po River as well as several small streams and they were totally frozen. It was a cold January! Cremona seemed like a delightful small city. We walked around a bit, saw the front of the large cathedral, and the statue of Stradivarius, but did not linger. The weather was clear, but very cold, and we were still fighting jet lag. There is a museum dedicated to Stradivarius and his violins, but we're saving that for a warmer visit.

Earlier in the morning we wanted to make reservations at one of our two favorite restaurants. I never could have remembered where it was located, but Roger drove precisely to a road near the restaurant and then backed down the street to park practically in front of it. He's so Italian!I think he was switched at birth!

The previous April we had been in Piacenza on Liberation Day. This holiday in Europe is a bank holiday, the beginning of a long weekend, and the occasion for many Europeans to get away for a few days. We drove to Pavia through extremely heavy traffic. Two days later the newspaper reported that an estimated ten million Italians took to the road for the week-end, with the heaviest traffic in the northern regions of Piedmont, Lombardy and Emilia. After walking through Pavia and seeing the partially opened Duomo, we continued on to the highly recommended Certosa monastery. Very large crowds were everywhere enjoying the lovely day; we too appreciated the park surrounding this noted institution as we sat outside for a light lunch, bought several small ceramic pieces from a local artisan, walked through the fresh greenery, and drove home through the legendary rice growing area of more than 200,000 acres. Pavia is known as the "risotto" capital of Italy; this wonderful food, slowly and carefully prepared is a gourmet treat in its many manifestations.

Emilia-Romagna has a well-deserved reputation for its gastronomic excellence. Many first time tourists are unfamiliar with this area in their understandable zeal to see the fabled cities of Rome, Florence and Venice. But those who are very interested in gourmet food do tend to make pilgrimages to cities in this interesting region. This is undoubtedly true; we have eaten supremely well in Parma, Bologna, Modena and Piacenza. We haven't spent much time in Parma or Bologna in more than ten years, not because we have avoided them, but simply because we have acquired so many favorite places and kind friends in other areas and as we re-visit these places and people, we find that there is simply less time to explore, even though we seem to happily continue expanding the amount of time we spend in Italy.

We were guests at a warm, lovely home several years ago in the city of Imola. Not having been there before, we had a lovely time exploring. The city of 65,000 is impressive, green and tidy. Our hosts, Gloria and Gianluca had invited us and could not have been kinder. Their home is surrounded by a private garden, has ample bedrooms and bathrooms plus a wonderful living room with fireplace and a great kitchen. Gloria is an amazing cook and we were spoiled with special pastas, stewed rabbit with green and black olives, eggplant, salads, fresh pineapple and cakes. One evening Gianluca made an antipasto of smoked salmon on buttered crostini. We tried to take them to dinner at a restaurant, but because Gloria was about due with her second child, they declined.

Gianluca gave us a tour of this town in his car. The weekend following our visit the Formula One race with the famous Michael Schumacher is scheduled to be held here and preparations are in high gear throughout the city. The huge track is five kilometers around and the stands are vast; thousands of fans are expected.

After breakfast the following morning we walked through the town and stopped at the local tourist office, but were told that all the local museums were open only on weekends during the cold months. We spent an afternoon sipping tea in front of their fire and talking with their beautiful three year old daughter who is adorable and a true *principessa!* She is gradually warming up to us and likes me to read the book about rhinoceroses which we brought to her. It is written in English, but she seems to enjoy my enthusiasms as well as the lively illustrations.

The Po Valley, running through Emilia is rich, flat farmland; there are acres and acres of vines, grains and espaliered fruit trees. This area is the part of Italy which produces Parma ham, Parmigiano cheese and the famous and delectable pastas.

The Romans built the Via Emilia through this region as they secured the entire area and gained entry to Gaul. For some reason this district has always been known as a seat of dissension and discontent. Although not historically proven, or perhaps only slightly accurate, a legend suggests that this situation exists because the Romans "rewarded" the retired soldiers of their legions by granting them plots of land along the Via Emilia. This land was swampy and required extensive labor to drain before anything could be grown on it; the old soldiers were angry at this disrespect for their loyalty, and according to many, this feeling has lingered and has been passed down to the present. Towards the end of the Second World War, as the Germans were retreating to Italy's north, there was much activity by the partisans, and today, especially on April 25, the anniversary of Liberation, those Italians who were sacrificed are honored. All through Emilia there is evidence of the terrible reprisals by the Germans on the Italian partisans; many were shot in groups in the town squares; today those martyred men and women are recognized in the town squares with named memorials, and frequently with photographs.

Many Italians affirm that the very best pasta in their county is found in Emilia. I've enjoyed pasta all over Italy and won't commit about what is "best," but I will not argue with those who maintain its perfection is superior to all others.

Parma is a city very well worth visiting. The Farnese Palace, now an art gallery, is filled with interesting and wonderful Renaissance paintings; many are by the famous artists of that period, but others by those not immediately recognized except by serious students of art history. At the top of this building is the absolutely magnificent Farnese Theatre. This room, originally designed to seat four thousand people, was built at the behest of Duke Ranuccio I Farnese de Porto. The structure was severely damaged in the Second World War, but has been meticulously restored, even to using the original splintered pieces of wood wherever it was at all possible. Constructed entirely of wood, it is an architectural gem. I was delighted to read that for the first time in more than two hundred years it opened for the Verdi centennial; as part of this celebration, two of Shakespeare's plays, AS YOU LIKE IT, and THE TEMPEST were also presented as a tribute to the author whose works influenced the composer.

The five stories of pink marble of which the baptistery is composed is famous throughout Italy. When we were there we were not able to enter as it was closed for the noon meal. This happened more than fifteen years ago, and as many other traditions in Italy are changing, this may no longer be true. We have observed that although the formerly iron-clad rules about opening and closing hours and days are being bent in the larger cities, most are still observed and maintained in the small towns.

Our visit to Modena was sentimental; our favorite Italian professor was originally from there—it was "his city." We had stopped here on two occasions before, just for lunch, but had never stayed. This time, in his memory, we stayed on for several days. After dinner on our first evening we took a long walk and got lost looking for our hotel. Finally, we stopped in a bar and asked for directions and discovered that we were within twenty feet of it a half hour before.

The following day we toured "La Galleria Estense di Modena" which had a large and most interesting collection; unfortunately none of the signs with explanations were in English and the brochures were gone, so much was lost in the absence of translation. We saw two groups of children, I'd guess about the age of second graders, being given art history lessons by museum guides; the Italians are so good about getting children around to their important monuments and works of art and this is so impressive.

There were railings in front of many of the paintings as we have seen in some American museums, which protect them from anyone getting too close. Roger inadvertently bent over one rail to look at a painting more closely and a very loud alarm sounded. No one seemed to get excited about this except us in acute embarrassment.

One of the most interesting circumstances we have observed is the constant upward movement in the Italian economy and standard of living; an amazing upward spiral has been consistent since our first visit here in 1971, and even more dramatic if one considers the drastic ruin of this country at the end of the Second World War. Shops today are filled with expensive designer clothing; portions in restaurants, especially of meat, have tripled in twenty-five years, and although many people still use bicycles or motor scooters for convenience especially for parking which can be a formidable problem, cars have proliferated.

The Northern industrial machine grows ever more enormous; we are constantly awed by the changes each year shows, and to compare this with 1971, the differences are enormous and gigantic.

Two things stand out in my mind about Bologna; the towers and the food. Only a few of the several hundred towers originally built are left, and some of these lean so far that if the Tower in Pisa were not so outstandingly beautiful, its list would not be noticeable compared to one or two in Bologna. The famous "Bolognese" foods need no explanation; these also must be the dishes from the celestial menu. Many of the sidewalks in this city are arcaded, making it pleasant to walk under a covering from the hot sun or winter rains. Art and churches abound; the university is famous, especially for its famous sons Galvani, Marconi, and those who were first to teach physical anatomy from human bodies, previously a forbidden and dangerous assignment to those practicing or teaching this science.

Long before we began to travel, I heard older people in our town boast of the great bargains in food and clothing they were able to get in Italy. This now varies, depending on the exchange rate of dollar and euro. This does not matter very much to us as we do not travel in order to shop, and in any case, almost all manufactured items from Italy can easily be purchased in the United States. We go to Italy for the ambiance, the food, the hospitality, the interesting paradoxes, the art, the wine, the anachronisms, the enchanting views of land and sea, but most of all for the many fine, fine friends we have come to know and love.

About ten years ago as we were driving toward Mantua in Lombardy my dear husband was yet again hungry and looking for lunch. We stopped in a small town, Casalmaggiore, and asked a policeman where he might suggest we lunch. He directed us and this led to three hours of a gourmet extravaganza. The owner of the restaurant had worked in England and hence had excellent

English; somehow he was taken with us and proceeded to bring course after course to us without having us order anything. We had three different kinds of pasta, risotto, veal piccata, salad, cheeses and fruit. He gave us a tour of his establishment; there were twenty-five rooms as he was developing a hotel along with this excellent restaurant. Another great Italian experience for us!

A footnote to our lunch; we returned to our car, satiated with our divine lunch to find we had left the window open. Parked in the piazza, unlocked, we discovered Roger's wallet on the front seat with money sticking out of one end. Untouched. Incidentally, he thought he had lost it; I had to buy lunch!

The main reason that we left Emilia-Romagna was because Mantua was the place I wanted to see. Perhaps it was originally because Romeo had gone there when he was ordered from Verona; then again, I might have been influenced by a book a friend gave to me about the Gonzaga of Mantua. Whatever the reason, we were going there. We stopped first in the tiny town of Sabbioneta, known in the Renaissance as "Little Athens" and built by Vespasiano Gonzaga. It boasted the first roofed theatre, built purely for dramatic purposes, a ducal palace, and was an entire town conceived to be the "Ideal" and home to writers, philosophers and artists.

Arriving in Mantua we were immediately impressed; it boasted lovely piazzas, palaces and many other handsome buildings. Our hotel was filled with antiques, Persian rugs, huge ceramic vases more than four feet high, flowers everywhere and exquisite furniture. I had time to admire all this as I remained in a second floor lounge, reading and writing, too full from that glorious lunch to accompany Roger to dinner, or his search for a few thousand more Italian calories. We stayed in this town for several days, touring palaces, viewing yet more art, and simply wandering around inhaling the historical past and imagining the drama of Shakespeare.

Lake Como, or *Lago di Como,* is a magical place. Legendary since Roman times, its grandeur never fails to take my breath away. My brief notes from our first visit in 1975 stress the mountains which seem to drop right down into the lake, the picturesque towns along the borders and our first hydrofoil ride to the city of Como. My memory includes the profusion of flowers that seemed to be everywhere, a hotel room overlooking the lake, and a feeling of tranquillity after the rapid pace and rhythm of Milan. Although we had spent several days enjoying the sights and tastes of this delightful spot at that time, we had not returned until 2000, and what a wonderful return it was. Our dear friends in Rome have two homes here in the tiny village of Nesso and invited us to share some time with them. The younger part of the family could not be separated from their restaurant, so we were the privileged, and I might honestly add the spoiled guests of the mother and father of our good friend, Fabio.

The effect of the lake area is enchanting; I state that not from personal experience alone, but from the results of the many creative people who have derived inspiration from this magical place for centuries. Musicians such as Liszt, Rossini, Verdi and Bellini were supposedly stimulated by this, one of the most beautiful of lakes, and a number of Romantic poets breathed in the air and exhaled the verses.

We followed directions to their small hamlet and at the first turn, the father, dear Rino, was parked and waiting for us. We followed his car up a precipitous road, then to a driveway to their houses. Perfectly constructed with luxurious windows, doors and woodwork, each was a small work of art. The kitchen and bathroom areas were ultra modern with every convenience;

the furnishings impeccable. These thoughtful, gracious people had furnished "our" small house, very close to their larger one, with tea, coffee, milk, butter, bread, wine, mineral water, fresh fruit and all the paper and soap products one might need for six months. The added attraction was a bowl of fresh camellias on the table.

I did no cooking for the entire stay; Rino, a talented and enthusiastic cook as Fabio's wife Tiziana stated, who loves to feed those he likes, made many delightful lunches and dinners, and when that didn't happen, he insisted on taking us out for meals to unusual places we never would have found on our own. We tried to resist or reciprocate, but he would not hear of it or even discuss it. Like a general, he was directing this operation and would not heed dissent. If I am describing this kindly man like a tyrant, I do him disservice. He was the essence of generosity and hospitality. He wanted to do this as a gesture of friendliness and he and his lovely wife Giuseppina succeeded on every level. He explained that during the previous summer their granddaughter had visited us on Cape Cod for three weeks, and during that time, her father, their son, had also joined us for one week. He and his beloved wife had picked them up at the airport when they returned, and he said they emerged from the plane with large smiles and said they had a wonderful time and that we were so good to them. This was their way of thanking us for his family, he said.

On the day we arrived lunch was prepared and served "at home;" prosciutto, salume, veal chops, artichokes, cheese and fruit. Dinner consisted of the most delicious pasta with a sauce of bacon, tomatoes, peas and cheese.

We had a date with this wonderful pair for ten one morning and we walked on a stony path, built by the Romans to the site of a 2000 year old Roman bridge. Never would we have found it on our own. The walk could be described only as magnificent as it edged along the lake with the other side of the path abundant with trees, flowers, evergreens and stately buildings. Two huge ravines with gushing water and ending in waterfalls completed this viewing of a side of Nesso not usually viewed by the casual tourist. This village is thinly populated, I believe he said about two thousand full time inhabitants, but now, with the economy of Europe so improved, many of the older houses have been renovated and become summer residences and vacation homes. Rino was brought up here; the land and his houses standing on them once belonged to his mother.

We felt we had not been taken care of so thoroughly and solicitously since either of us were infants! We were instructed on arrival that breakfast would be on our own each day, but lunch and dinner would be provided by them! We enjoyed so many special meals, not only in our friends' house, but in the extraordinary places they brought us. One restaurant, well-known throughout the region and overlooking the lake, specialized in serving lake fish, and yes, we were stuffed yet again!

After we rested and recovered from our hearty repast, we took another long walk with Rino up through the village on an old road by another waterfall and on to a beautifully arched old bridge. The countryside, green and sweeping upward towards the mountain background, he informed us, was formerly the home, food and grounds used by three or four thousand cows; cow sheds, now abandoned, are sprinkled all over the mountains, but now, unlike the days of his youth, not even one cow remains.

We next passed a concrete shelter next to the waterfall which housed deep sinks fed continually by flowing water. This was where housewives did the family laundry in days gone by, but actually not that far back. Rino, who remembered this rather vividly, grumbled that the women all gossiped constantly while the laundry was done! This is deeply embedded in his memory. Automatic washing machines or even the old type with wringer rollers were not a usual item here until fairly recently.

Invited for a "light" supper, we feasted on homemade minestrone, followed by four kinds of cheese, radicchio, pickled *cipolle,* or small sweet onions, roasted peppers, and fruit. Each night we brought wine to their home as they would hear of nothing else we could do.

Special plans were in order for the next day. Rino's brother and his wife live next door to their home, and they, together with their grown son and his wife as well as two grandchildren, were all going up into the mountains for a special local meal. This would feature polenta, typical of the region. I must admit to a certain anxiety about the trip as I know it would entail an ascent on curving mountainous roads with precipitous drop-offs not always having guard rails. However, even after Roger warned me, I decided to go. Here I was in Italy with people, not only that I honored and trusted, but who had been born and brought up here and who wanted to show us things and places we would never find on our own. I instinctively knew I'd never have a chance to see or do this again, so off I went. We had a caravan of three cars as up, up and up we went! And I have never regretted it for an instant!

Climbing through forests with only an occasional chalet, or an abandoned or restored farmhouse near, I was amazed to suddenly view a small village, but we continued to climb. Suddenly I saw a bar! Up here? Who attends ? But then signs appeared for other restaurants, agriturismos, hotels and a camp group for travel trailers. The area was obviously becoming an idyllic mountain retreat for vacationers. We reached our destination and pulled into the parking lot of what turned out to be an incredible restaurant. The owner was a childhood friend of Rino's and the reception was truly warm; the dining room was huge, decorated with animal horns, a stuffed fox, paintings of mushrooms indigenous to these mountains and other items in keeping with the local rustic motif. Large windows enabled diners to see huge, yet seemingly close snow-covered mountains. A fireplace glowed at one end of the room, but the radiators were also pouring out heat. If anything, it was surprisingly warm; I had not expected this as it was much colder outside in this altitude than it was down at the village by the lake.

The main course of the meal arrived and it was something to behold. We sat at a long table set up for ten diners; the waiters brought out extremely large dinner plates and placed one in front of each person. One half of each plate contained a large slab of tender and delicious veal, covered with rich gravy and smothered with local mushrooms; the other half imitated the snowy mountains. Two huge mounds of polenta, dripping butter, with avalanche imitating coverings of melted mozzarella flowing down the slopes completed the offering. This would have appeased the crankiest of mountain gods even on a bad day! Of course I could understand the need for this kind of high caloric meal when people had to chop wood, climb miles into the mountains to care for and milk the cows, or as Rino said, he had to go to work each day on bicycle—a trip that today takes more than a half hour by automobile. Now this kind of meal is nostalgia food, delicious, but enjoyed only on occasion by those who remember, or who have shared their parents and grandparents memories of a time gone by. It reminded me of the huge Thanksgiving feasts we enjoy once a year in the United States. It would be more than dangerous, completely foolhardy, to indulge in this more often, however we were so grateful to have been honored to share in this experience.

The family houses we were privileged to share are high enough from the lake so that the seaplanes appear to be at eye-level from the windows, and when outside, seem to appear even lower. Looking from a window on the east side of the lake toward the west, I notice the mountains and only momentarily acknowledge their height as well as the distance across Como. My quick assessments of height and distance are acutely wrong; I question the evaluation as I worry about my reality. The buildings next to the lake on the western side must be made of pastel Legos, all with orange colored terra cotta roofs, I decide. And then dawn breaks! I stare at the structures, some five or six stories, or as the Italians say, *pianos,* high. My original estimate of distance and height could not be more wrong. My career choice of high school literature and Shakespeare teacher was so much more appropriate to my qualifications than surveyor, architect or geographer.

We often take boat rides, mini-cruises, on the lake and then I see the "real" houses, villas, apartments, hotels and restaurants in actual size, making the scale of distances more real. Many private boats sail these waters in the warm weather, but these pleasure boats are at rest or in dry dock in the colder months; the large ferry as well as the smaller hydrofoil pass by several times a day during all seasons although their schedules are diminished after the heavy tourist season.

I had requested, perhaps begged for a light supper after the gargantuan repast at the Sunday lunch. Amazingly they agreed and we finished the minestrone from the night before. Of course that wouldn't really please them, people who want to do more for you, so Roger was talked into a veal chop; I don't think his arm had to be twisted. Naturally there was salad, bread, cheese and wine.

Roger and I had to make a trip to Malpensa airport as we were trying to change our ticket date and we had a continual chuckle about the bureaucratic mishmash we encountered. Terminal #1 or Terminal #2? Which one held the Swiss Air desk? We took a chance and bet on #2, but of course, that was wrong. After parking in long term, another error on our part, we enjoyed yet another comedic scenario. The booth attendant had to write down everyone's license plate number and then engaged all in an animated, gesture-driven conversation. It seemed quite inefficient, but he seemed to be friendly and enjoying himself; who can understand all of the Italian ways? We then took a free bus to Terminal #1 and a no-nonsense gentleman at the Swiss Air desk told us it would cost us fifty Swiss francs to change the ticket—at the time, about thirty American dollars. He suggested we go to Delta; the slight confusion was due to the fact that we had booked with Delta, but had flown on their then partner, Swiss Air. We did and found it unmanned as the agent was helping to board the flight to JFK that was about to depart. We waited and finally she materialized. We told her we wanted to change our return flight date; informing us that there was a charge only for change of destination but not of dates, she called the Swiss Air man and in rapid Italian gave him what I think were instructions, and sent us back to him. He mellowed a bit and said she really should have made the changes herself, implying that she was a trifle lazy. At first I thought he might have been the Dean of Men at Bergen-Belsen, but after awhile he had melted into an almost sweet "G-man" who had just captured public enemy number one. Actually, by the time he finished changing our tickets, he smiled, well, almost.

When we returned, our gracious hosts were awaiting us, but said we should rest before dinner at their home at 7:30. Had yet another incredible meal! What a talented man Rino is! Wonderful pasta with tomato sauce, roasted chicken and artichokes followed by strawberries and four kinds of mouth-watering cheeses was the total offering of this evening.

Our wonderful hosts planned a special trip in the area of the Valtilenna to the town of Talamona, which is Giuseppina's childhood home. Originally we had all planned to spend the night there, but they felt our time was growing short and a day trip would be more appropriate.

We drove to Bellagio to get the *traghetto,* or ferry for Varenna. Lake Como is like a two pronged fork; the two prongs stick out toward the south, and Bellagio is located where the prongs would meet the handle if it were a real fork. We needed to cross to the far eastern side of the lake. Upon arriving in Bellagio we found we had just missed the boat, but another appeared in a half hour. We walked around a bit and reminisced about our stay here twenty-five years ago. We were fascinated to find out that Rino had worked at a lake front hotel here as a young man before he entered the restaurant business in Rome. Additionally, his son Fabio, our good friend had been employed at the same place as a teenager. Interestingly, we had stayed at the very same hotel. Bellagio itself, still special and as beautiful as ever, has, just as the rest of Italy has, become ever more upscale. Many of the shops were displaying expensive pieces of silver, crystal, china and jewelry. The clothing stores appeared quite different from the high fashion emporiums, sometimes bordering on the almost outlandish, of Florence or Rome. These lake front shops for both men's or women's apparel seem to be more of Talbots married to Brooks Brothers than those of the nouveau chic. It was delightful to walk around with our friends and to take pictures of the hotel just as it was, or almost just as it was on our memorable first visit.

After our pleasant crossing by ferry, we continued on to the valley of the Valtillena, and I was amazed. Huge supermarkets and large factories dotted the countryside. I think I was expecting small villages, THE SOUND OF MUSIC style, with sheds and two cows and four goats. Wrong!

We stopped at the most sumptuous and palatial gourmet store stocked with specialties of smoked salmon, jars of gorgeously arranged artichoke hearts, onions, mushrooms, bags of dried porcini mushrooms and so much more. I was dying to buy some specialty food items, but felt I might be committed if I had to carry even one more thing home! Rino bought salmon for supper and some delectable condiments. Then Giuseppina stopped at a bakery for very special local bread.

Of course it was lunch time again and we went to a special restaurant for another memorable meal and one that again we never would have found on our own. Even if we had by some remote chance, we would not have known what we should have ordered. The local regional speciality was something called "*pizzoccheri della Valtellina.*"

Composed of dark noodles made with a type of what I believe was buckwheat flour, potatoes, sweet cabbage, lots of oozing butter, and the cheese known as "grana saraceno." the result was absolutely delicious, and needless to say, different from anything we have ever had before or since. This was followed by *tagliata all brace,* a type of broiled beefsteak served on a bed of my favorite green, arugula, often known as "rocket," and we finished with fresh pineapple and strawberries.

The restaurant was huge and capable of holding eight hundred people as it specializes in weddings on the weekends. Rino told us it was impossible to come here on a Saturday evening or for Sunday lunch if you had not booked months in advance. Now, at lunch it was filled with businessmen. I was still amazed at the extent of industry in this area; Giuseppina told us that when she was growing up there was nothing here but cows.

After our lunch we visited Giuseppina's childhood home in Talamona. Ten years ago it was totally restored and is in perfect and exceptional condition, as are their other two homes in Nesso. How perfect this place would be for a party or for a group of friends who might ski during the day as it contains two complete modern kitchens, fireplaces, bedrooms, bathrooms and living rooms upstairs and down. This large house is occupied by the family for perhaps one week of the year, while the ones in Nesso are never used for more than two weeks. They explained that these houses are the ones in which they grew up, although now vastly modernized and customized; they appreciate the roots and memories of their early lives and that preservation is important to both. I said Americans were not like that; as a people we have always shown so much mobility and our real estate is not usually treasured enough to retain. They said they were aware of that and understood that their granddaughter's generation would be more like us. We had coffee and a small taste of a delicious dessert wine from Pantelleria before we left this special house.

I saw family pictures in this house and recognized one of a son they lost, Luca, at age three. He would have been in his mid-thirties at this time, and seeing him, I felt so sad looking at this beautiful and adored child, I began to weep. He would have had so much pleasure in this wonderful family.

We drove to say a quick hello to Giuseppina's sister; in her house I saw a photograph of the two sisters, probably circa 1940, and they could have been in an Andrews Sisters movie, their clothing and hairstyles were so in keeping with that era.

It was time for us to leave Nesso; our plane to Boston was scheduled for the next day and we had booked a hotel next to the airport as the flight was early. We exchanged sincere, hearty and emotional farewells with our more than generous hosts. Many kisses after a farewell supper of fabulous salmon enlivened with an excellent bottle of French champagne. As parting gifts, we were given a silk tie for Roger and a scarf for me, both from the shops of Como, the silk center of Europe.

Stopping in the city of Como for a brief look at the cathedral, we were surprised to see two statues; one of Pliny the Elder and another of Pliny the Younger, his nephew. The older was born in Como and many things in the area are named for him. I was surprised to see two "pagans" enshrined in the cathedral facade, but a guide book stated that these men are placed here because people of the Renaissance believed noble intellectual ancients as revealed through their writings, were considered "honorary saints."

To save time on the following flight morning, we turned our rented car in at the airport after checking into our favorite hotel which is very near Malpensa; the concierge at the hotel said they had arrangements with nearby restaurants whose drivers would come by and take you to their restaurant, and when finished, would return you to the hotel. So we did, and it worked out very well indeed. While we were at the restaurant I enjoyed a good, grandmother experience.

Near to our table there was a large family celebrating the birthday of a young girl of eleven or twelve. She looked so much like one of our granddaughters, not only in looks but in action and expression. Seated next to her was a little fellow of about four who was absolutely adorable. At Roger's urging I went over to say hello to the grandparents and to show them photos of our grandchildren. At the end of the evening when we were ready to depart, I returned to their table, wished them well and said good-night. The little boy had his father bring him out to the front door so that he could kiss me good-bye at the door. I shall never forget that! A great gesture!

We returned to Nesso the following year at the kind behest of our hosts and benefactors. We apparently had passed muster and we not only were on our own, but were given the larger house to use! At the risk of being redundant, I have to emphasize that the views of Lake Como are stupendous. Looking across the water at the seemingly minute houses, one is reminded of illustrations of perfect, if imaginary structures, in childhood books of fairy tales. On one of the mountains across the lake, there is a tiny village perched high on the slopes looking as if it were simply pasted on by a glue-wielding youngster having cut its image from a postcard. Magical is the feeling.

We had fun watching a project going on in front of the property of this compound. A crew was re-building a stone wall and seeing the men at work reminds one of the excellence of knowing how to do something well. The Italians certainly are experts in building with stone! New gas lines were also being installed at the same time and this job made it more difficult for us to drive in and out of the narrow driveway as it was filled with equipment and stones, but we made pals of the pleasant workmen and they went out of their way to assist us when we were leaving or returning.

This, our second visit to Nesso, was in the month of May, and I don't know whether this is typical or not, but the weather was extremely rainy. Clouds hung heavily over the mountains in front and behind the lake; at times the fog was so thick the lake was not visible and often we couldn't see the houses on the mountain or across the lake. At night we would listen to the rain continually pour, often accompanied by loud bursts of thunder. A gushing torrent coming down from the mountain near to our wonderful borrowed house could be heard as well. One afternoon we walked up from the lower village, crossing a narrow footbridge above what I called the "torrent in the crevasse" and even six days after the rain ceased, the water continued to gush down the mountain.

Cruising on the lake is a must; we took the "slow boat" from Bellagio to the city of Como passing amazingly beautiful scenery, villas, hotels and spectacular gardens. Returning, we took the *aliscafo* or hydrofoil for a quick ride back. It is enclosed and used by many local people for commuting, but for the scenic route and especially in good weather, I prefer the slower boat while sitting outside. However, obviously this is a godsend in the cold months.

Another cruising experience occurred when we drove up on the opposite side of the lake through Cernobbio up to Mennagio and took the car ferry back to Bellagio. The road seemed better and to me, less curvy than on the Nesso side. The short ferry ride was interesting nevertheless as we watched scenes of the mountains, some snow-covered, while crossing the lake.

During our stay two events in Italy occurred drawing national attention. Soccer is an obsession and during June of 2002 Italy beat Ecuador in the World Cup. This seemed very fortunate in averting a country-wide depression.

The other important day was June 2, 2002 which is the "*Festa della Repubblica*" celebrating the fifty-sixth anniversary of the national referendum after the Second World War that "turned the monarchy of Italy into a republic." A huge parade was televised from Rome with representatives from all parts of the Italian military. Thousands attended; The President of Italy, Carlo Ciampi, who reinstated the parade in 2001, was in the reviewing stand as well as the Prime minister, Silvio Berlusconi. Many bands, some with elaborate uniforms, paraded along with one hundred and eighteen military formations. We watched this grand spectacle on and off, later reading the translation of the prime ministers's remark, "A splendid day that makes us feel proud to be Italian!"

We decided to visit a trattoria where we had dined in 1975; because we are both "squirrels" and tend to keep more things than are necessary, Roger brought the dinner check from the trattoria that year with him. The man who waited on us, the son of the original owner from '75, was very friendly, had perfect and totally colloquial English, so Rog decided to show him our old dinner bill. It was 6400 lire; without missing a beat, he said, "It's the same thing now—64 euros!" We laughed, but he was impressed and asked if he could show it to his mother who was busy in the kitchen. He did and then she came out and greeted us. He then took it into the kitchen to show the chef. Later a young woman who is the bookkeeper for the restaurant came in and he asked if he could show it to her also. When she looked and saw the date, she gasped and said, "Mamma Mia!" We were the hit of the dinner crowd that day!

The man who was so intrigued by our check was two years old when we first had dinner here. We remembered the restaurant well as the table the proprietor had in front of his establishment held a huge bottle of grappa, and pasted outside of the bottle was a drawing of a large skull and crossbones!

Since then we have returned many times with great pleasure. The young man who was two in 1975 and his mother have become friends of ours, and in true Italian style, invited us to make an reservation for a certain night as it would be filled with local people; by special order only, the chef will make a gourmet delicacy, *zuppa di pesce,* a rich soup—almost stew—of many fish varieties. The month was October and it was much colder than usual; actually the mountains surrounding the lake were totally snow covered and the TV weather people devoted much coverage to this unusual northern spectacle. We arrived at the restaurant too early for our special meal and knowing that, we waited outside the trattoria. Aurelio, the proprietor, spotted us and insisted we come it from the frosty evening. We were the only ones there, but it gave us time to leisurely chat with him for more than thirty minutes.

At between seven thirty and eight o'clock, an interesting phenomenon occurred. Since Bellagio seemed suddenly devoid of tourists, the patrons who were arriving were all local. We knew that not only because they all seemed to know each other, but because a majority carried large pots, kettles or other containers for the special fish meal as "take-out." Most were men who had been sent by their wives to bring home the special delicacy. The fish soup wasn't quite ready until almost eight-thirty, but no one was stressed. The gentlemen sat at tables as they waited for the chef to finish his masterpiece; some had a glass of wine while others had a small hors d'oeuvre and a few had nothing but conversation. All of these families knew this evening was the special offering and had ordered ahead.

When we were served we appreciated the interest in this wonderful and rare meal. Each morsel was succulent! Aurelio told us that he had driven to the city of Lecco early in the morning to purchase the fish. He has started the special menu evenings which have generated so much interest among the local people as well as with tourists during the season and they have become a great success. He told us that several weeks before he had a Tuscan menu evening with prime beefsteak from that province and had to purchase twenty-six kilos of beef. We were sorry that we wouldn't be here the following week as he was planning a *bollito misto,* a delicious mix of different meats simmered in broth as that night's special menu.

So many business owners in all parts of Italy have complained to us about Italian bureaucracy. As visitors, we don't come into contact with those kinds of problems, but we listened to Aurelio and his complaints were so similar to so many we have heard before. He wants to expand his restaurant and improve his kitchen as it is extremely small and inefficient for the present time. He presented his project to the governing board and they said it was okay, but did not put it into writing, and until they agree to do this, he is not allowed to begin and cannot go to the bank to borrow the money to achieve the project.

We became acquainted with another young man and his mother who run a restaurant in the small village of Nesso. We enjoyed the excellent cooking and superb pizza prepared there, and when the weather was good, in the late spring, we enjoyed meals on the terrace next to the lake.

Chatting with him one evening after dinner, he asked us to wait a moment and returned with a tee shirt for me with the logo of his restaurant. We stopped there for a coffee the next morning and I wore it to show him! Roger had gotten one from the restaurant in Bellagio, so now we were even, having each received one from two charming young men, each at his own restaurant.

Although I have never been there, I have been interested in the city of Bergamo for a long time. One reason is that Italian people always say that the dialect from here is almost unrecognizable to other Italians, but the other and main reason the name has fascinated me comes from Shakespeare's most wonderful comedy, THE TAMING OF THE SHREW. In a funny scene in which Lucentio's father Vincentio is confronted by his servant Tranio who pretends to be his son Lucentio and comments that he is able to dress finely and live well thanks to his father; Vincentio yells, "Thy father! . . . he is a sailmaker in Bergamo!"

We decided to drive to this mysterious town, but set out too late. When we reached it having driven through an area which reminded me of the more unattractive industrialized parts of New Jersey, Bergamo itself seemed good-looking, modern and bustling with activity. A castle was perched high above the city, but we checked our watches and knew we had to return in time for our dinner reservations, so we did not get out of the car. I regret this, but in time, I am sure we will give Bergamo its due.

Although we now live in Massachusetts, we lived in a small city on the Hudson River in New York State for most of our lives. During one Italian visit, we had a goal. Go to Milan and find a bronze horse which had been cast in a town on the east side of the Hudson in the town of Beacon, and which was originally designed by Leonardo da Vinci. An American man discovered that this horse existed only in design plans, and he was determined to have it cast. This effort took place over many years and cost him a small fortune. The statue of the horse was a gift from him to the people of Milan.

The search took several hours; at the airport where we had been to change our flights there was a tourist center. Here we were given a general idea of its location and we began. We parked our car near the huge sports center and hippodrome. The first person we asked about the horse's location didn't have a clue; then a young man we saw said he knew and walked with us for quite a way and pointed out of direction between the stadium and the race track. We walked and walked and walked, but found no horse. We then stopped at a bar and asked; we were told it was around the other side of the stadium. We continued walking; the day was hot. When we arrived on the other side of the stadium, there was no horse. We saw a well-dressed gentleman who turned out to have excellent English skills and we asked him. He immediately pointed in a direction and said it was in the "Fiera" area about three kilometers away. We walked to our car and began to drive away when suddenly Roger said, "There it is!" Directly across from where we had parked, the horse stood in front of an impressive building enclosed by a sturdy fence, the gate of which was fortunately open. On the building there was a large incised caption: "Leonardo da Vinci's horse." Success! Much larger than I had envisioned, it is a magnificent sculpture.

In the Prologue of HISTORY, Book XXI, sec. 30, Titus Livius, or Livy as he is generally known, wrote, "Beyond the Alps lies Italy." When I think beyond those majestic mountains, I first visualize two lakes—Maggiore as well as Como. The town of Stresa on Lake Maggiore has been our first stop many times when we have flown into Milan. A haven of quiet, restful and scenic, it is an ideal spot in which to recover from jet lag, which seems to be more of a problem as one accumulates birthdays!

The hotel room we have occupied on many occasions overlooks the lake and I never stop enjoying the changing scene. Sightseeing boats go to the Borromeo Islands and a more pleasant way in which to recover from the time change, I cannot imagine. The town is filled with magnificent gardens, villas, hotels and restaurants. A glass enclosed porch on which breakfast is served in this lake front hotel is a perfect start for morning; sipping coffee while gazing at the perfection of Maggiore is at once calming and blissful.

Maggiore is about forty miles long and two miles wide; surrounded by mountains, the scenery is spectacular. I've been intrigued by the palm trees in the gardens by the lake as they lie in the shadow of snow-covered mountain peaks. A mini-Mediterranean climate exists because of the large, deep lake. This atmosphere contributes to the grandeur of one of the most beautiful gardens in Europe, at Villa Taranto. A Scotsman, Captain Neil McClaren who had acquired a great fortune, bought a villa surrounded by vast lands and he spent the rest of his life creating an English garden on hundreds of acres. Meticulously manicured, the mild temperature allows many species of palms and other exotic plants from around the world to exist though Switzerland is only about fifteen miles away. Thousands of huge trees, flowers, and several ponds and fountains are spread about in an orderly and very planned manner. The flowers are changed according to season;I took a number of photographs of them and have framed some so that I might vicariously continue to enjoy the Captain's gardens while at home. He is buried on the grounds, and interestingly, his first name on the sarcophagus is "Antonio." In response to a vow he became baptized and a convert to Catholicism and took this name at that time.

Two nearby towns to Stresa are Cannobbio and Domodossola. We have visited each on several occasions. Situated on the lake front, Cannobbio is an old and very charming town. We have lunched there on several occasions and have enjoyed walking through and around the village. I have special memories of an after lunch cheese tray which we were served at an enchanting lake front restaurant. A large dinner plate arrived with ten pieces of cheese arranged on the circumference. Instructed by our waiter to begin at "six o'clock" and then to continue counter-clockwise around the circle, we complied. It was a gastronomic adventure! We both loved the first eight pieces, turned our noses up slightly at number nine, and loathed the tenth! But, we'd do it again in a minute!

Domodossola is not a tourist mecca for Americans, although this changes in the winter ski season. We viewed mountain peaks, snow-covered and dramatic, making the scenery unimaginably attractive. We tend to drive around and explore and often find it most interesting to stop at places not noted for tourist attractions. Walking around a small town and stopping for coffee and or lunch is an experience which often is unique to you alone.

Several years ago in Stresa, we were taking an after dinner walk. Passing a bar we glanced in and looked at the television; it was Thursday evening at a little past ten o'clock. The program "ER" was being broadcast, dubbed in Italian. What a hoot to see George Clooney and the cast emote in perfect Italian! This reminded me of turning on TV in a hotel room and seeing a Tom and Jerry cartoon, again in Italian.

During the 1980's we decided to visit *Isola di Ponza,* or the island of Ponza. As with many of our travel decisions, it was based purely on an emotional response. In the town on the Hudson River in New York State where we lived for most of our lives there was a restaurant we really loved. It was informal, the antithesis of elegant, but the food was fabulous and the people who owned it and worked there were the best. They were originally from Ponza; why not go there, we said? Why not, indeed?

I had an attractive and very bright young lady in my tenth grade English class. On parents' day, a young man in his twenties arrived as a surrogate for the parents of this girl. An older brother, he explained that his parents did not speak English well and he was standing in for them. As we talked I realized that his family, father, mother, aunt and uncle were the principals in the restaurant of which we were very fond and visited almost weekly. He had finished college and was beginning to relate to the restaurant himself. After the school visit, we always had so much to talk about when we were at this restaurant. The parents, although not fluent, were perfectly able to understand and converse in English. Their daughter, together with the great meals, became a topic of conversation whenever we were there. Eventually when she was in senior year, she began to help out on weekends and it was always great to see her. This continued for years, through her final high school year and during college as well. She came home from college every weekend for four years to help her family.

The parents often spoke of Ponza and planned to return there when they retired, so it simply became a destination for us, from curiosity or the desire to have another Italian experience.

Ponza was used as a place in which to stash political prisoners during the terrible Fascist years, but recently has become a popular summer resort for Italians as well as other Europeans. We took a hydrofoil from an embarkation area near Anzio. As soon as the boat landed, a man with rooms to rent rushed up to meet and greet us, and to convince us to book a room from him. We did and it was interesting and quite adequate. Our room was immaculate, airy and comfortable. We had to cross a small courtyard, private only to us, for the shower, but, for the most part it was agreeable. After two nights we decided to move into a regular hotel so that we might have the use of their swimming pool and breakfast. This hotel overlooked the sea and we had a great view of it from the bedroom as well as from the bathroom. I recall standing in the shower and looking out into the vastness of the very intensely blue water. One evening there was a heavy windstorm and the height and power of the waves were impressive. Since then we have found out that this is a weather phenomenon in Ponza which occurs from time to time.

Some of the best swordfish I have ever eaten was found in Ponza. We watched the boats bring these fish in from the sea; unfortunately, since that time I have become aware of the dwindling supply of these creatures from over-fishing. Many are being caught young, even before they have been able to breed. I do not eat them anymore, but at the time I remember their excellence and the perfect way in which they were cooked. At a restaurant on the first evening on this island, I wanted to order swordfish, but the menu was written in Italian and I didn't know the correct word for it. Roger, who can draw quite well, took a sheet of paper from the notebook I always carry, and drew a picture of a fish with the large "sword" and showed it to the waiter. He enjoyed the "translation" of *pesce di spada,* and I got the fish.

We enjoyed our brief sojourn in Ponza, relaxing, swimming and enjoying the cuisine. When we left we took the large ferry boat, much slower than the hydrofoil, but decided we weren't in that much of a hurry as it was a beautiful day for a voyage, and besides, the boat boasted a dining room. First things first !

Many years ago we had a quick day trip to Assisi with a group of students, but in May 1996 we were invited to go there for a special gathering planned by our friends we've been fortunate to have since junior high school, Susan and Terry. Several of their California friends were meeting in this medieval town, especially because one woman, whose family was from Italy, was related to a gentleman who had a most unusual restaurant here. The four of us left Tuscany for Umbria where we had made hotel reservations. That night was one we shall never forget.

Susan and I had packed a picnic lunch, and when we arrived we drove up Mount Subasio to Eremo Delle Carceri, an "oasis of peace and silence" according to the brochure, and the favored retreat of Saint Francis. The views were unbelievably breathtaking; we walked on the paths and through the building, and then feasted on our provisions—cheese, prosciutto, eggplant, apples, bananas and bread.

After checking into the type of hotel we favored, probably vintage 1930's, with large rooms, wide halls, but all re-done with wonderful tile baths and a tiny balcony, we walked around the town. Stopping at a shop filled with paintings and prints, I fell in love with a painting of Assisi on wood. The artist had done a total of five in a total panorama of the town, and this was the only one remaining. I called the style, "cubistic, abstract realism;" the proprietor smiled vaguely at that, but didn't disagree, probably because I bought it. I also purchased a tile of Assisi as I have from most of the places we have visited in Italy. At the time I planned to have them permanently placed in my kitchen at home, and since then, the tile man has installed all where daily they remind me of delightful and pleasing memories.

What an industry Saint Francis is for Assisi; I wondered if he would be horrified as the son of a rich man who gave all away to live an ascetic life, if he knew that his town was filled with pilgrims of the tourist type and not of a religious ilk, and that he had become the major local industry.

That evening we met the other couples at their hotel and took a long uphill walk to the restaurant where we were expected. Located in a medieval building, it was magnificent in every respect. The owner gave us a tour of his edifice; behind the facade of the aged but perfectly restored structure, an entirely modern and efficient plant existed. There were extensive specially cooled wine cellars, an on premise laundry for table linens, a computerized inventory system and the most modern kitchen one could dream of.

The owner and chef, cousin of the charming woman from California, gave us enormous attention. As each dish was presented, he explained exactly what it was, the ingredients it was made from and precisely how it was prepared. We sat for hours in what I can only describe as an orgy of food beautifully prepared and served. I recall with extreme pleasure each presentation; the first courses consisted of tortelloni stuffed with veal, risotto with porcini and truffles, and local twisty pasta with fresh tomatoes, asparagus and parmigiano cheese. The second courses we enjoyed next were, first, the most tender lamb morsels simmered with long stemmed artichoke hearts, and second, beefsteak fiorentina with herb sauce. Salads and vegetables were offered, and we finished with plates of fresh fruit. Some of our party also had richer desserts, but we couldn't manage it. It was a banquet fit for the gods!

The morning after the wonderful dinner we did the sightseeing tour, and I have been so grateful that we did in light of the devastating earthquake that so damaged this town and the surrounding region the following winter. The Basilica of Saint Francis is nothing less than magnificent. The frescoes attributed to Giotto, as well as to many others of the greatest painters of the 13th and 14th centuries make this realm a treasure. I was fascinated by the fact that the Saint's tomb below the lower church was not discovered until 1818. He died in 1226, but his faithful friend and protector, Brother Elias, later designed a crypt, obscure and hidden, and had the remains re-interred, so that the body would never be disturbed or stolen during the frequent uprisings which occurred in this area through the medieval and Renaissance eras.

In October of 1997 we returned to Assisi, hoping that the earthquake damage would by now not be severe enough to prevent us from once again enjoying and appreciating the area. It turned out to be a mixed experience. From Urbino we telephoned the hotel we had used the year before; there was no answer. We asked an Italian friend to call for us, thinking that perhaps we did not do it correctly. Again, no response. But, we decided to see for ourselves.

The road towards Fossombrone and ultimately Rome, was new, straight and beautifully engineered. Totally new to us as we had never approached Assisi from the Marche', we enjoyed the hillside country. Suddenly the new road evaporated and the old one, twisty and narrow appeared. Our pace was slowed but we decided to stop in the town of Nocera Umbra for coffee. That was when we first began to realize the dreadful impact of the earthquake on the entire area. Many buildings here were damaged and uninhabited; hundreds of temporary trailers could be seen all over the countryside providing shelter for those who had lost their homes.

Although we had never spent the night in Nocera Umbra, we had several fond memories of it, and the damage was somehow more sad, knowing this small, medieval town with steep streets from other visits. The first time we had ever been there we were traveling toward Urbino from Rome. Roger spotted a tiny trattoria, high above the highway; we exited and it took some searching, but his stomach led him to this delightful small restaurant. Several years later, we stopped for our morning cappuccini and spoke to the barman where we had enjoyed coffee on the last visit. When we told him we were going to Rome, he was full of concern and eagerly warned us of the dangers of a large city. We assured him that we would be careful; we were reminded of those in our own country who warn others of the dangers of New York City, Chicago or Miami.

When we arrived at the Portal San Giacomo in Assisi we had to enter on foot as cars were blocked off from entering. There was a trattoria at the entry and we walked in for lunch. The proprietor was extremely fluent in English and explained what had happened to his city since the catastrophe. The Church of Saint Francis is the reason people come here, he told us, and because it is closed off for extensive and needed repairs, the tours have canceled and we have become a ghost town. We readily discovered that he was totally correct. Of the many hotels, only three were open, and the one we found would be closing within four days. This building was part of a four hundred year old palazzo, built on a hill so that we entered on the third floor and took the elevator down to the first floor for our room. The restaurant where we had so happily dined seventeen months before was shut tight, as was the hotel we had stayed in on that occasion. Most stores were closed; I looked for the shop where I had bought the painting and it was empty. There were virtually no tourists in the town which is usually filled to capacity.

That evening we experienced one of the more minor results of this tragic situation. At the only restaurant still open and miraculously undamaged, we had a meal that was unusual as it was far from the Italian culinary standards. We were told later that most of the city residents had gone to stay temporarily with relatives or friends in other towns, leaving very few people to carry the workload in the few places remaining open. The first and second courses were brought to the table simultaneously; the artichokes Roger had ordered were forgotten; the meat, overcooked. Not a terrible situation, but one so different from the typically excellent Italian meal service. We guessed that the usual employees had disappeared and that the replacement cooks and waiters most likely had been commandeered in a high unemployment area and had been promised a good income if they worked in this depressed town.

At this time though, the police were in constant evidence, patrolling to prevent looting. Building damage was apparent everywhere; supports were erected on hundreds of buildings to prevent further destruction. At the main Church of Saint Francis, there was an army of workmen repairing the extensive earthquake harm. Enormous scaffolding was built, complete with an elaborate stairway to the top. A crane was in place. Inside the basilica we were told there were a large number of art restorers trying to piece together as much of the terribly damaged frescoes as possible.

Business was almost totally crippled, if not at an end in Assisi. Normally the tourists come in hordes from April until December.

We chatted with the young man in charge at our under-populated hotel. He told us that the hotel has forty-six rooms, and counting ours, only four were filled. On duty all night, he asked what we would like for breakfast and at what time, as he would be bringing it to our room. He apologized because, in his words, "Our famous dining room is closed."

He told us there were actually three quakes; the second was the worst, but fortunately, almost all of the population were out of doors following the first one, and thus personal deaths and injuries were much fewer than if the first one had been the worst. Some small villages had been totally annihilated, and often inhabitants were still living in tents.

The Roman Temple of Minerva was undamaged as far as we knew and we were able to enter its museum located in part of its underground; we thought it most interesting. The temple, built here in the first century B.C.E., is an impressive sight; its six columns front a wide piazza which last year was filled with people enjoying themselves, and this year with cranes and machines repairing the vast damages.

We have not returned to Assisi since that time; we will again, but in the meantime, the news is that this historic place is very much again hosting eager tourists. I hope the Saint understands.

Most of the traveling we have done in and around Italy has been in rented or leased cars; several times we have flown between cities if the distance was great and the time was short, and twice we have traveled on overnight boats. We had heard of the Pendelino, a modern express train which goes fast, is on time and makes few stops. Roger wanted to try it, so one day while we were renting an apartment in Florence, we decided to take this famous train to Rome to surprise our friends at their restaurant. To make a good comparison of the features, we bought first class tickets to Rome and second class return. The ride was great! We arrived in less than two hours.

We took a taxi to our friend's restaurant, but it was too early for guests; the staff was having lunch. We walked around for a half hour and then entered. We certainly surprised everyone which was exactly what Roger had hoped for; it was so pleasing to them and fortunately the entire family was there that day; we were given a great welcome. We sat and talked for several hours; they promised to visit us when we got to the small rented cottage we had reserved in Tuscany for October. The train ride back to Florence was perfect; we decided that on this train, second class was perfectly adequate. The only difference was that for a larger price in first class, one was given cookies and coffee.

Michelangelo was born in a small village now known as "Caprese Michelangelo." The small museum there was opened in 1964 honoring the artist on the four hundredth anniversary of his death. I had heard of this settlement and finally we were able to visit it. The museum contains photographs of most of the artist's works and reproductions of many of his most famous sculptures. A film also shows the life and works of this giant; except for the wonderful scenes, most of the dialogue was lost to us because of the language.

Painters from Florence have created twenty-three scenes from what his life might have been like. Some are very human as the first, which depicts the artist's mother fallen from her horse while pregnant, but being safely delivered of her son on March 6, 1475. Others, perhaps a trifle fanciful such as the one in which a pope has Michelangelo sit next to him while the cardinals remain standing. Against the background of the small house and museum are remnants of the medieval castle, part of which holds old reproductions of the master's works. Modern sculptures are also displayed both in and outside of the museum. The visit was a worthwhile detour on our way to Urbino.

Situated on a hill about a half an hour's drive above Florence sits the town of Fiesole. One summer in the mid 1970's we discovered this town as we tried to escape from the brutal heat of Florence and moved into a higher elevation. Originally Etruscan, but typically conquered by the Romans, we discovered a large theatre in the center of this very attractive town built by the Romans several hundred years B.C.E. Walking around after dinner we noticed a group of people going into this theatre and intrigued, we followed, led by curiosity only, not having any idea what to expect. What was going to happen was the showing of an aged Russian documentary film.

What the heck, we decided; we had nothing planned and so to sit in this open ancient theatre, now cool in the dark of night, was an opportunity not to be missed. We entered, sat, and soon the film began. Interesting, it really was not. The topic was Russian agriculture and cattle raising. The commentary was neither in Italian nor English and I can only assume it was Russian which, from the comments heard near to us, was not understood by anyone.

One scene vividly stands out in my mind. A single cow is led into a primitive slaughterhouse, is then summarily butchered and cut up into various pieces of meat. It was at this point that the film's projectionist must have become incredibly bored and most likely sensed that the audience was as well, because a few people had begun to leave.

He momentarily stopped the film and then unbelievably began to run it in reverse. We watched as the various pieces of potential stew meat, hamburger, roasts and soup bones were miraculously put back together, the animal's head re-attached, the hide replaced, and the finale, the cow walked backwards out of the barn-like building.

The audience burst into applause; the lights were illuminated through the theatre, and as if by signal, we all exited with smiles.

A few years ago, aided by the ever skillful computer, Roger took our photo of this theatre and superimposed a cow in its midst. I giggle at the memory each time I see it.

Fortunately there are so many places in Italy which remain to be visited by us—Trieste, Torino, Sardinia are only a few; many others where we have been for a brief time but wish to return, including all the places discussed in this section as well as everything in the other chapters as well. Although the character Pistol states in THE MERRY WIVES OF WINDSOR, "the world's mine oyster," we would shorten that to, "Italy's our oyster" where we feast with eyes, ears, taste, and very grateful hearts.

ITALY! WE REALLY LOVE YOU!!
LAKE COMO

Between steep, seemingly sculpted mountains
Lies the deep blue vastness of Lake Como.
This water, named by the Italians here
As *"Lago di Como",* are correctly
Proud of its intense, deep, beautiful and
Incredible form. The mountains cradling
The vast depths are imperious, stark, bold
And composed of limestone and solid earth.
Mostly tree-covered, these natural titans
Rise majestically toward the sky
And appear to my amazed, bewildered
Sight, off-balanced by the severity
And awe of the spectacular greatness,
As a supernatural creation.

But reality intervenes and I
Look from the vantage point of our friend's house
Located high above the dark waters
And see ferries, pleasure craft and sailboats
Delightfully navigate the blue below.
This is the true reality—not the
Fantasy imbedded in excited
Imagination. Then I look over
And spy houses, churches, docks and roads
As tiny as children's toys remembered
From eons past. These structures are not real;
They're too small! Yet I was there yesterday
And know they do exist. Distance across
The lake fools the eye and mind to pretend
They are not real. Night falls and suddenly
Lights blaze on the opposite mountainsides.

Now I understand the logic of scores,
Perhaps thousands of silvery, immense
Transmission towers put in places I
Believe impossible, defying laws
Gravity wise, and to me, common sense.
How do they get there and how do they stay?
Technological engineering is
Not my forte, so I just acquiesce.
Because of them, villages can twinkle
And punctuate the mountain's bleak darkness.

I see and appreciate tiny towns near
The lake's edge as they alight. What I don't
Understand at this latitude are palms!
Yes, palm trees of various kinds blithely
Grow and thrive among pine and leaf filled trees!
Near the mountain top I spy villages.
I question their real probability.
How do they exist? How does one get there?
Do roads penetrate woods and altitudes
For people who live there? And how survive?
Are there butchers, bakers, grocers, not to
Even think of doctors, pharmacists or schools?
But exist they do, and gently survive.
I'm impressed, overwhelmed and a witness
To this near-heavenly situation.

When speaking of heavens, I'm reminded
Of the ubiquitous sea planes flying
Over the lake at levels I see low;
Actually the aircraft fly altitudes
Completely normal, but we are so high
We must look down to view these flying things—
These impressive airborne machines! A most
Unusual and most exciting sight.

Abodes, bordering the lake and above
Are alive with persons displaying life.
Necessities acquired; rugs hung on
Railings bordering balconies are made
Fresh; sheets and towels dry in the breezes;
Dogs bark, cats creep, car horns pierce the air, and
Remind one and all that Italian life
Exists, survives and thrives as we admire.

Beloved Lake Como and citizens
Who live there—bravo! Continue in joy!
I never tire of observing mountains
Grand, some snow-covered, others only green
As they envelope, guard, and dominate
The valley of the *Lago di Como!*